THE ULTIMATE BEGIN

ELECTRIC GUITAR COM TE

Keith Wyatt • Nick Nolan • Colgan Bryan

INTRODUCTION

The electric guitar is one of the most enjoyable instruments you can play. With this book and DVD, you will learn all the basics you need to start playing and have a solid foundation that will enable you to play blues and rock.

The Guitar Basics section will get you started learning about the guitar, how to tune, how to read music and TAB, picking techniques, and much more. You'll also learn chords and get an introduction to soloing.

The Blues Guitar section teaches you the basics of playing the blues. Topics include the blues progression, "call and response," bending, vibrato, and the slow blues, to name a few.

The Rock Guitar section gives you everything you need to play rock. You will explore power chords, picking techniques, scales, and lots of rock licks. There are also tips on playing with a band.

Also included are play-along tracks featuring legendary recording artists that will enable you to instantly apply the new rhythms, techniques, and licks to music.

Let's dig in and get started playing electric guitar.

The included DVD contains MP3 audio files of every example in the book. Use the MP3s to ensure you're capturing the feel of the examples and interpreting the rhythms correctly.

To access the MP3s on the DVD, place the DVD in your computer's DVD-ROM drive. In Windows, double-click on My Computer, then right-click on the DVD drive icon. Select Explore, then double-click on the DVD-ROM Materials folder. For Mac, double-click on the DVD icon on your desktop, then double-click on the DVD-ROM Materials folder.

Alfred Music
P.O. Box 10003
Van Nuys, CA 91410-0003
alfred.com

Book and DVD (without case)
ISBN-10: 0-7390-5617-4
ISBN-13: 978-0-7390-5617-2

Cover photographs:
Blue energy © istockphoto.com/Raycat
Guitar courtesy of Fender Musical Instruments Corporation

CONTENTS

GUITAR BASICS

BLUES GUITAR

ROCK GUITAR

CONTENTS

Section 1: The Basics

The Three Basic Guitar Types

Nylon String Acoustic (Classic Guitar)

The nylon string acoustic guitar has a nice mellow tone and has several advantages for beginners. The strings are much easier to press to the fretboard so they don't cut into your fingers the way steel strings do. Also, the neck is wider than on a typical steel string guitar which makes fingering chords a little easier. The classic guitar is perfectly suited to intimate, unaccompanied guitar performances.

The Steel String Acoustic

The steel string acoustic guitar is perhaps the most versatile and common guitar type. Although it is a little bit harder to play than the nylon string guitar, the steel string acoustic has a loud, bright, ringing tone that clearly projects to the listener. This guitar is excellent for backing a singer.

The Electric Guitar

The electric guitar has come to dominate popular music. It is an extremely versatile instrument capable of producing everything from mellow jazz tones and biting funk riffs to the screaming, over-the-top, dizzying pyrotechnics of rock's reigning guitar virtuosos.

Parts of the Guitar

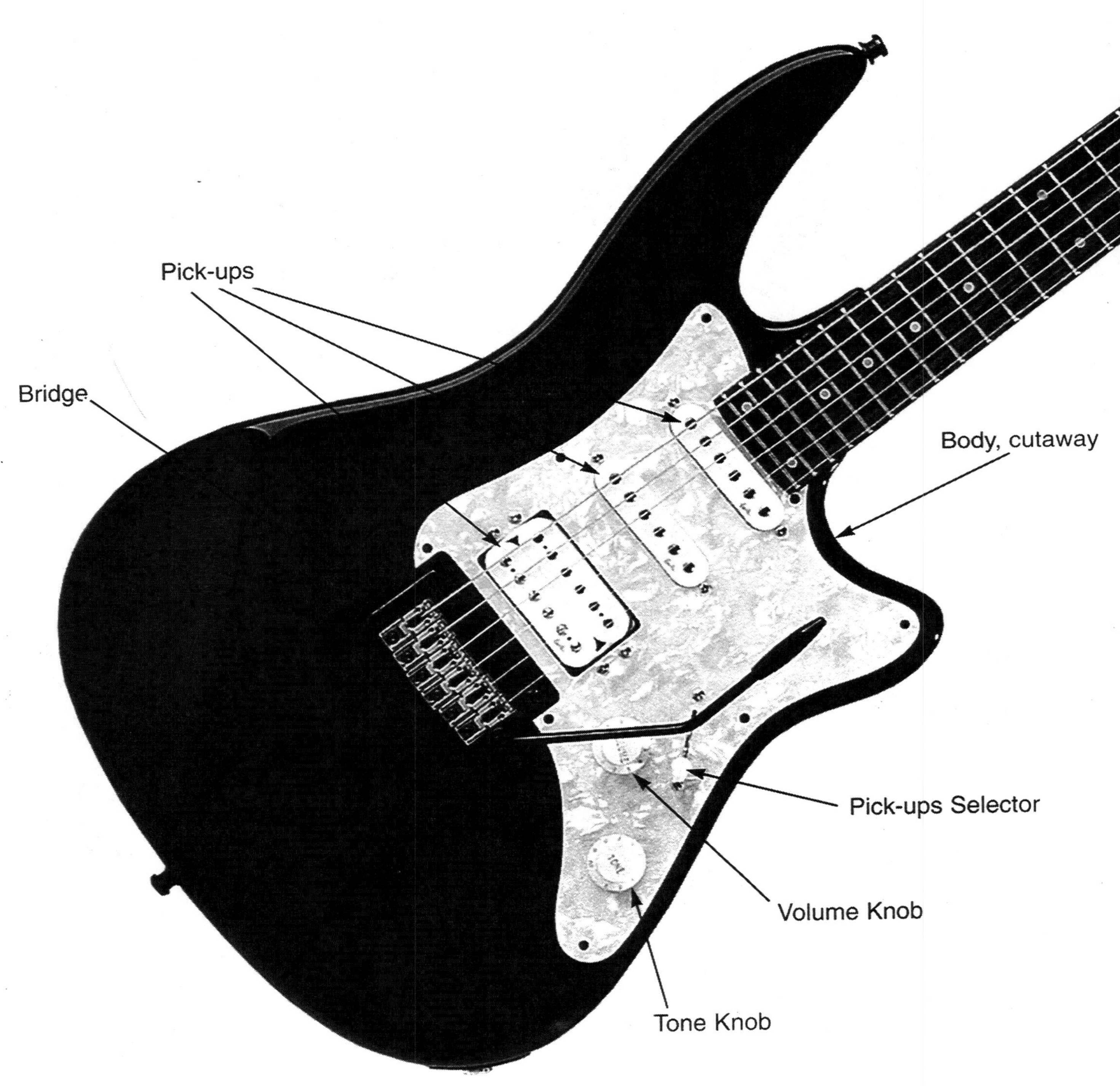

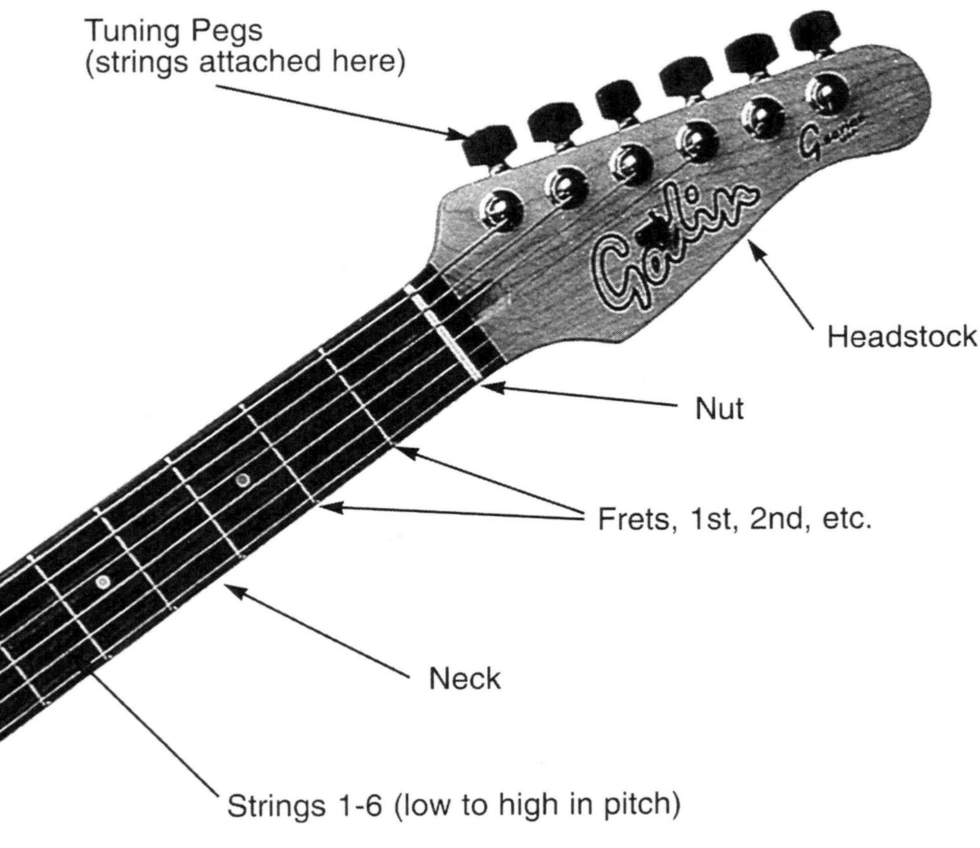

Strings: Strings are available in three basic gauges, light, medium and heavy. I suggest you begin with light or medium gauge strings.

Picks: Picks come in many shapes, sizes and thicknesses. For acoustic guitar, I recommend light to medium thickness. For electric, the thicker picks seem to work best. Experiment to find the size and shape you are most comfortable with.

Tuning Methods

Tuning to a Keyboard:

The six strings of a guitar can be tuned to a keyboard by matching the sound of each open guitar string to the keyboard notes as indicated in the diagram.

Note: You will hear the intonation better, and your guitar will stay in better tune, if you loosen the strings and tune them **up** to pitch rather than bringing them from above the pitch and tuning down.

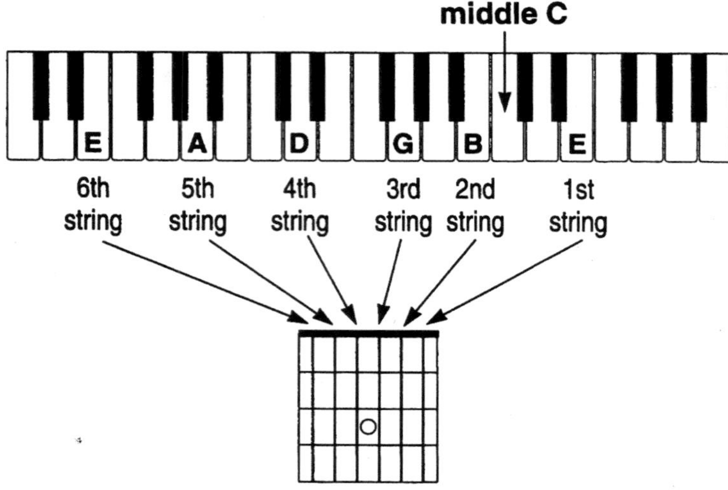

Electronic Tuners:

Many brands of small, battery operated tuners are available. These are excellent for keeping your guitar in perfect tune and for developing your ear to hear intonation very accurately. Simply follow the instructions supplied with the electronic tuner.

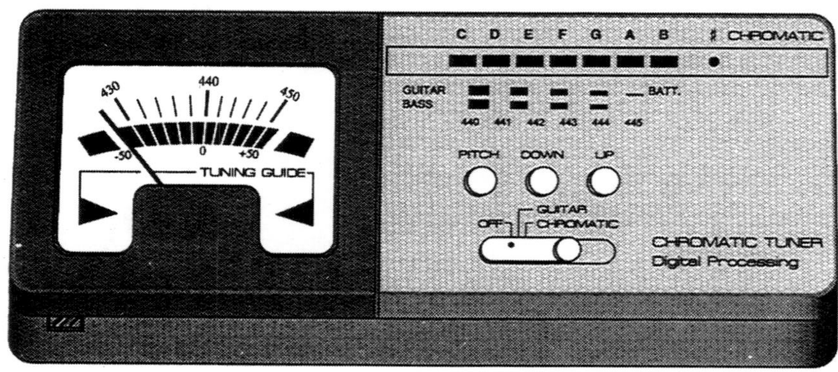

Tuning the Guitar to Itself – The "Fifth Fret" Method:

1) Tune your 6th string "E" to a piano or some other fixed pitch instrument.

2) Depress the 6th string at the 5th fret. Play it and you will hear the note "A," which is the same as the 5th string played open. Turn the 5th string tuning key until the pitch of the open 5th string (A) matches that of the 6th string/5th fret (also A).

3) Depress the 5th string at the 5th fret. Play it and you will hear the note "D," which is the same as the 4th string played open. Turn the 4th string tuning key until the pitch of the open 4th string (D) matches that of the 5th string/5th fret (also D).

4) Depress the 4th string at the 5th fret. Play it and you will hear the note "G," which is the same as the 3rd string played open. Turn the 3rd string tuning key until the pitch of the open 3rd string (G) matches that of the 4th string/5th fret (also G).

5) Depress the 3rd string at the 4th fret (not the 5th fret as in the other strings). Play it and you will hear the note "B," which is the same as the 2nd string played open. Turn the 2nd string tuning key until the pitch of the open 2nd string (B) matches that of the 3rd string/4th fret (also B).

6) Depress the 2nd string at the 5th fret. Play it and you will hear the note "E," which is the same as the 1st string played open. Turn the 1st string tuning key until the pitch of the open 1st string (E) matches that of the 2nd string/5th fret (also E).

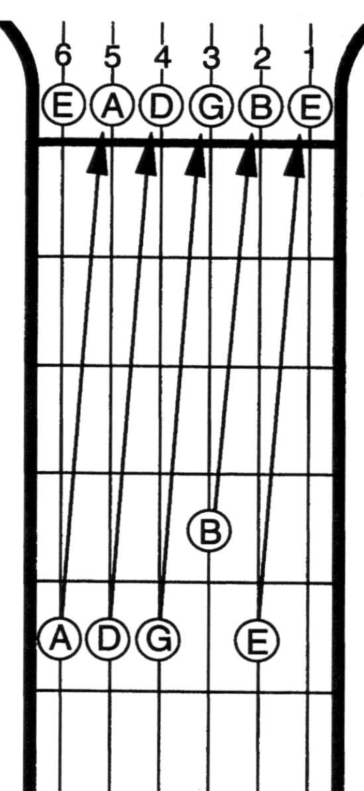

Changing Strings

Eventually, whether because a string has broken on its own, or because through repeated use it is no longer "tunable," you will have to change your strings. Be prepared! Always keep in your guitar case:

1) A set of extra strings
2) A pair of wire cutters
3) A string winder

All available at your local music store.

Changing Strings:

1) First, remove the old string. If the string has broken you will have to remove the "ball end" from the bridge and unwrap the other end from around the tuning peg.

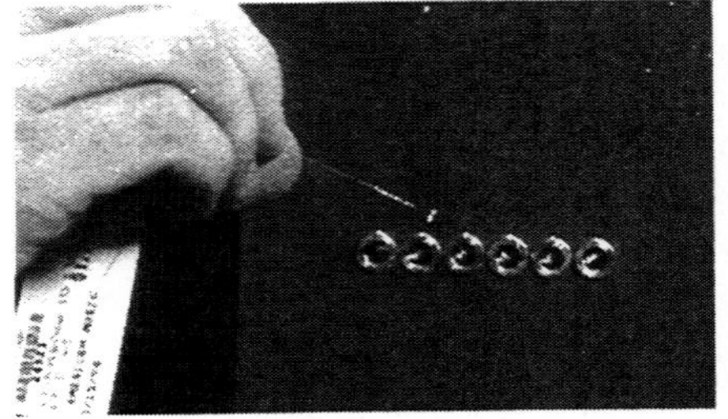

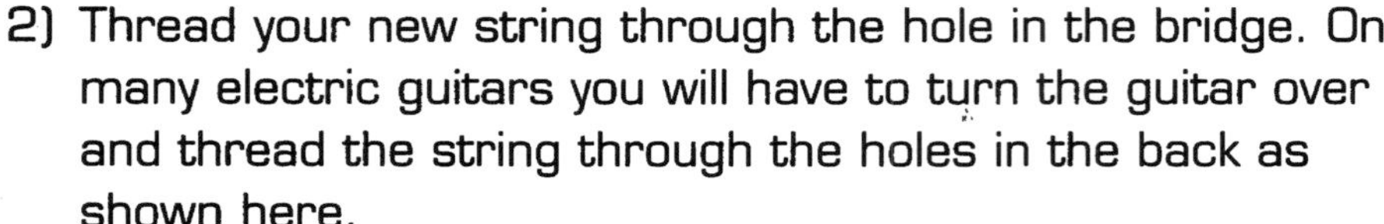

2) Thread your new string through the hole in the bridge. On many electric guitars you will have to turn the guitar over and thread the string through the holes in the back as shown here.

On other electric guitars the string will thread directly through a hole in the bridge.

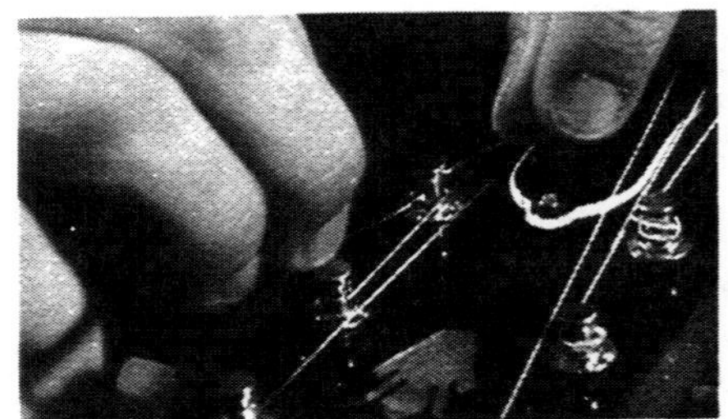

3) Once the string has been threaded through the bridge, feed the other end through the hole in the tuning peg, making sure to leave some slack in the string.

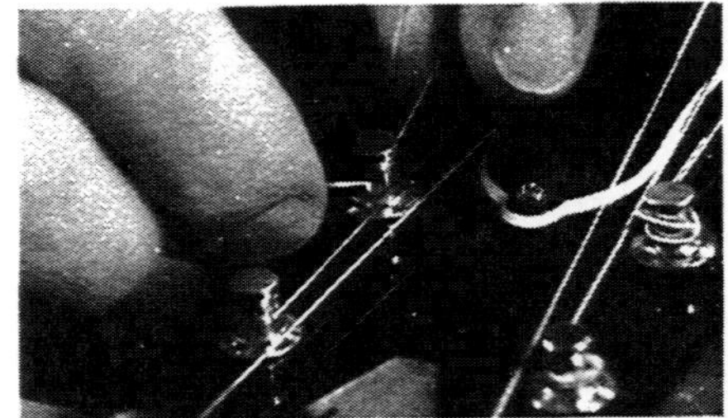

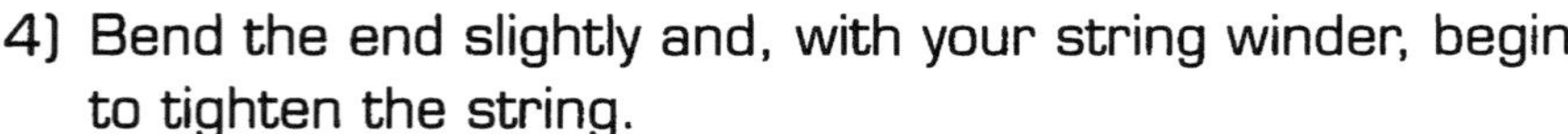

4) Bend the end slightly and, with your string winder, begin to tighten the string.

5) Trim the excess string off with your wire cutters.

Reading Rhythm Notation

At the beginning of every song is a time signature. 4/4 is the most common time signature:

4 FOUR COUNTS TO A MEASURE
4 A QUARTER NOTE RECEIVES ONE COUNT

The top number tells you how many counts per measure.
The bottom number tells you which kind of note receives one count.

The time value of a note is determined by three things:

1) note head:

2) stem:

3) flag:

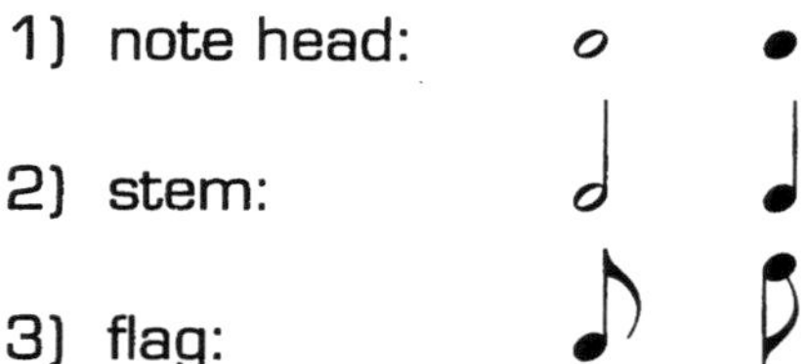

𝅝 This is a whole note. The note head is open and has no stem. In 4/4 time, a whole note receives 4 counts.

𝅗𝅥 This is a half note. It has an open note head and a stem. A half note receives 2 counts.

♩ This is a quarter note. It has a solid note head and a stem. A quarter note receives 1 count.

♪ This is an eighth note. It has a solid note head and a stem with a flag attached. An eighth note receives 1/2 count.

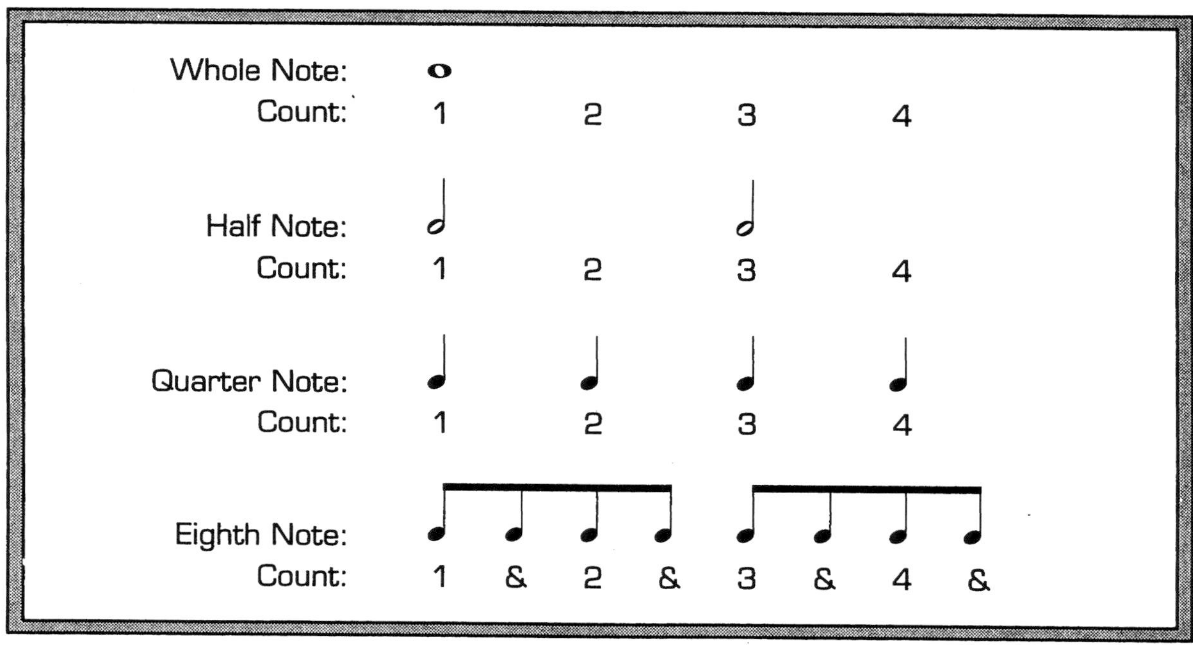

Reading Music Notation

Music is written on a **staff**. The staff consists of five lines and four spaces between the lines:

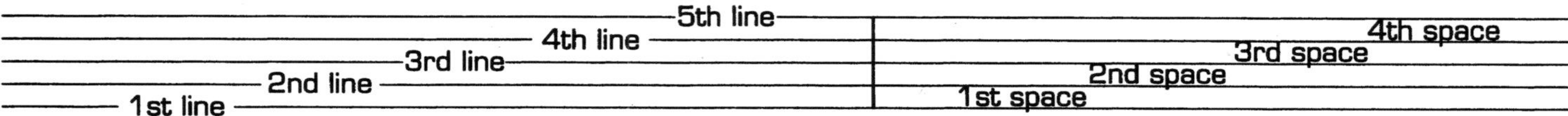

The names of the notes are the same as the first seven letters of the alphabet: A B C D E F G.

The notes are written in alphabetical order. The first (lowest) line is "E":

Notes can extend above and below the staff. When they do, **ledger lines** are added. Here is the approximate range of the guitar from the lowest note, open 6th string "E," to a "B" on the 1st string at the 17th fret.

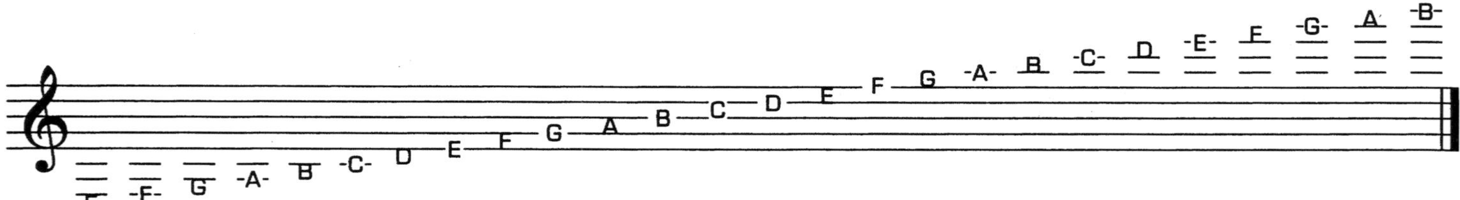

The staff is divided into **measures** by **bar lines**. A heavy double bar line marks the end of the music.

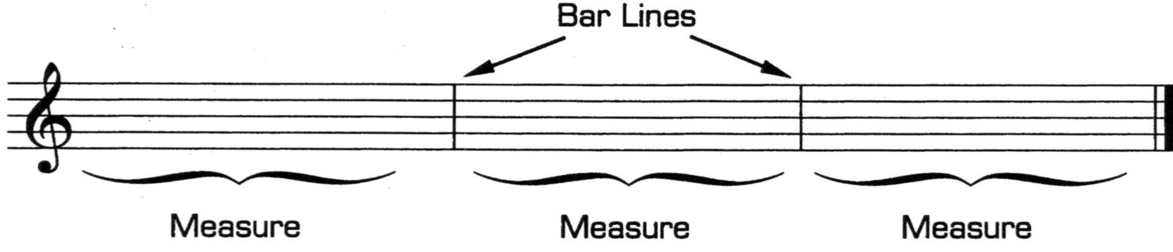

Reading Tablature and Fretboard Diagrams

Tablature illustrates the location of notes on the neck of the guitar. This illustration compares the six strings of a guitar to the six lines of tablature.

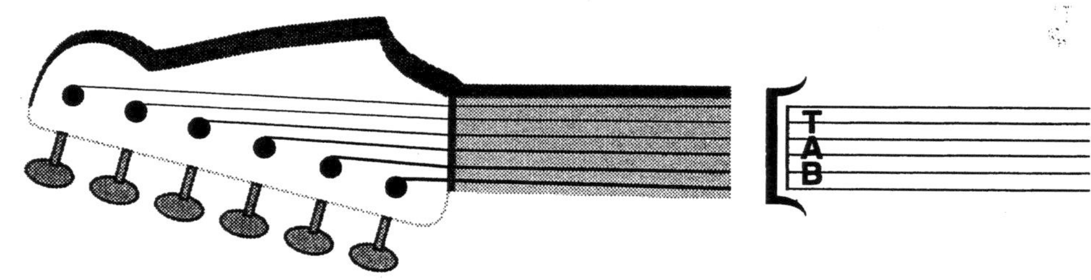

Notes are indicated by placing fret numbers on the strings. An "O" indicates an open string.

This tablature indicates to play the open, 1st and 3rd frets on the 1st string.

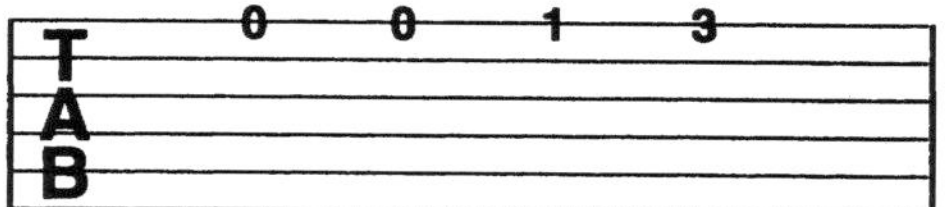

Tablature is usually used in conjunction with standard music notation. The rhythms and note names are indicated by the standard notation and the location of those notes on the guitar neck is indicated by the tablature.

Chords are often indicated in **chord block diagrams**. The vertical lines represent the strings and the horizontal lines represent the frets. Scales are often indicated with guitar **fretboard diagrams**. Here the strings are horizontal and the frets are vertical.

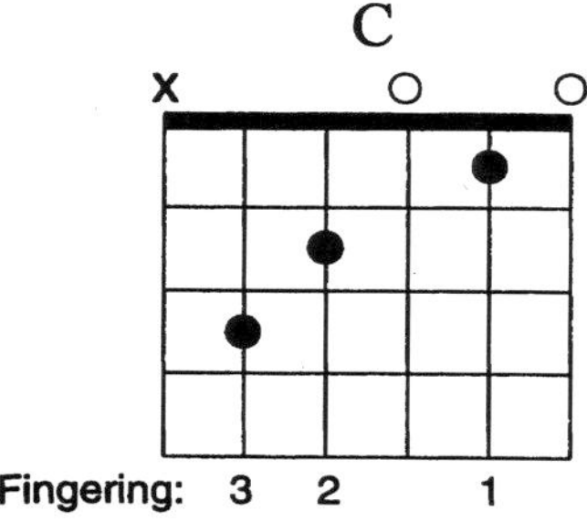

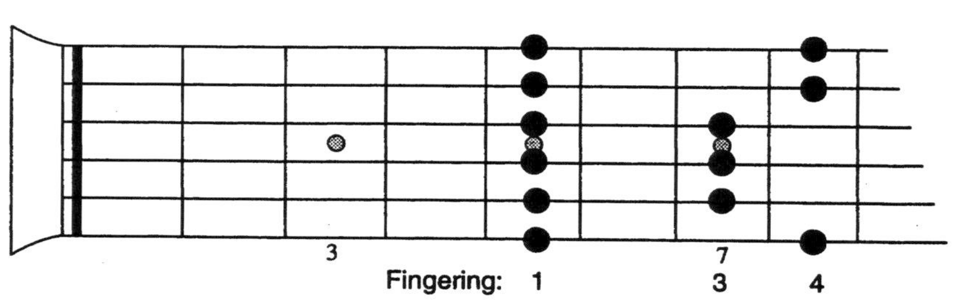

Section 2: Open Position Chords

The Six Basic Open Position Chords

These are the most fundamental chords to all styles of guitar playing. "Open" position chords contain open strings which ring out loud and clear. The sound of a ringing open chord is probably the most identifiable guitar sound there is. Whether you play acoustic or electric guitar, these six chords will be some of the main chords you will use throughout your lifetime.

The E Major Chord

The dots indicate which notes to play with your fingers, the open circles indicate open strings and "x" indicates a string that should not be played. Play the E chord. Make sure you get a clear sound without any buzzing or muffled notes. Your fingertips should be placed just behind the fret—not on top of it or too far behind it. Also, the fingertips should be perpendicular to the fingerboard; if they lean at an angle they will interfere with the other strings and prevent them from ringing.

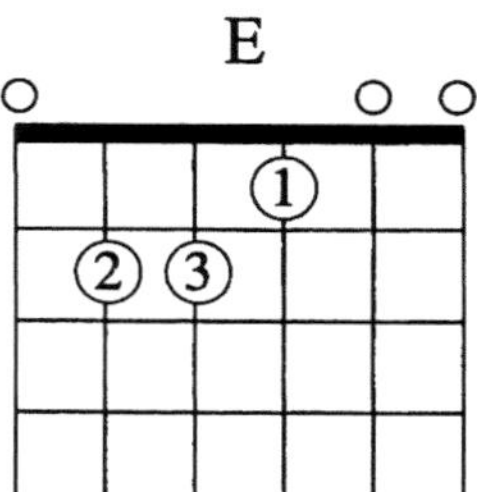

The A Major Chord

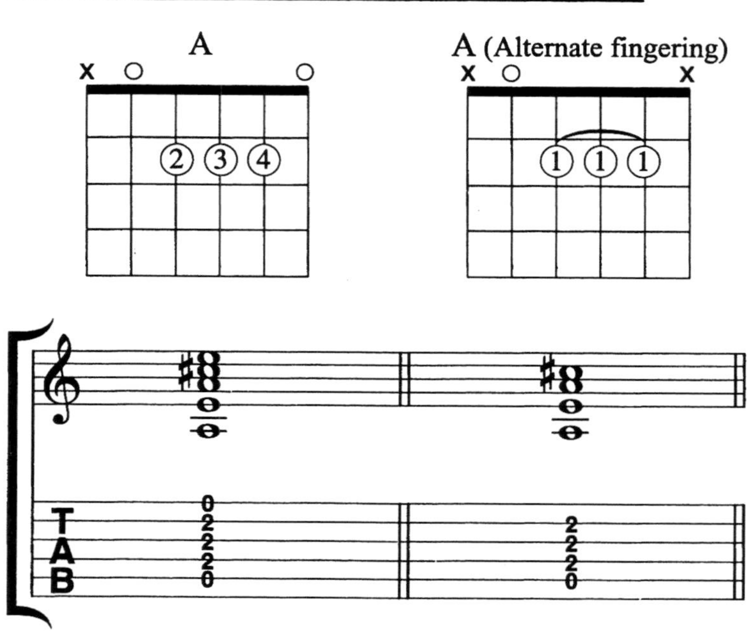

Notice that in the alternate fingering there is no 1st string E. This is OK, it's still an A chord.

The D Major Chord

The D chord uses just the top four strings. Play the chord making sure you can get a good, clear, ringing tone.

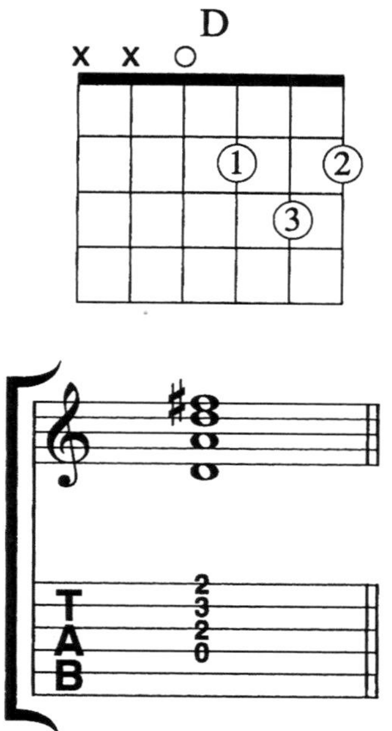

Strumming:

Relax your left hand and strum with a constant down-up motion from your wrist.

Example 1: First Strumming Pattern

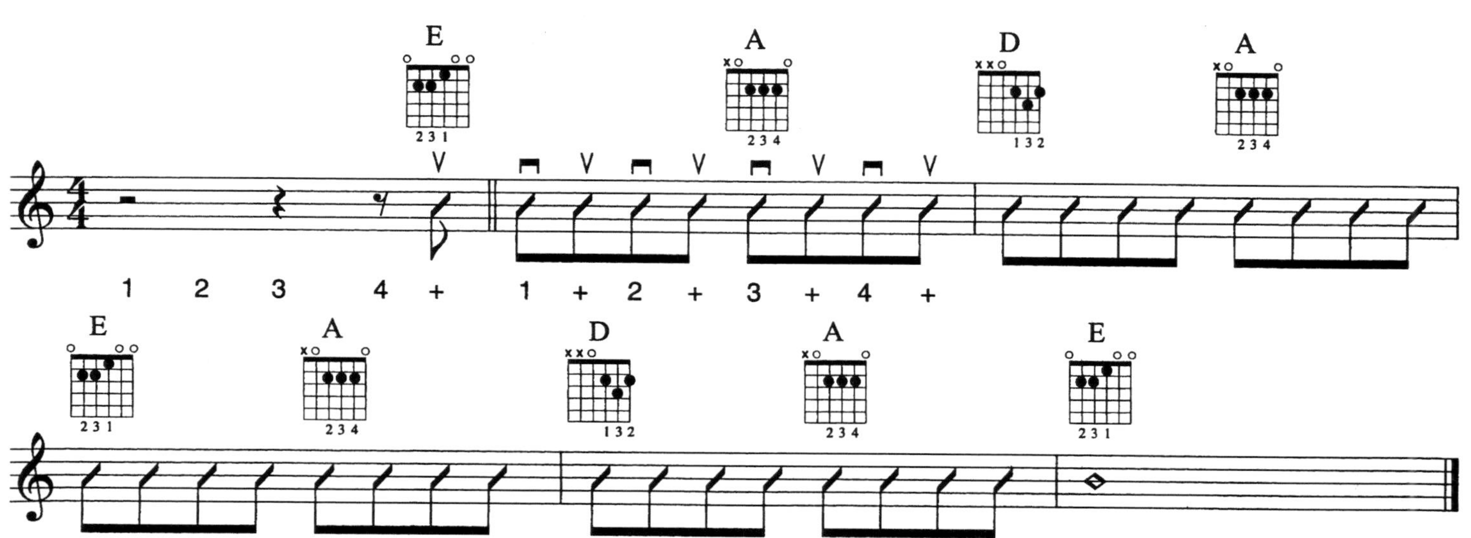

Note: Down-strums are indicated with this symbol: ⊓. Up-strums are indicated with this symbol: V.

G Major

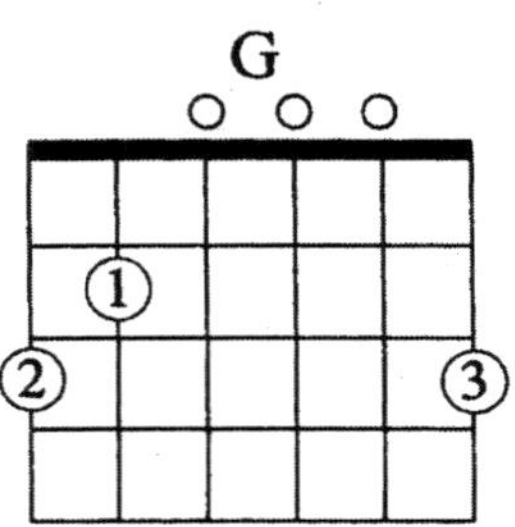

Tip: In order to play this chord cleanly, it is essential that you play on your fingertips, holding your fingers perpendicular to the neck. Keeping your left hand thumb down in the center of the neck will help keep your fingers in the best position to avoid interfering with the other strings.

Example 2

Now try combining the G chord with the D chord. Notice both chords use the same three fingers:

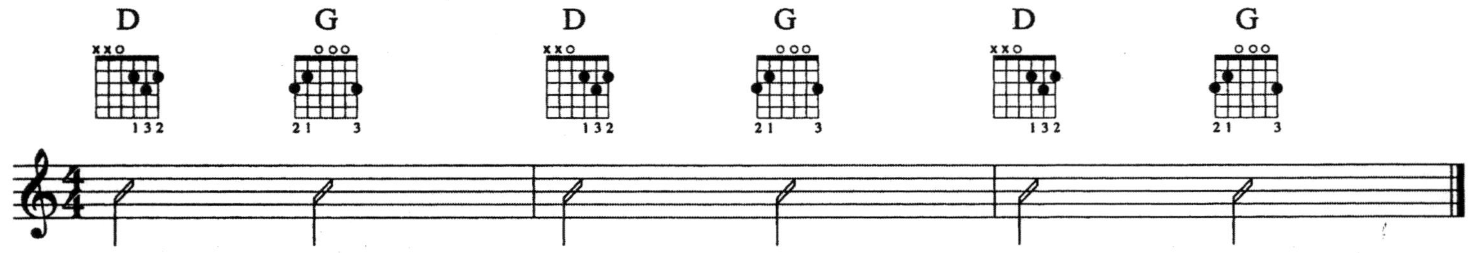

C Major

Remember: Hold your fingers perpendicular to the neck making sure they touch only the strings they are playing and do not interfere with the other strings.

Example 3

Practice moving back and forth between the C and G chords.

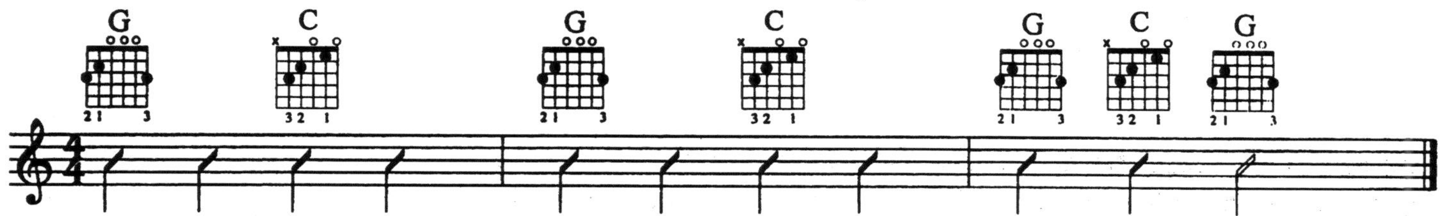

B7 Chord

The G, D, C and E chords each contain three different notes. The B7 is a four-note chord (B, D♯, F♯, A).

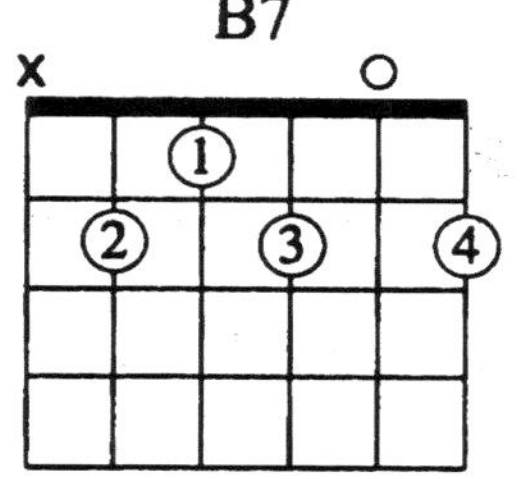

Example 4

Now try this next example which switches between the E and B7 chords.

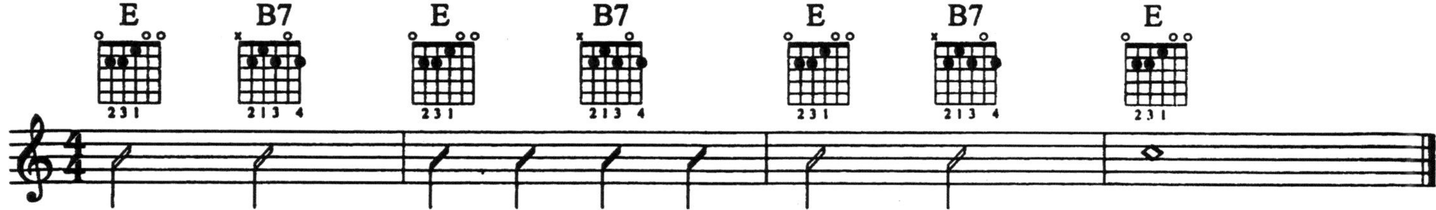

The Blues Progression (in four keys)

The blues progression is the most common chord progression. The typical blues progression is 12 measures long and uses the 1st, 4th and 5th chords of the key. To find the 1st, 4th and 5th chords (usually indicated with Roman numerals: I, IV and V) simply count up through the alphabet from the key note.

For Example:

Blues in the key of "A":	A I	B	C	D IV	E V	F	G	A
Blues in the key of "G":	G I	A	B	C IV	D V	E	F	G
Blues in the key of "E":	E I	F	G	A IV	B V	C	D	E
Blues in the key of "D":	D I	E	F	G IV	A V	B	C	D

Example 5: Strum Pattern A

The next progression can be played with a variety of "strum" patterns. First try this simple "quarter note" (one strum per beat) pattern.

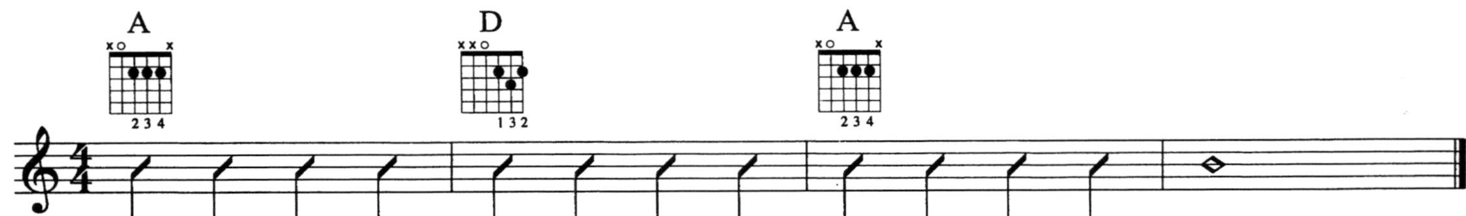

Example 6: Strum Pattern B

This next pattern uses both down- and up-strokes of the pick. Your right hand should maintain a constant down-up motion, but you'll hit the strings on both the down-stroke and on some of the up-strokes.

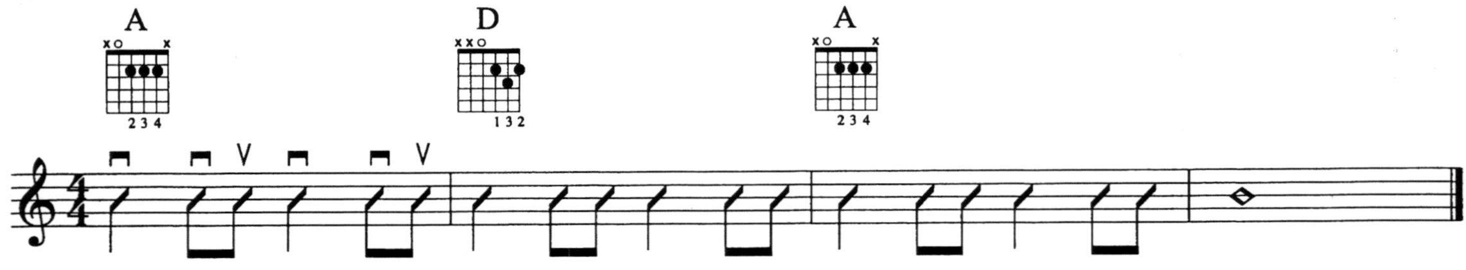

Example 7

This strumming example takes the blues progression through four keys: A, G, E, and D. It uses just the six chords you've learned so far: A, D, E, G, C, and B7. Play along with the video using the two rhythms you've just learned. When you're comfortable with the chord changes, try making up some rhythms of your own.

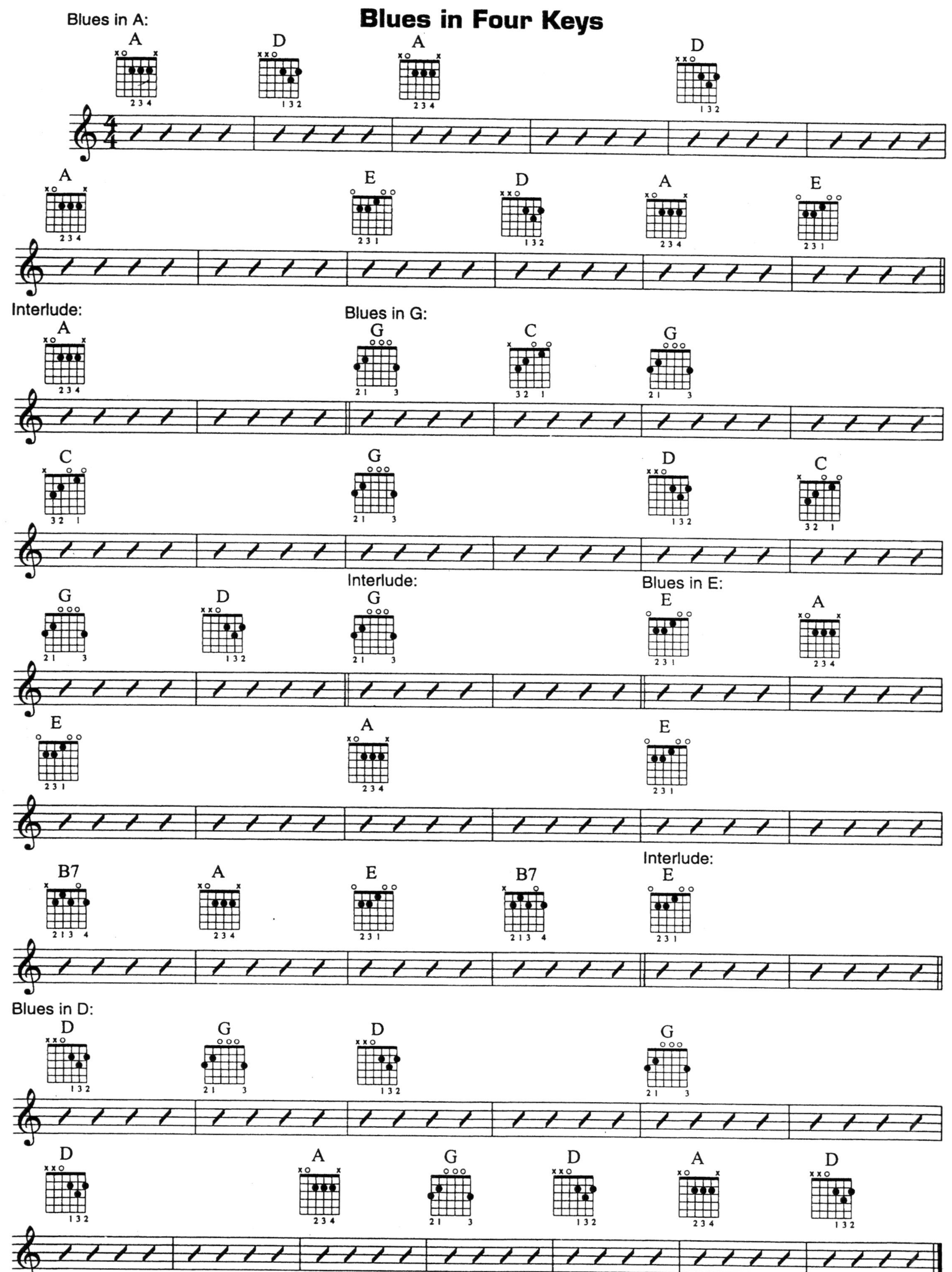
Blues in Four Keys
Blues in A:
A D A D
A E D A E
Interlude:
A
Blues in G:
G C G
C G D C
G D
Interlude:
G
Blues in E:
E A
E A E
B7 A E B7
Interlude:
E
Blues in D:
D G D G
D A G D A D

Chord Categories

There are three categories of chords: Major, Minor and Dominant. With these three type of chords you can play basically any pop or rock song. You already know five basic open position major chords: E, D, C, A and G.

Minor Chords: Minor chords differ from major chords by only one note: the 3rd. (To find the "3rd" count up three from the root (1). By lowering the 3rd of any major chord one fret, it becomes a minor chord.

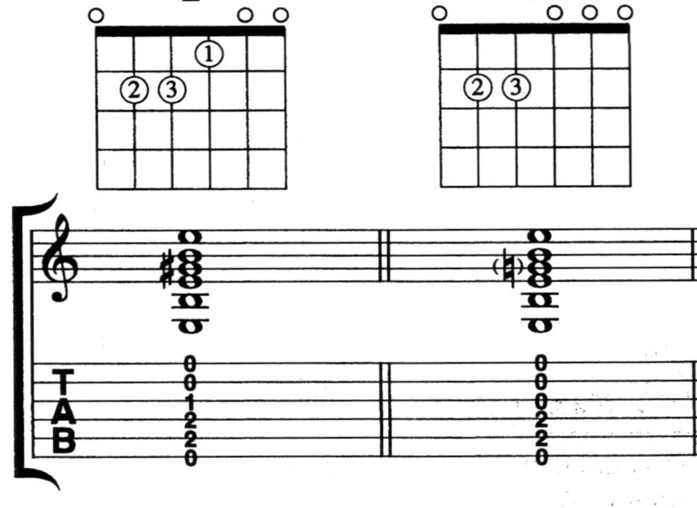

Example 8

Play back and forth between the E and Em chords:

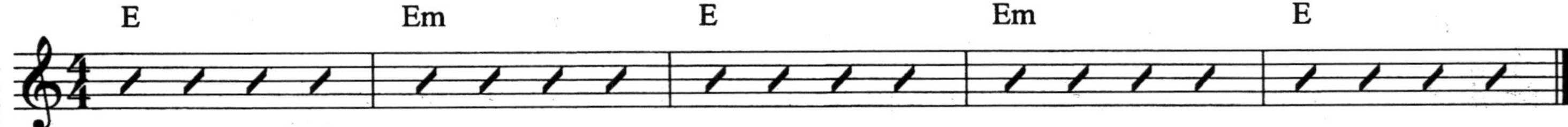

Notice again that the difference between the A and Am, and D and Dm chords is only one note (the 3rd).

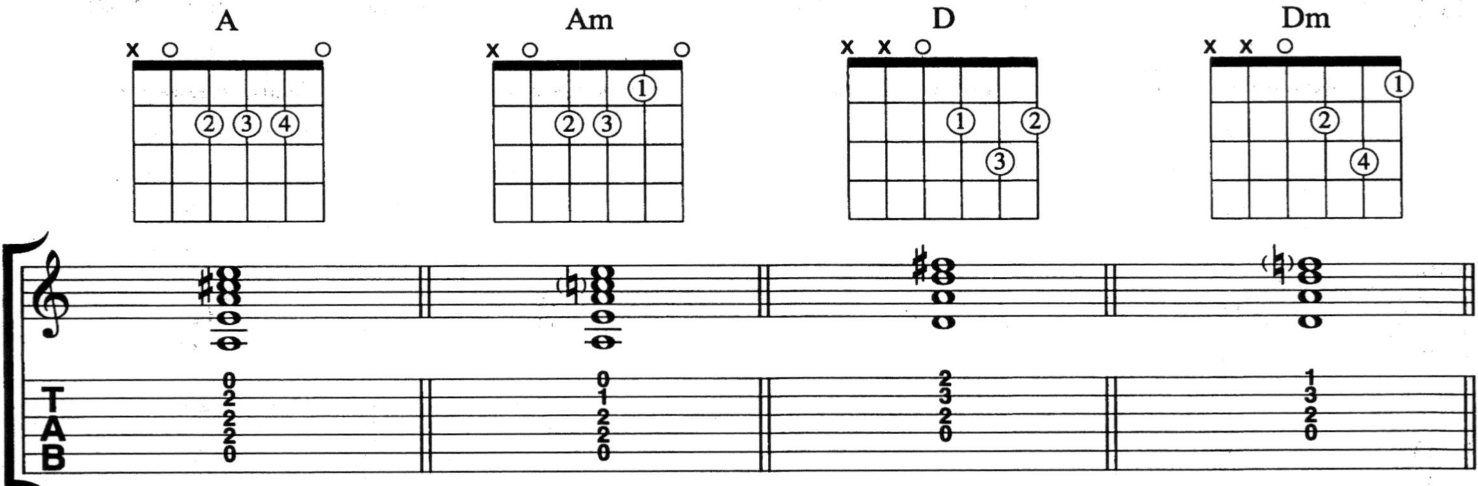

Example 9

Play back and forth between the A and Am chords:

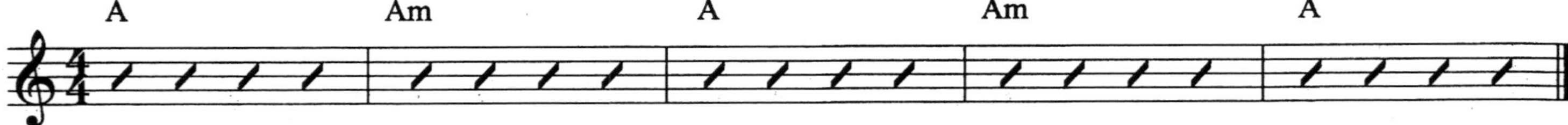

Example 10

Play back and forth between the D and Dm chords:

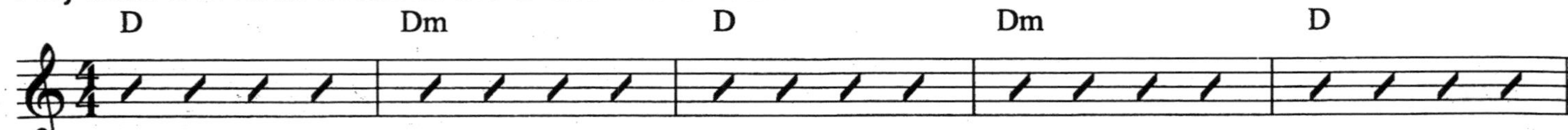

Dominant Chords: Dominant chords differ from major chords by the addition of one note: the 7th. To find the "7th" count up seven from the root (1). Adding the 7th to a major chord makes it a dominant 7th chord.

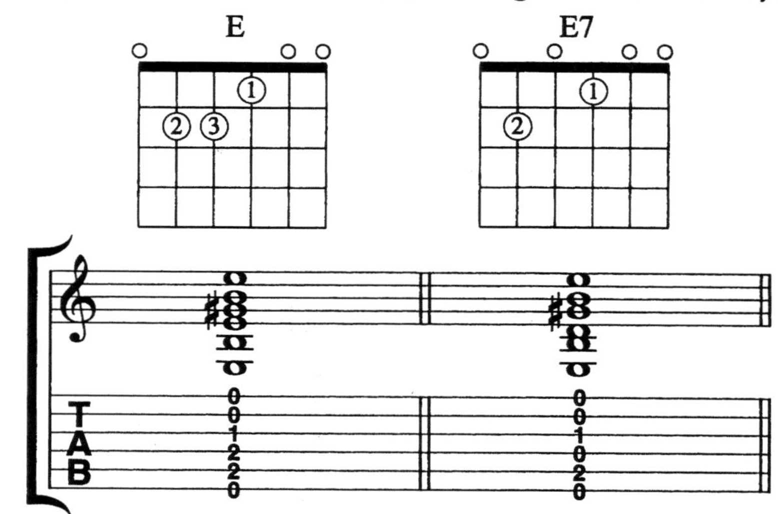

Example 11

Play back and forth between the E and E7 chords. Listen closely to the difference in sound the one new note makes:

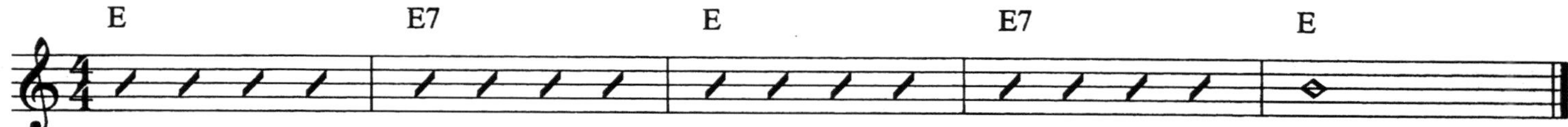

The difference between the A and A7, and D and D7 chords is again the addition of one note: the 7th.

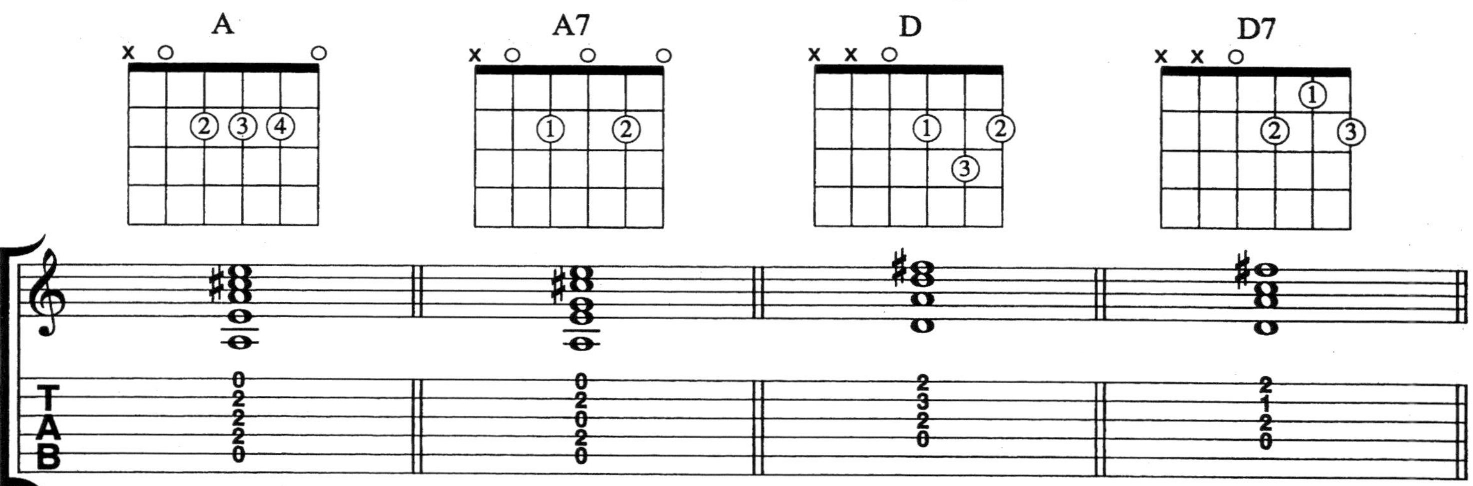

Example 12

Play back and forth between the A and A7 chords:

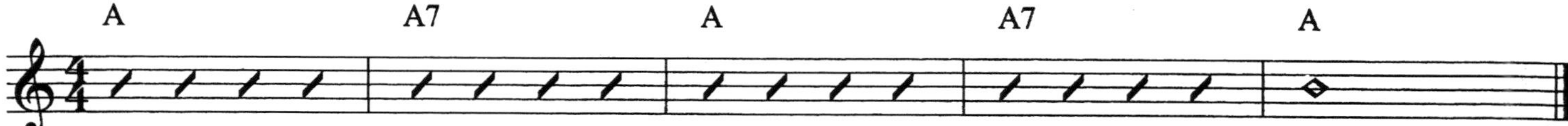

Example 13

Play back and forth between the D and D7 chords:

D D7 D D7 D

The open position G chord can be converted to a dominant chord as shown here. Try fingering the G chord with your 2nd, 3rd and 4th fingers. This will make the change to G7 easier.

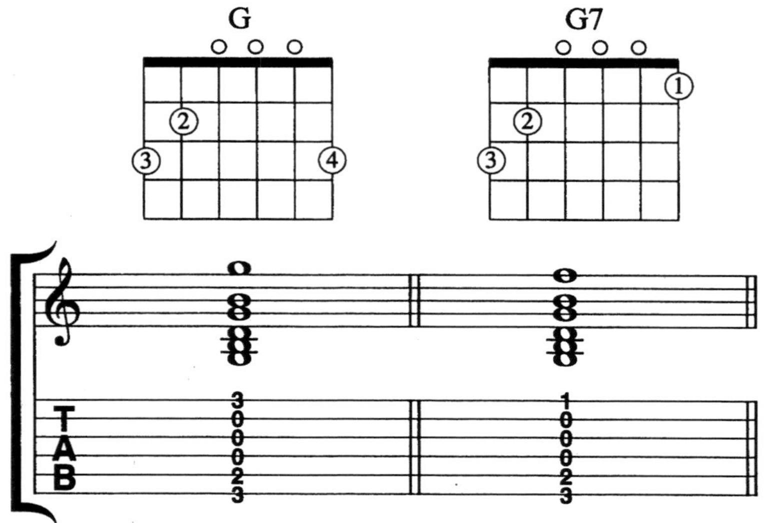

Example 14

Play back and forth between the G and G7 chords:

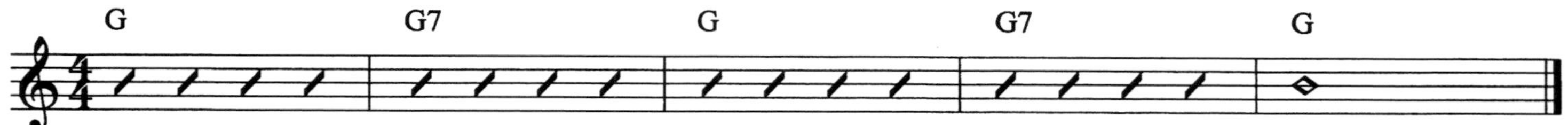

Now try converting the C to a C7. This is done by adding the 4th finger to the 3rd string.

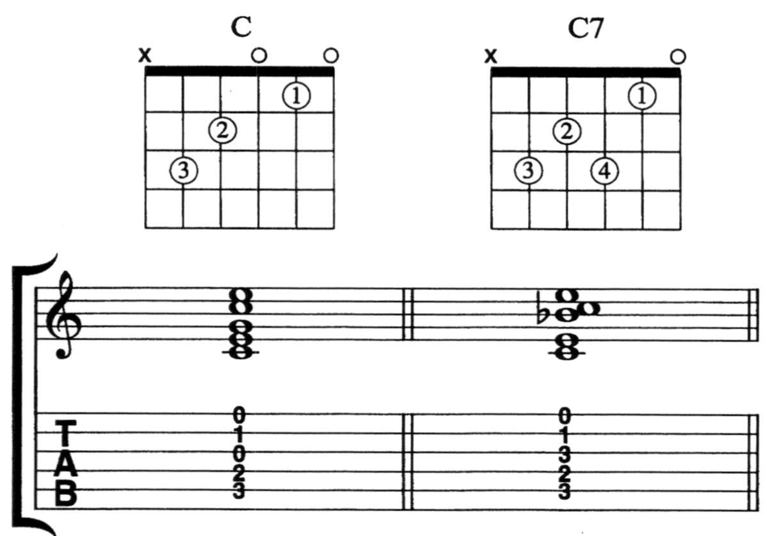

Example 15

Play back and forth between the C and C7 chords:

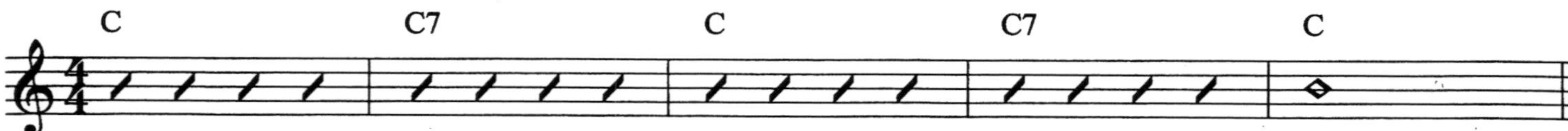

Section 3: Barre Chords

There are two types of barre chords: those with their root on the 6th string and those with their root on the 5th string. Before we learn the barre chords, lets first learn the notes on those two strings.

This diagram shows the location of the natural (no sharps or flats) notes on the 6th string. It is useful to remember that there is a whole step (two frets) between all adjacent natural notes except for "E - F" and "B - C" which are separated by a half step (one fret).

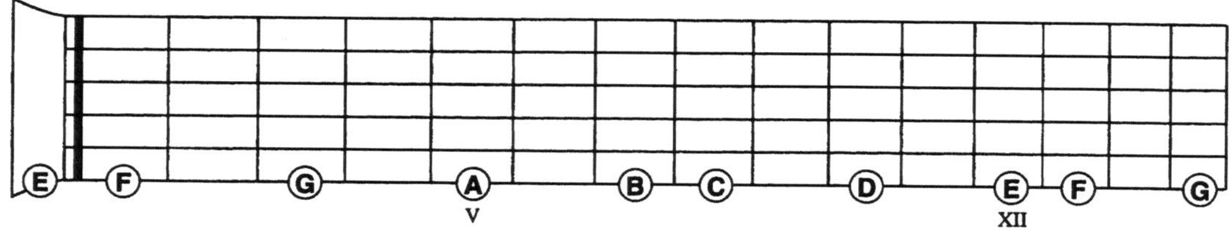

Here are the notes and tablature for the notes on the "E" string. Play these notes until they are memorized.

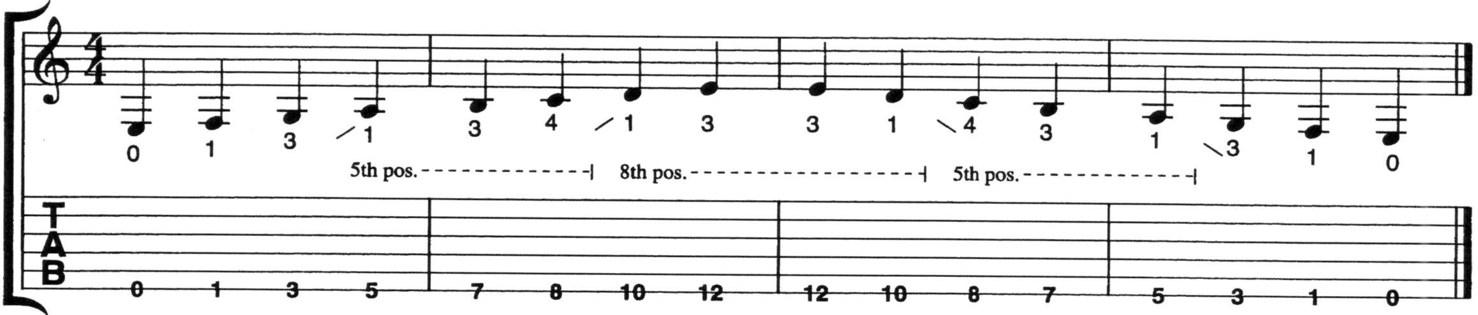

This diagram shows the location of the natural (no sharps or flats) notes on the 5th string. Again, remember that there is a whole step (two frets) between all adjacent natural notes except for "E - F" and "B - C" which are separated by a half step (one fret).

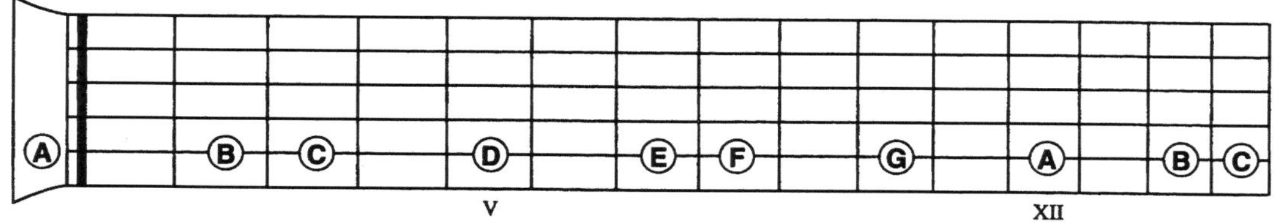

Here are the notes and tablature for the notes on the "A" string. Play these notes until they are memorized.

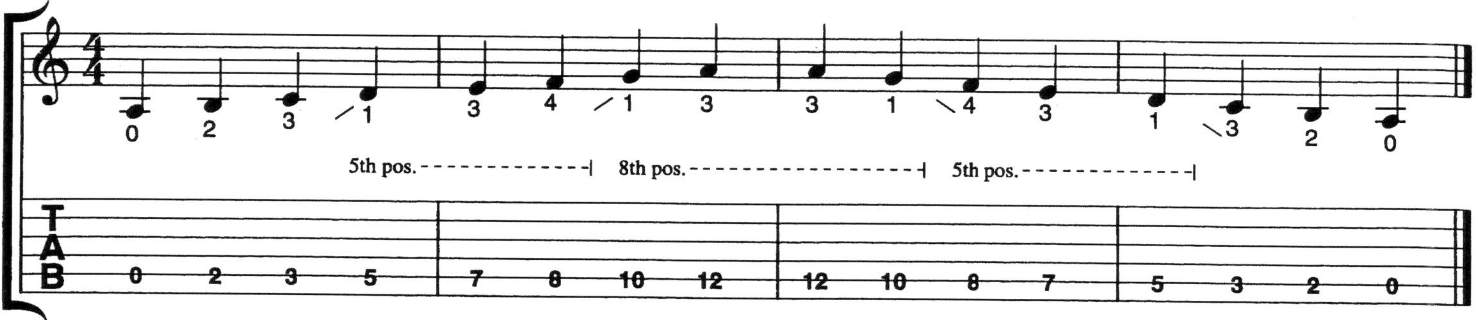

The "E" Type Barre Chord

So far we've only worked on open position chords. With barre chords you can leave the open position and play all around the neck.

Barre Chords: A barre chord is a chord in which two or more of the strings are played by one finger laying across those strings forming a "barre."

The most popular type of barre chord is based on the common E chord. To form the barre chord:

1) Re-finger the E chord with your 2nd, 3rd and 4th fingers.

2) Shift your fingers up one fret.

3) Lay your 1st finger across all six strings at the 1st fret.

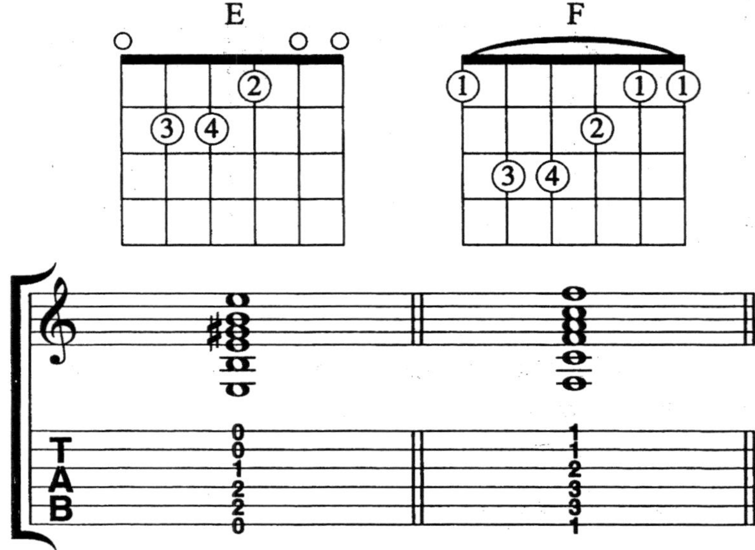

Tip: To add strength to your index finger barre, turn that finger slightly to the side so that the hard, outside edge of the finger forms the barre; not the soft, fleshy part on the inside.

Example 16

Practice playing each of the following barre chords. This could be painful at first. Just relax. Over the next few weeks you'll get the hang of it.

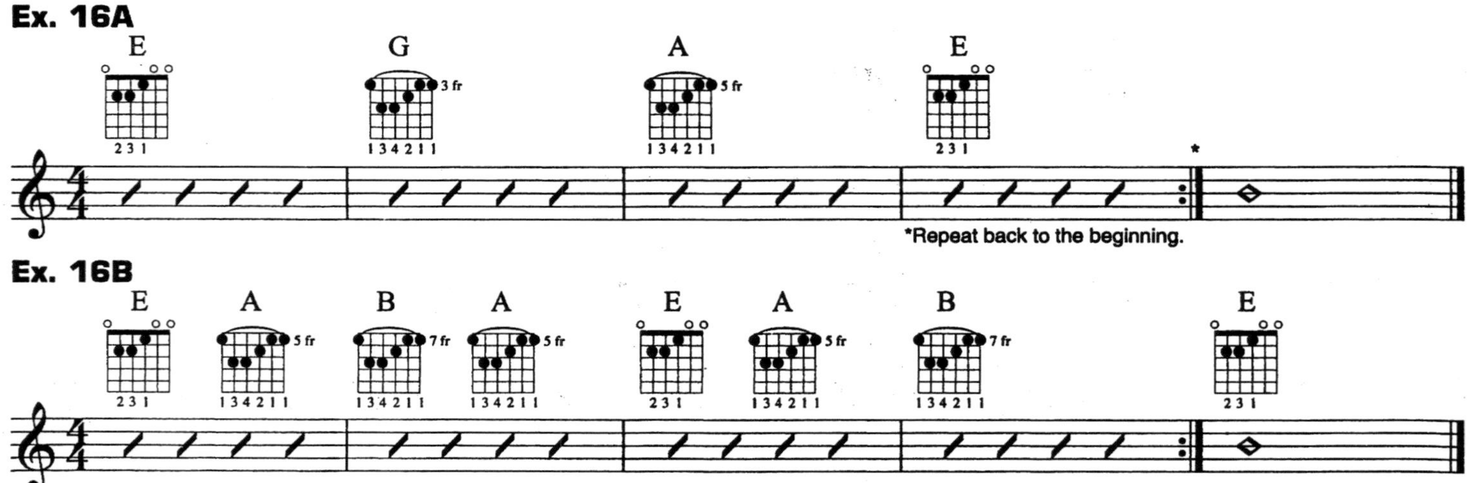

The "A" Type Barre Chord

The other popular type of barre chord is based on the common A chord. To form the barre chord:

1) Shift your 2nd, 3rd and 4th fingers up one fret.

2) Lay your 1st finger across the top five strings at the 1st fret.

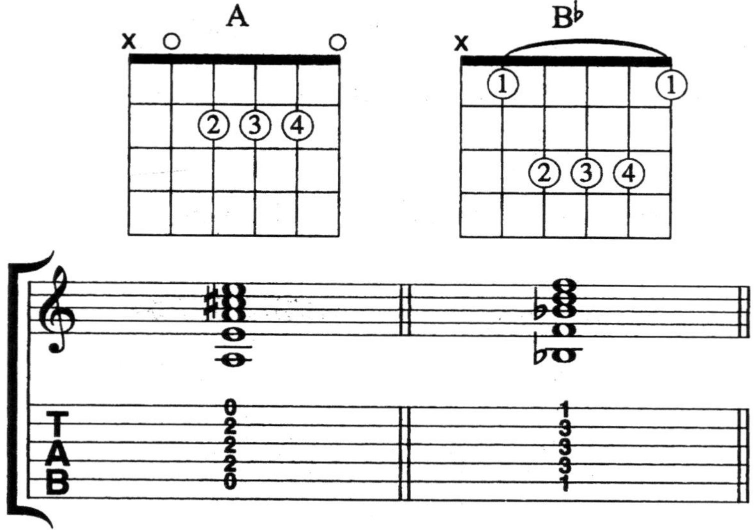

Note: If it is too difficult for you to play the top string you can leave it out and play this as a four-note chord. Here is another popular way to finger this type of barre chord:

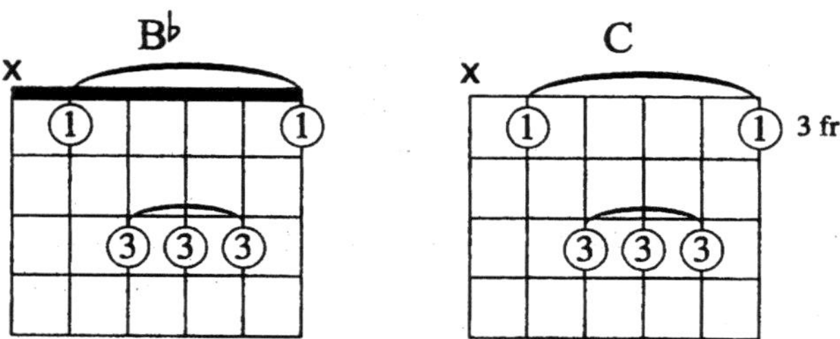

Example 17

This next example uses both types of barre chords.

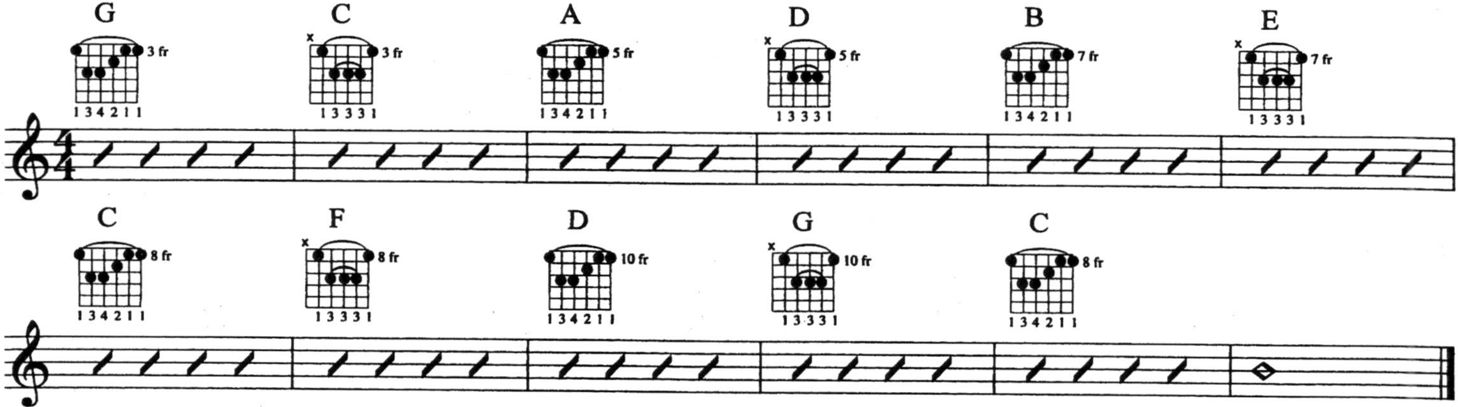

Minor Barre Chords ("E" Type)

Just as you converted the E major chord to an E minor chord by changing one note, you can do the same with the major barre chord.

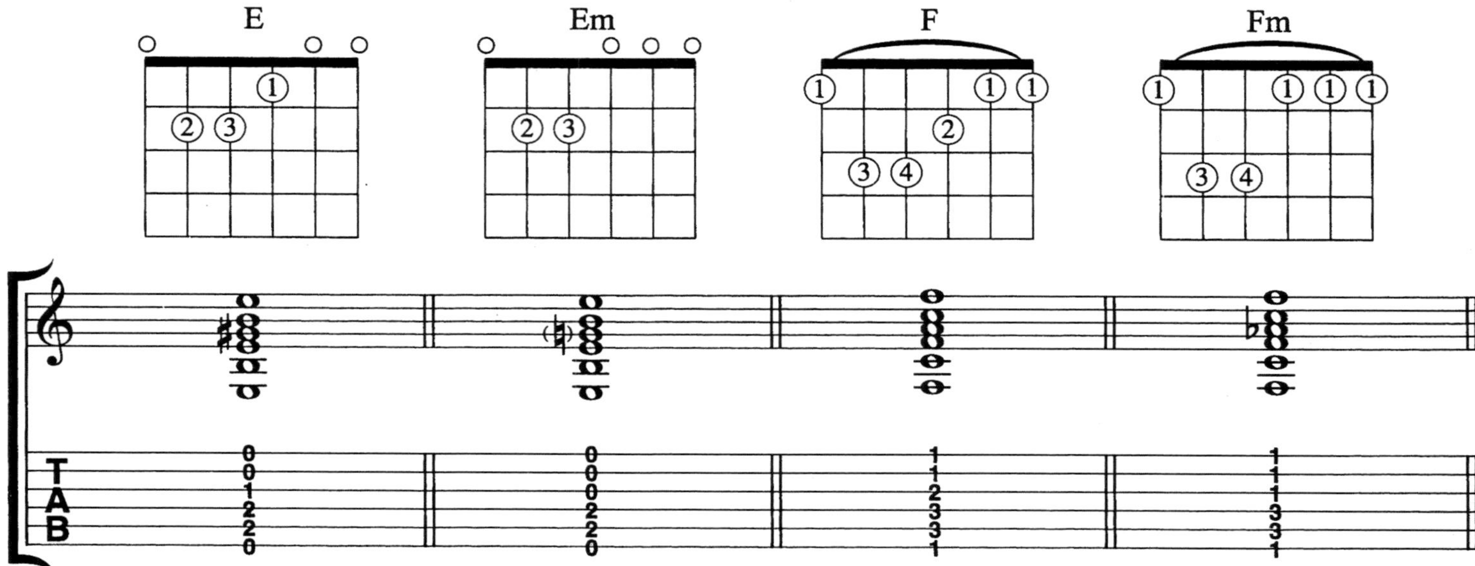

Just as with the major barre chord, the "E" type minor barre chord can be shifted up the neck to any key.

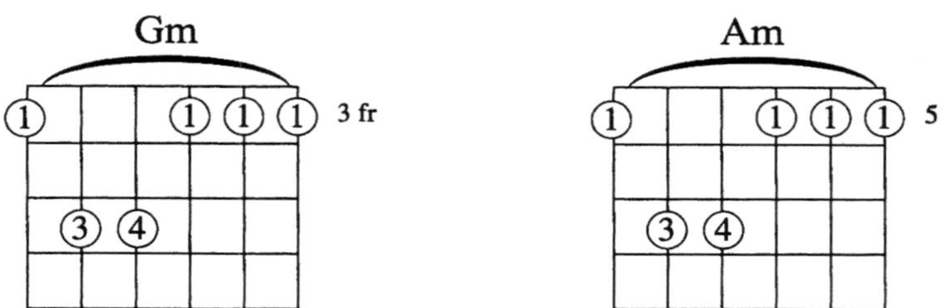

Example 18

Practice moving between these major and minor "E" type barre chords.

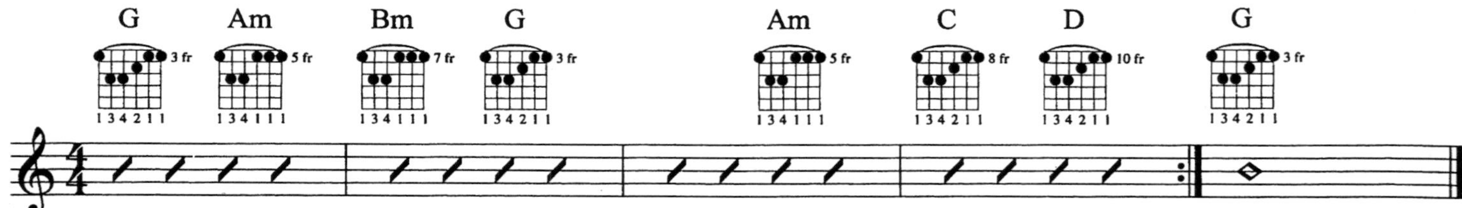

The "A" Type Minor Barre Chord

Now let's convert the "A" type major barre chord to a minor form.

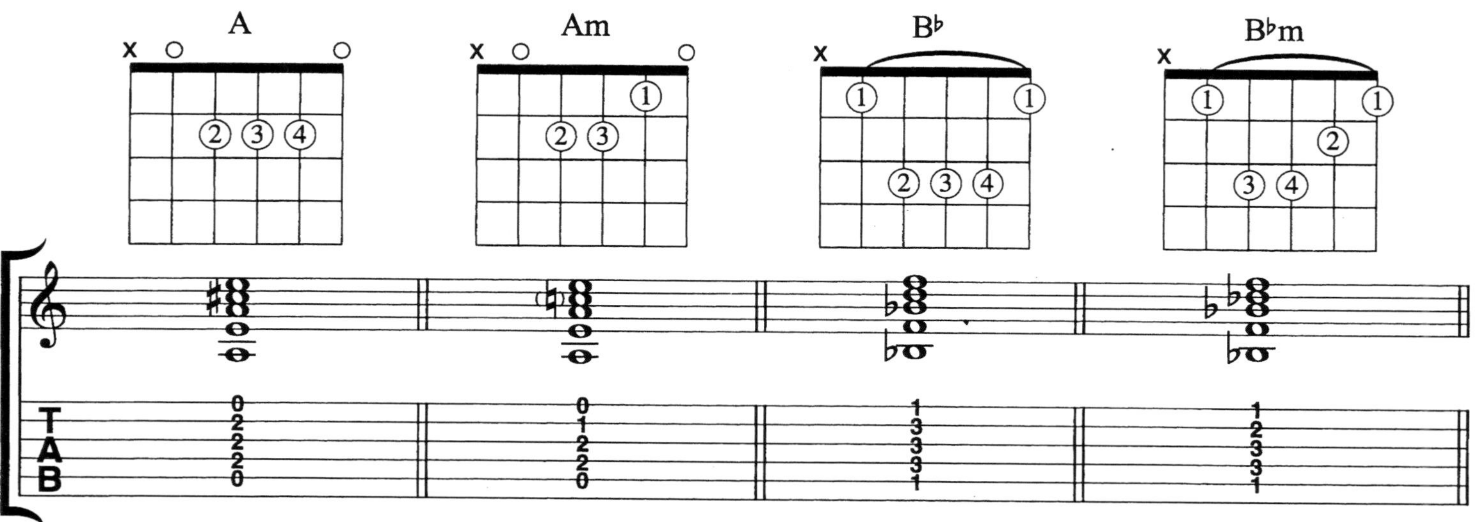

Again, just as in the last example, the "A" type minor barre chord can be shifted up the neck to any key.

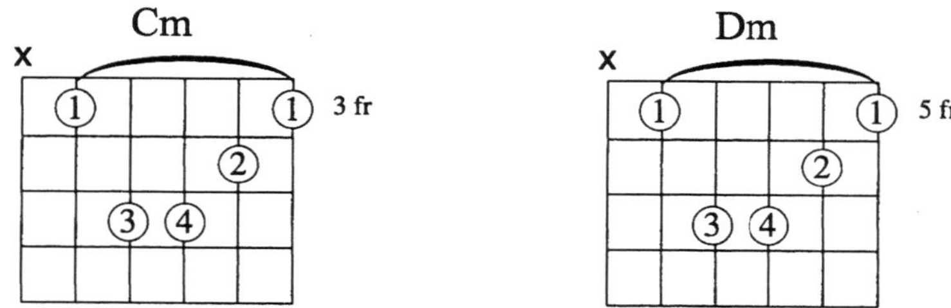

Example 19

Practice moving between these major and minor "A" type barre chords.

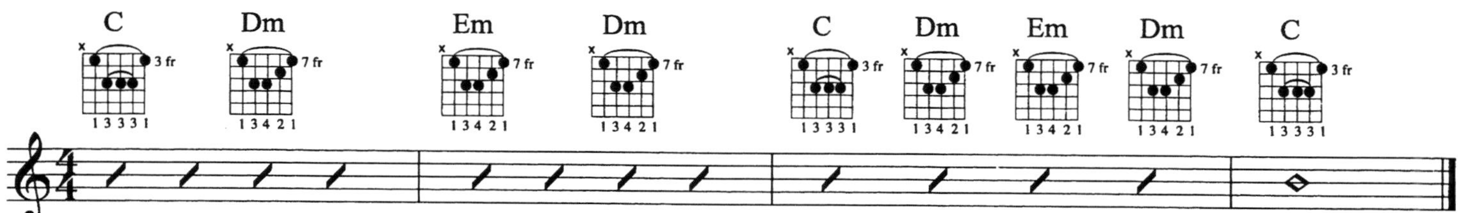

Example 20

This example combines each of the barre chord forms you've learned so far.

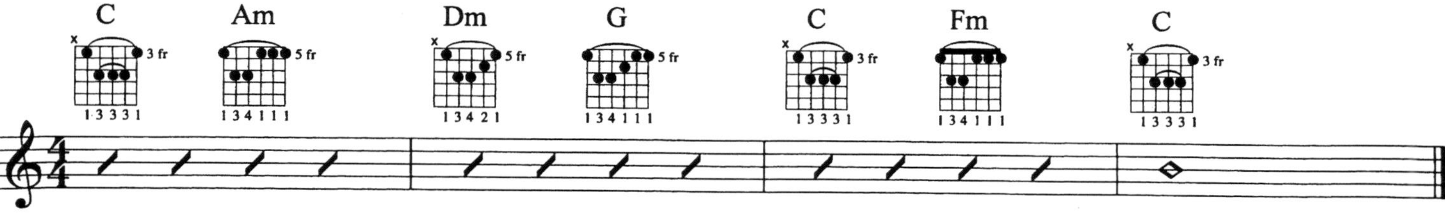

Dominant Barre Chords ("E" Type)

Just as you converted the E major chord to an E7th chord by changing one note, you can do the same with the major barre chord. To play the F7, hold an F barre chord and lift your 4th finger.

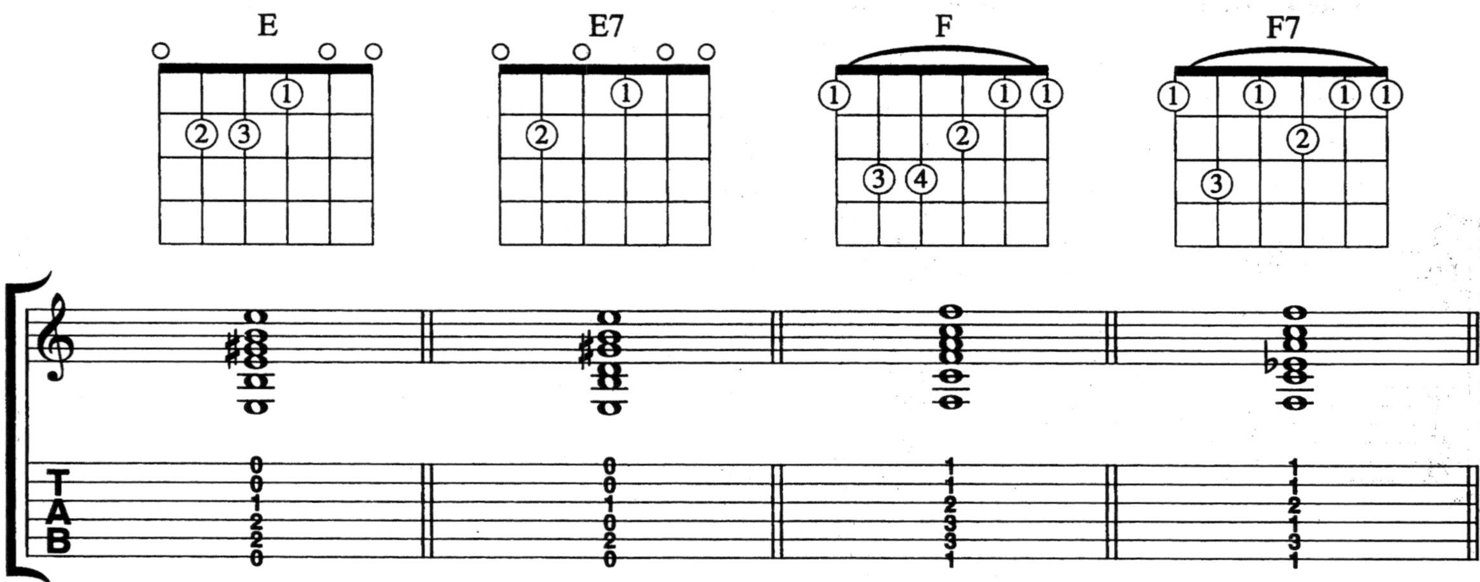

Just as with all the other barre chords, the dominant 7th major barre chord can be shifted up the neck to any key.

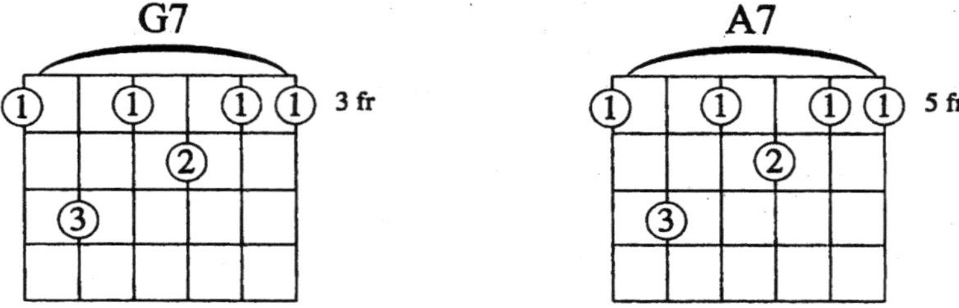

Example 21

This rock progression uses just dominant 7th chords.

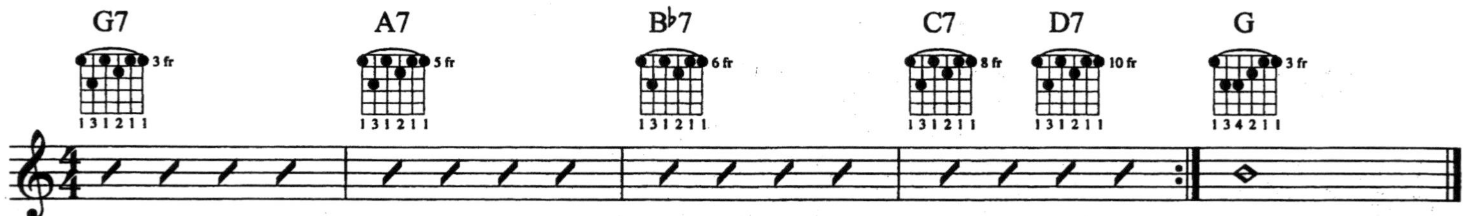

Dominant Barre Chords ("A" Type)

Now let's convert the "A" type major barre chord to a dominant 7th form.

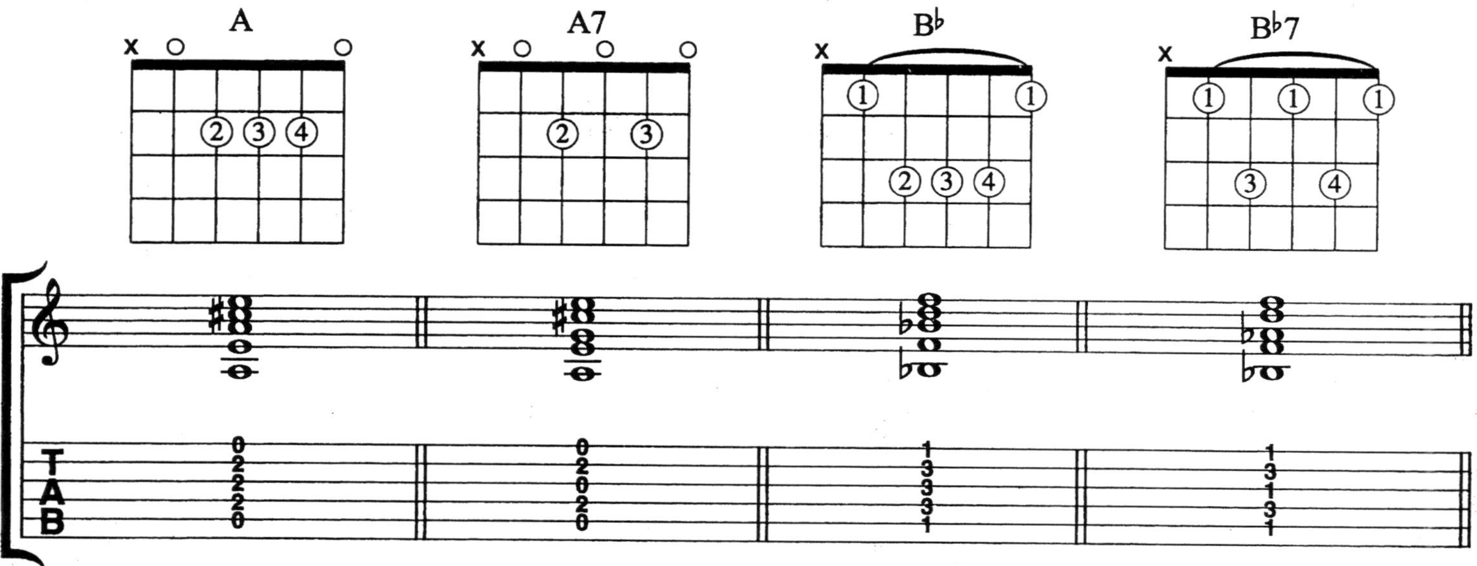

Just as in all the previous examples, the "A" type dominant 7th barre chord can be shifted up the neck to any key.

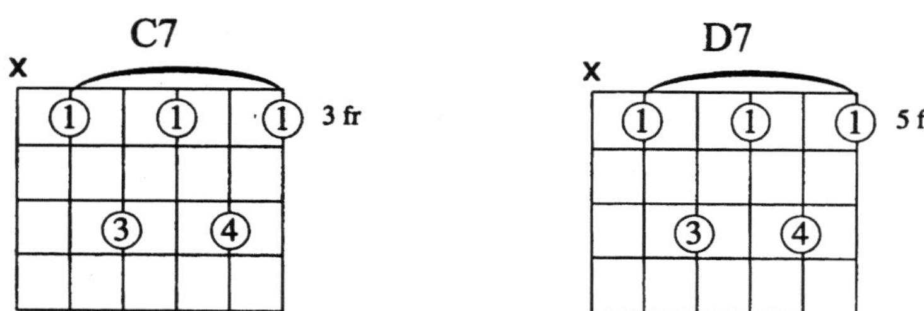

Example 22

This example uses just the "A" type dominant 7th chord.

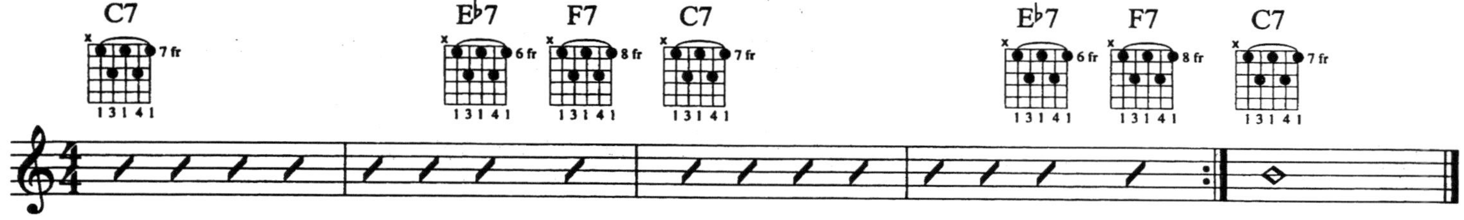

Section 4: Chord Progressions and Strumming

The chord progressions to most songs use combinations of major, minor and 7th chords. Using just the barre chords you've already learned, you can play the chords to almost any song. Here are a few common chord progressions.

Example 23

This first progression is one of the most common, in fact, it's probably the single most common chord progression found in old rock and roll ballads.

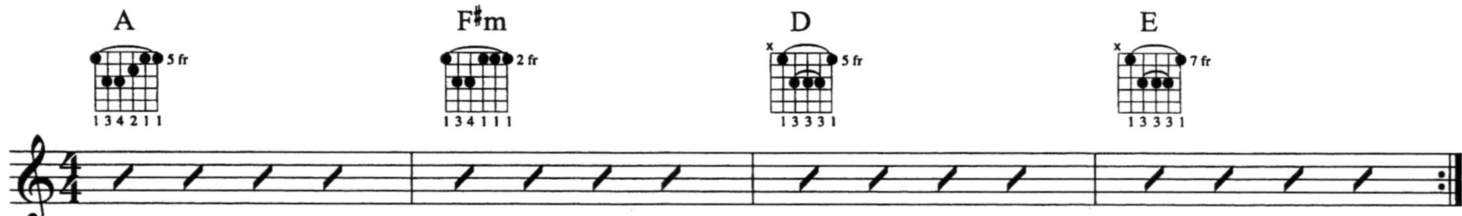

Example 24

Once you can make the transition from one chord to the next cleanly, try it with this strumming pattern.

Example 25

This next progression is designed to help you learn your dominant chords.

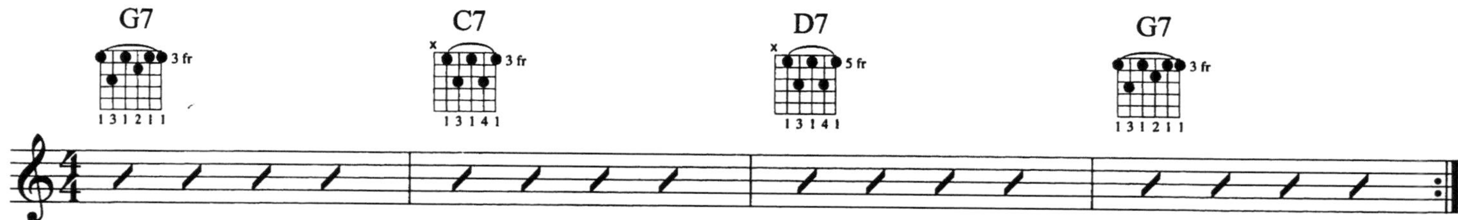

Example 26

Now let's try this chord progression with a new kind of strumming pattern. This pattern uses mostly downstrokes. On the 2nd strum, try **muting** by releasing the left-hand pressure on the strings. When you strike the muted strings you produce a short, muffled, slapping sound that adds a very driving, rhythmic effect to your playing.

Example 27

Now put everything you've learned to work in this next challenging chord progression. This one moves through every single key (12 in all).

* First try playing only major chords for the entire progression. (The major chord forms are shown above the music.)
* After you can play all the chords as major, then try to play only minor chords.
* Next try only dominant chords.
* Finally, experiment with mixing and matching the chord qualities (major, minor or dominant). See which combinations sound best to your ear. Note: Only the major form of each chord is indicated. Convert these to minor and dominant also.

The All Keys Progression

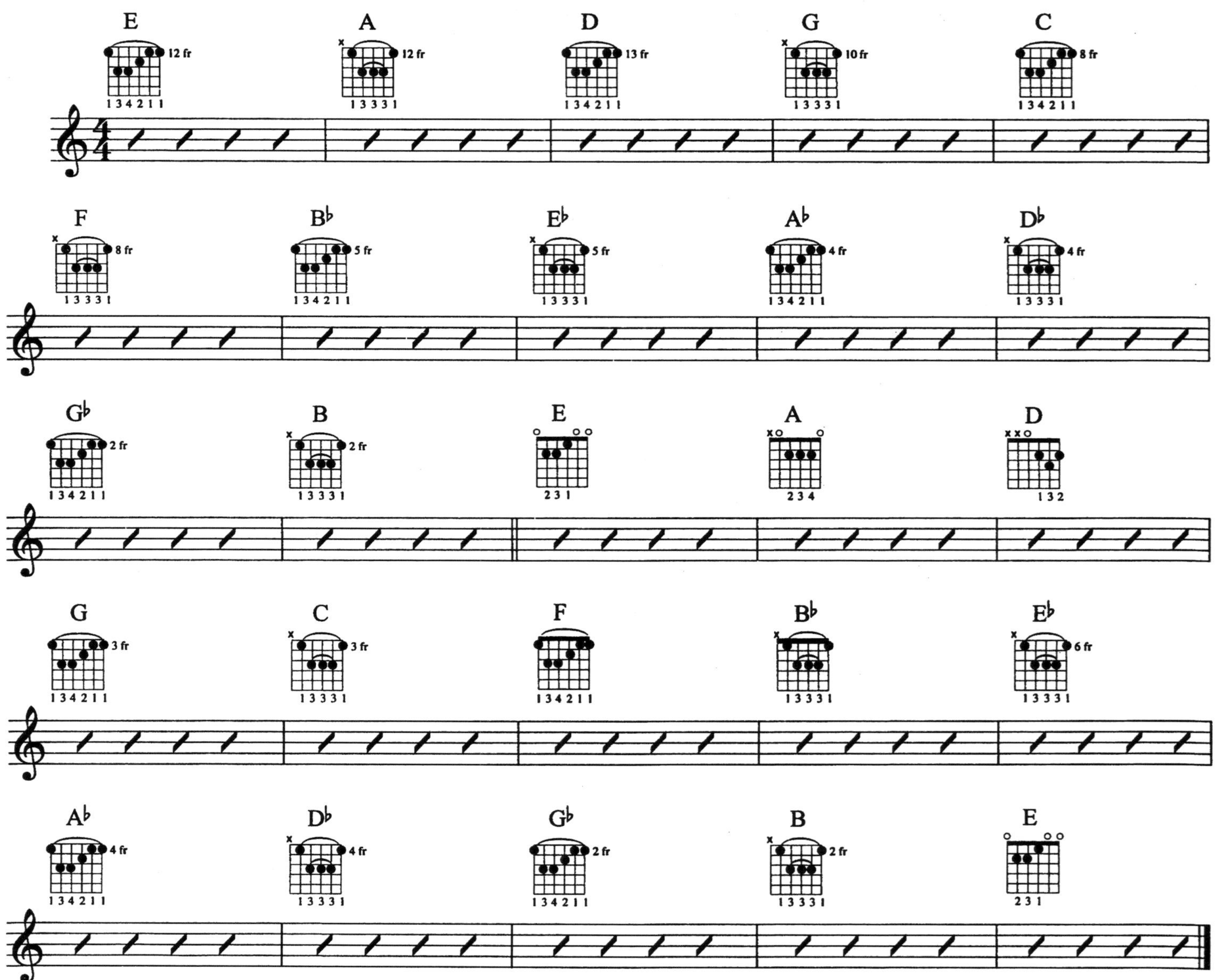

Section 5: Soloing and Picking

Pentatonic scales are found in all types of music, but they are perhaps most commonly associated with blues and rock.

The A Minor Pentatonic Scale

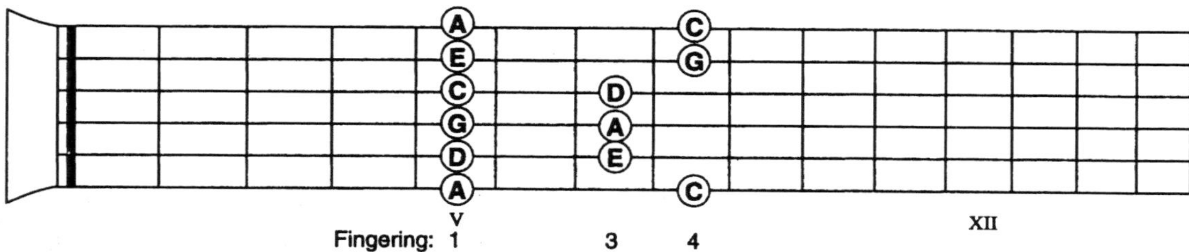

Example 28

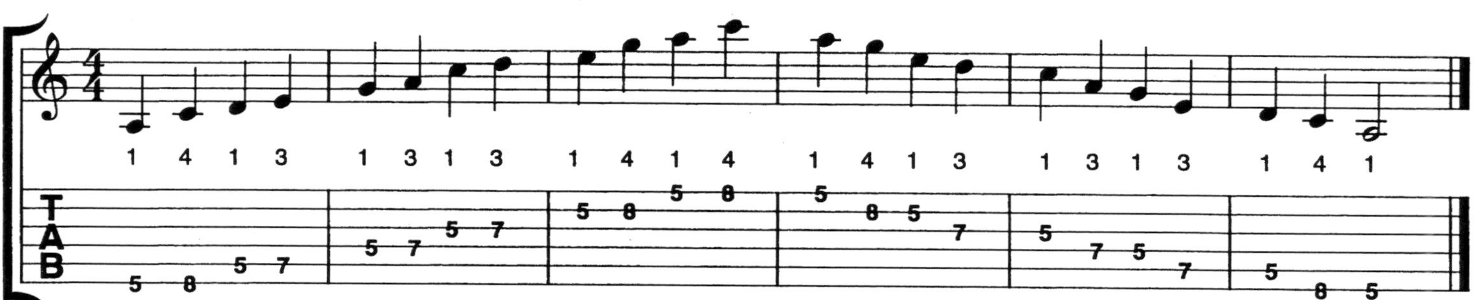

Example 29

Picking: There are three basic pick techniques:

1) The first is the down-stroke (⊓): Strike the string with a downward motion of the pick.
2) The second technique is the up-stroke (V): Strike the string with an upward motion of the pick.
3) Alternate Picking: Usually the down- and up-strokes are combined. The upstroke follows the down-stroke in one smooth motion—strike the string with a down-stroke and then strike the string with an up-stroke as the pick returns to the playing position.

Now play the A minor pentatonic scale with alternate picking.

Coordination Exercises

The most important aspect of developing good picking technique is the coordination of your left and right hands. You must get the pick to strike the string at the exact same instant that the fretting hand is pressing the note down. The following exercises are designed to help you develop good coordination between your left and right hands.

Example 30: The Group of Three

This first exercise involves playing through the minor pentatonic scale in groups of three. This type of repetitive pattern is called a **sequence.** (Note: the "3" above each each group of notes indicates a **triplet**: three notes in one beat.)

Example 31: The Group of Four

This first exercise involves playing through the minor pentatonic scale in groups of four. The tricky part to this pattern is that you often have to use the same left hand finger twice in a row. To do this you'll have to **roll** your fingertip from the first note to the second.

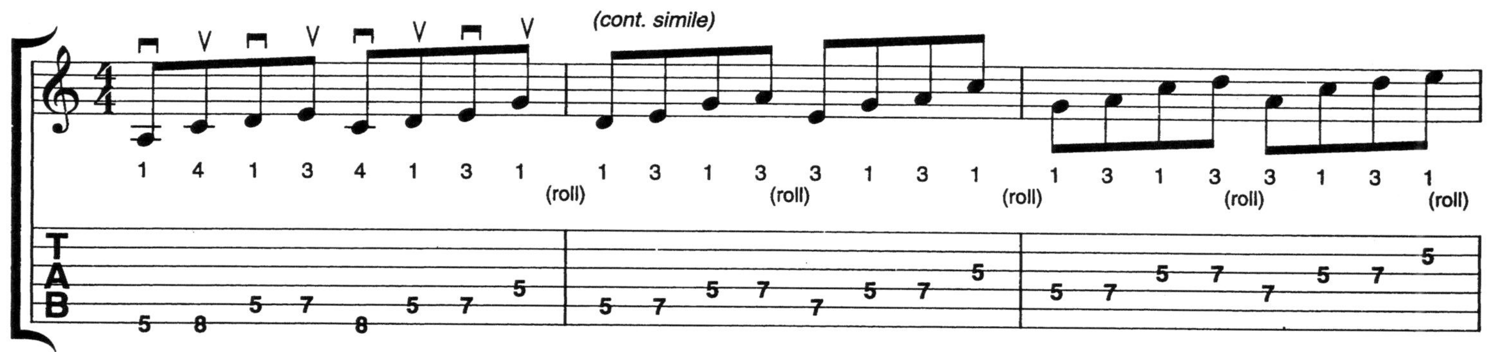
(cont. simile)
1 4 1 3 4 1 3 1 (roll) 1 3 1 3 (roll) 3 1 3 1 (roll) 1 3 1 3 (roll) 3 1 3 1 (roll)
T
A
B
5 8 5 7 8 5 7 5 5 7 5 7 7 5 7 5 5 7 5 7 7 5 7 5

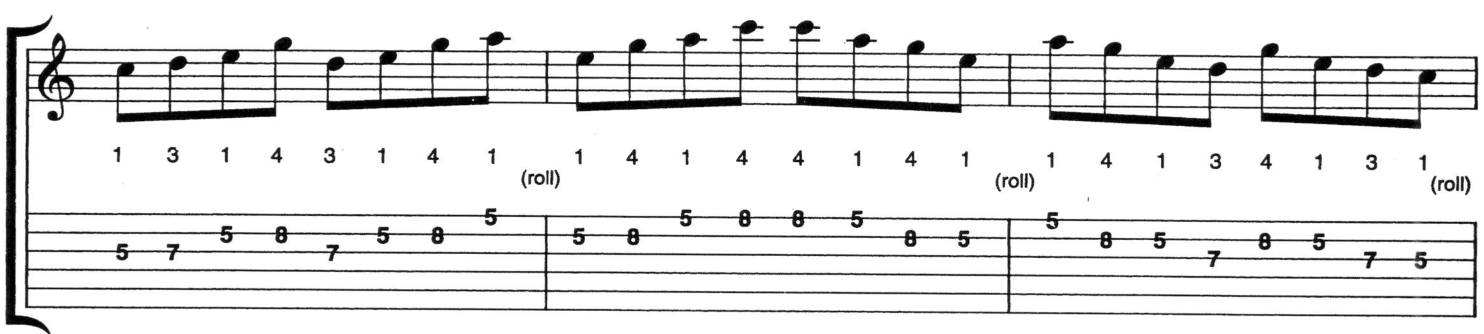
1 3 1 4 3 1 4 1 (roll) 1 4 1 4 4 1 4 1 (roll) 1 4 1 3 4 1 3 1 (roll)
5 7 5 8 7 5 8 5 5 8 5 8 8 5 8 5 5 8 5 7 8 5 7 5

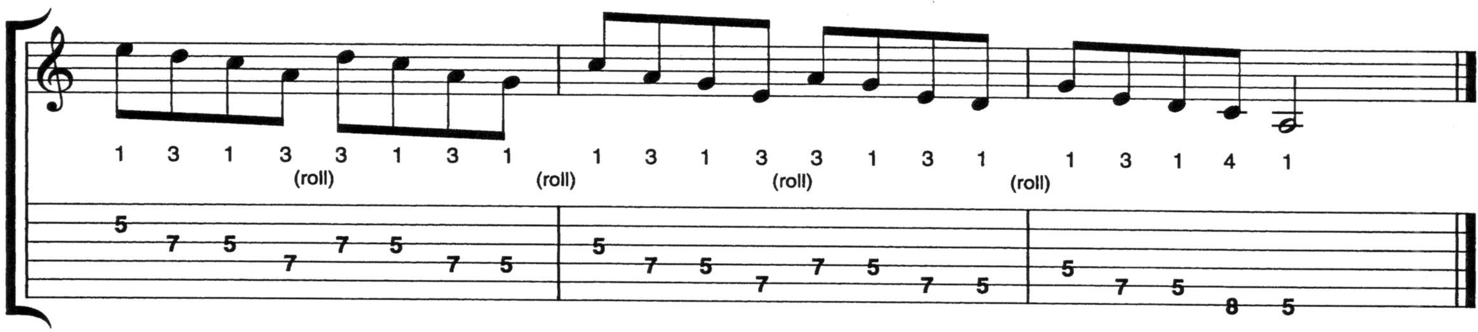
1 3 1 3 (roll) 3 1 3 1 (roll) 1 3 1 3 (roll) 3 1 3 1 (roll) 1 3 1 4 1
5 7 5 7 7 5 7 5 5 7 5 7 7 5 7 5 5 7 5 8 5

Lead Techniques

Hammer-ons, pull-offs and **bends** are three of the most important and guitaristic lead techniques to learn. All three of these are **slur techniques**, meaning that they allow you to play more than one note for each pick attack. Slurs give you a smooth, flowing sound. Picking every note tends to sound choppy and mechanical.

Example 32

Hammer-ons: Whenever you play two notes on the same string, instead of picking both notes, play the first note with your pick and sound the second note by "hammering" your finger down onto the neck. The impact of the finger striking the neck is enough to make a sound. This is actually easier than it sounds. Don't try to hammer too hard. With a little practice this technique becomes pretty easy. Note: You can only hammer "up" from a lower note to a higher note. Each "hammer" is indicated by a curved slur marking in both the notation and tab staves.

Example 33

Examples 33A and B are common A minor pentatonic licks that use the hammer-on technique. Try both picking patterns: all down strokes and alternate picking.

Ex. 33A

Ex. 33B

Example 34

Pull-offs: A pull-off is the opposite of a hammer-on. For example: Plant your first finger on the 1st string "A" at the 5th fret, now place your fourth finger on "C" at the 8th fret. Sound the "A" by pulling your fourth finger **down** off the string with enough force to sound the "A." Note that both the pull-off and hammer-on are indicated by a curved slur marking. **An upward slur is a hammer-on and a downward slur is a pull-off.**

Example 35

Here's a nice Jimmy Page lick. Practice this one slow until you can play it very evenly. Then push it as fast as you can.

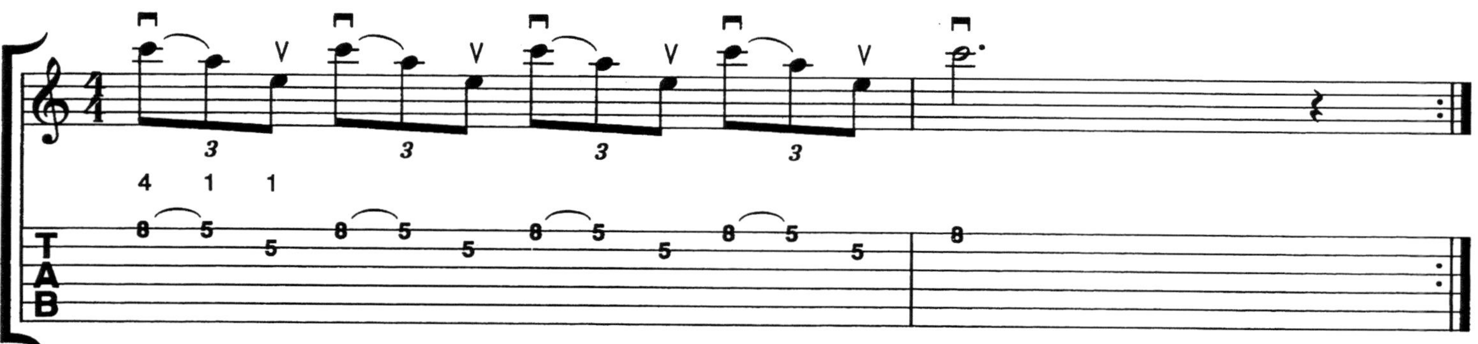

String Bending

String bending is probably the most unique and emotional sounding technique available to guitarists. Bends are used in all styles of electric guitar playing. When we bend notes we are actually imitating the human voice, which is one of the few other instruments with this ability.

This diagram illustrates the two most commonly bent notes in the minor pentatonic scale.

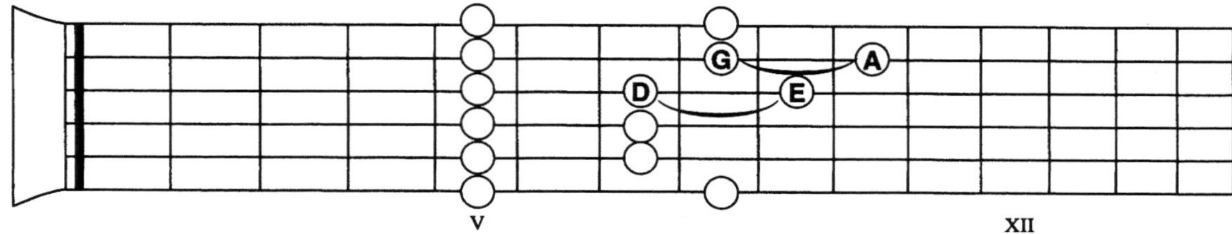

Example 36

First bend the 3rd string "D" up a whole step to "E" (Ex. A). This should sound similar to sliding from "D" to "E" (Ex. B).

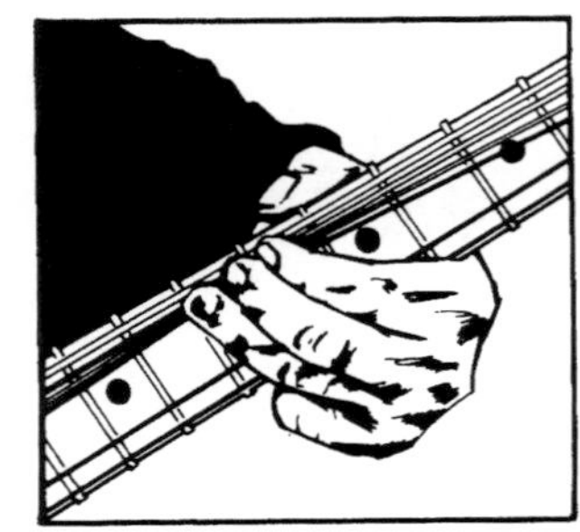

Technique: Don't just bend with your 3rd finger, place your 1st and 2nd fingers on the string also and push with all three. Also, hang your thumb over the top of the neck and bend the string by not only pushing up with your fingers but also by pushing down with the thumb.

Example 37

Now try bending the 2nd string "G" up a whole step to "A." You can use either your 3rd or 4th finger on the "G." Either way, support the bend with your remaining fingers. Again, the bend (Ex. 37A) should match the sound of the slide (Ex. 37B).

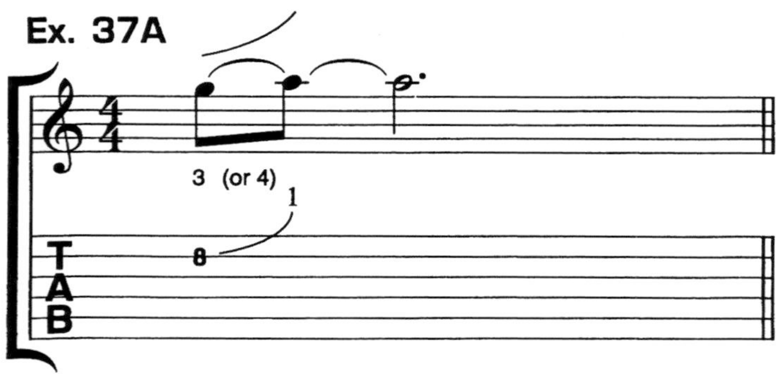

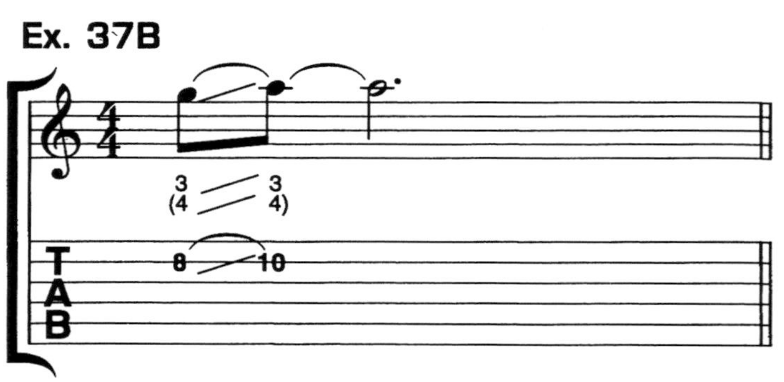

Example 38

You can also bend a string "down" (towards the floor). This is usually done on a 3rd string bend (the 1st and 2nd strings would get pulled right off the neck).

Example 39

Another common blues oriented bend is played with the 1st finger. Try bending the 3rd string "C" a half step (one fret) to "C♯." This is done with the 1st finger pulling down towards the floor. Often in the blues this bend goes only halfway to the C♯. This is called a quarter tone bend.

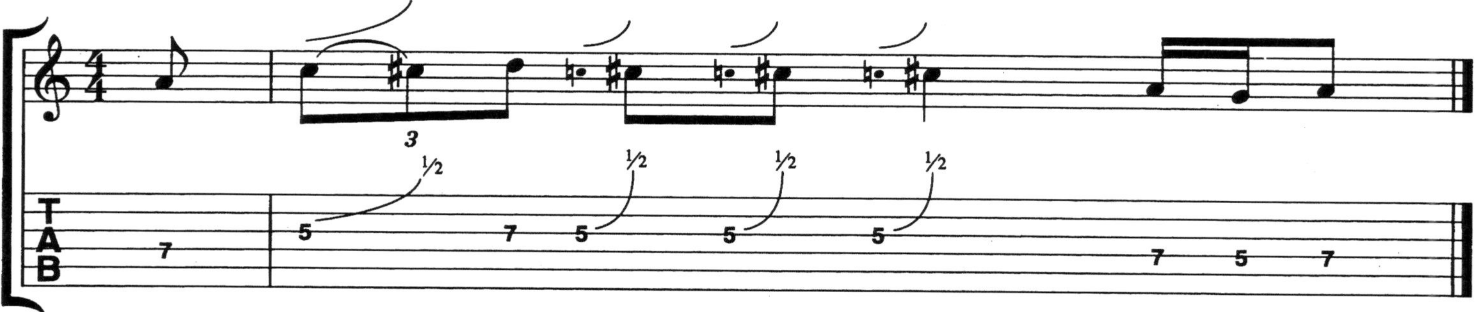

Example 40

Here's a common lick combining bends, hammers and pulls. The whole thing is derived from the A minor pentatonic scale.

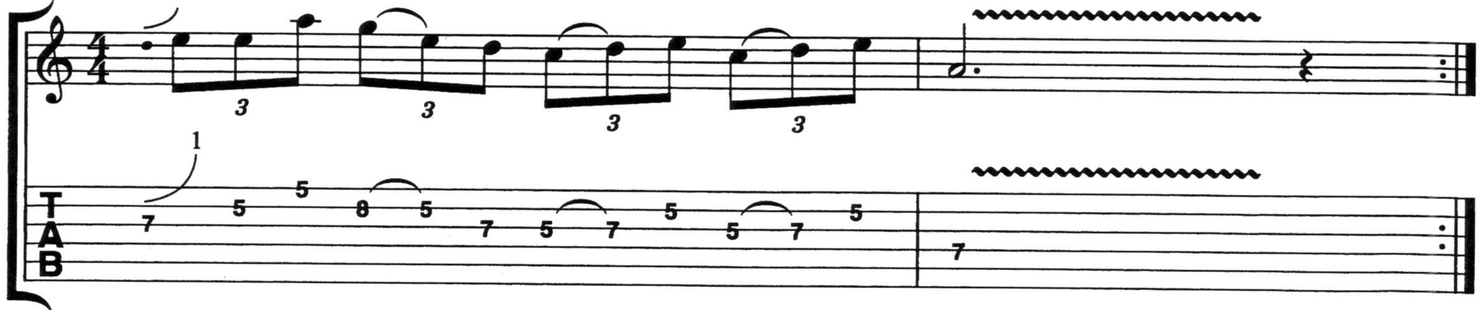

This jam uses everything you've learned so far. All of the notes are derived from the A minor pentatonic scale. Techniques such as hammers, pulls, and bends are applied throughout. Study the video and pick out your favorite licks. Then, use the tablature and the notation to practice until you can play them comfortably.

Ex. 41

The Final Jam

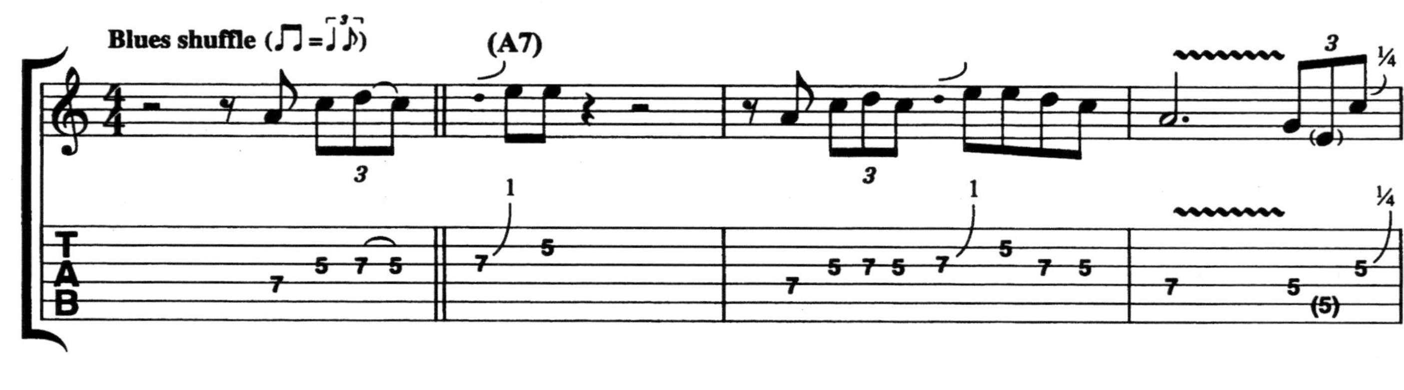

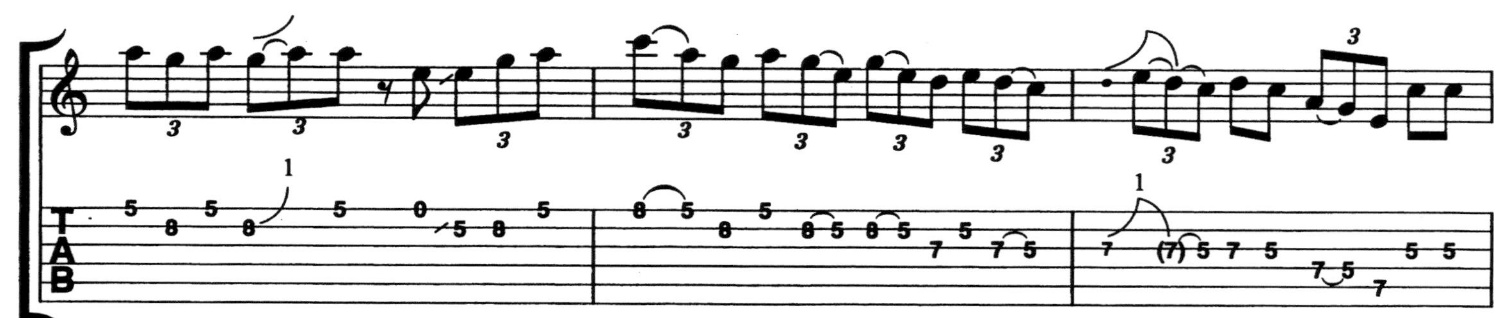

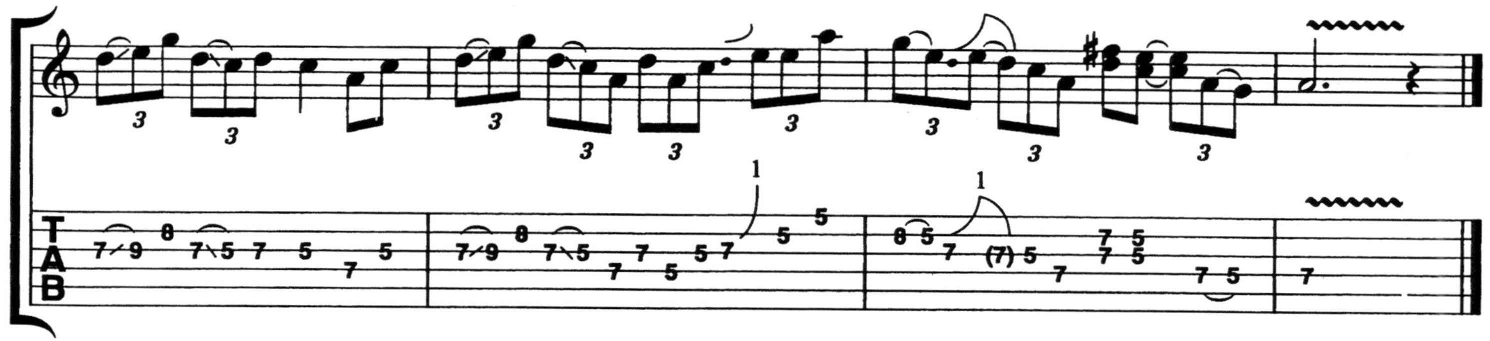

The most important thing in learning to improvise lead is to PLAY A LOT. Here is a blues play-along track in "A." Use the A minor pentatonic scale and all of the licks you've learned so far as you improvise to this track.

Slow Blues Jam

Ex. 42

A7 | D7 | A7 |

| D7 | |

A7 | | E7 |

D7 | A (A7/G D7/F♮ D/F | E7 B♭7 A7)

BLUES GUITAR

SECTION 6: RHYTHM GUITAR

Example 43

Rhythm is the driving force behind the blues. It may not take many notes to play good blues, but the rhythm must be strongly felt. The eighth note triplet is the most common rhythm in blues music. The eighth note triplet divides a beat (one quarter note) into three equal parts. **The shuffle rhythm uses the first and last notes of the triplet to create a smooth and relaxed feeling.**

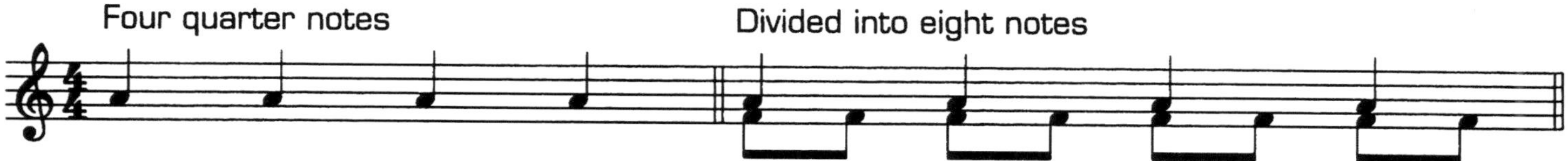

Example 44

Accenting the first note of each triplet figure brings out the natural, swinging quality of the shuffle. Let's also add palm muting with the pick hand by deadening the low E string. This makes for a percussive effect. Use only down-strokes.

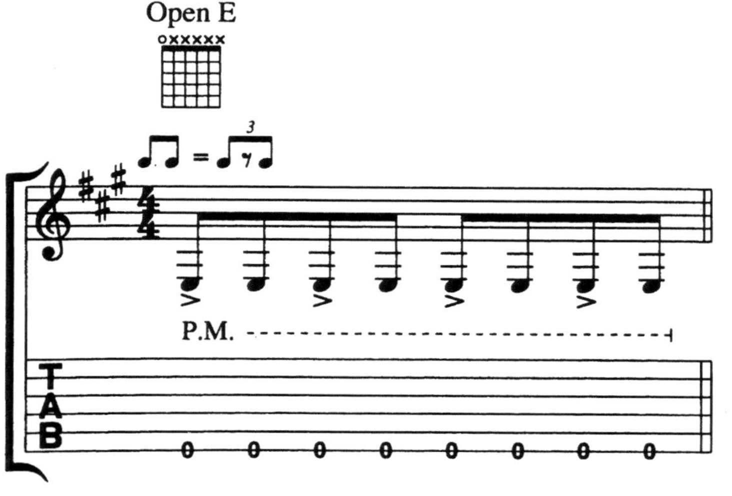

Example 45

Two and three-note chords are made by harmonizing the E note with notes on the A and D strings. This chord is known as E5 or an E "power chord".

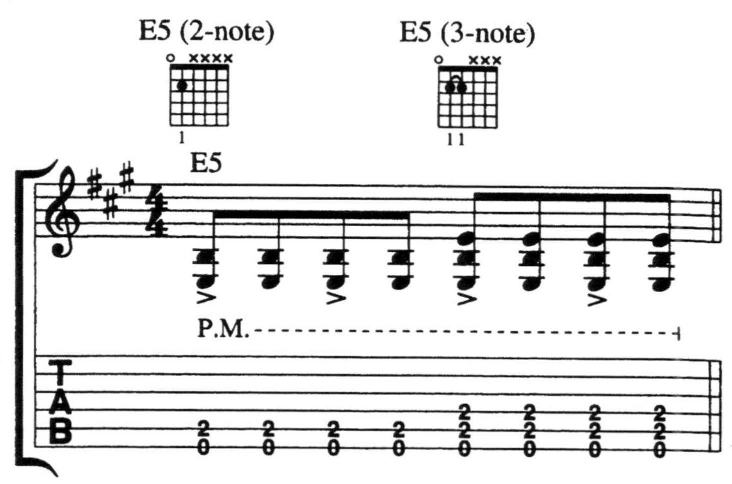

Example 46

Adding another chord (E6) helps us to play the main staple of blues guitar rhythms known as "the boogie". Continue to accent and palm mute. Note the up-stroke on the last chord of the bar.

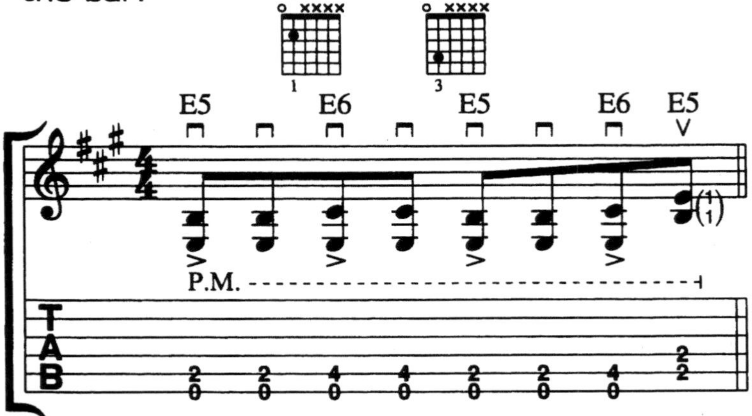

Example 47

If you transpose these "shapes" (E5 and E6) to the next two sets of strings you get A5 and A6 (on the 4th and 5th strings) and D5 and D6 (on the 3rd and 4th strings). These are all the chords needed for a typical 12-bar blues boogie pattern in the key of A.

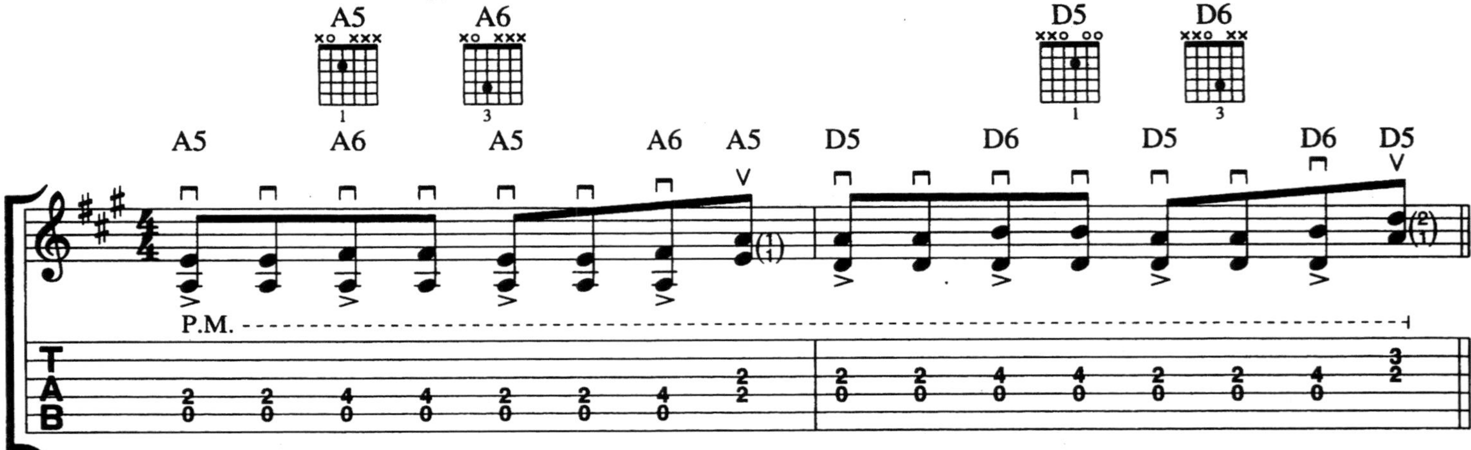

Example 48

In order to play in other keys, we must transform these open position chords into moveable barre chords. When played in 5th position, the A5, A6, D5 and D6 chords all sound identical to the open position versions, only now with new fingerings. The E5 and E6 end up being an octave higher than the originals.

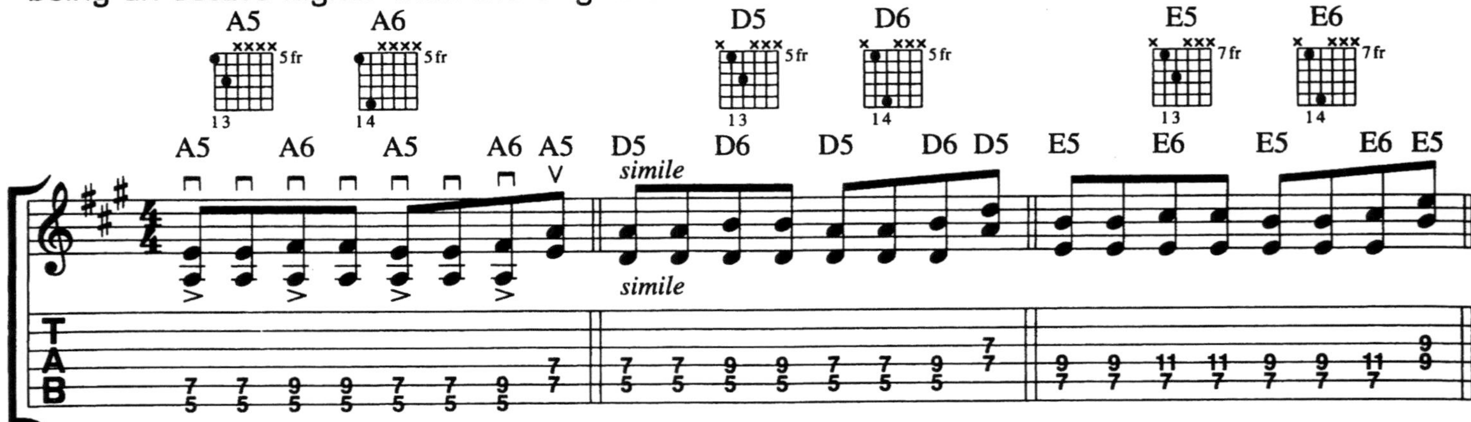

THE 12-BAR BLUES PROGRESSION

The 12-bar blues is the most common form of the blues progression. It is 12 measures long and uses the 1st, 4th and 5th chords of the key. Those chords are usually indicated with Roman numerals (I, IV and V) and can easily be determined by counting up through the alphabet from the key note. For example:

Blues in the key of A:

The A Blues Progression:

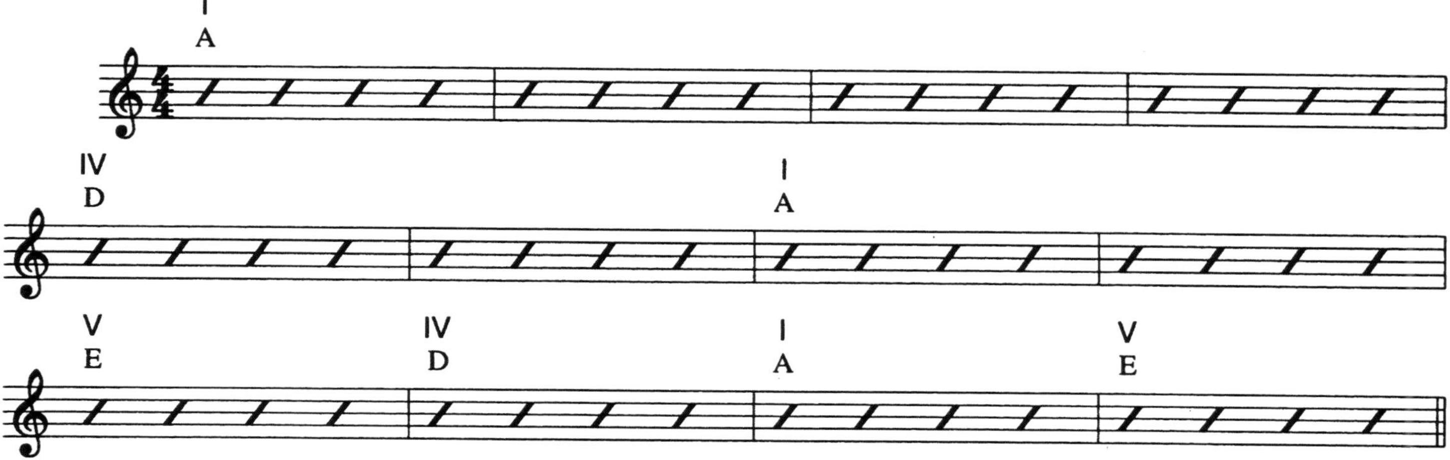

Example 49: The Turnaround

A common variation for the end of the progression is called a turnaround and it requires a new chord called E9. A turnaround marks the end of the progression and sets us up to repeat from the top. Notice how this last bar (bar 12) remains on the I chord for the first beat before an F9 is played on beat two, serving as a passing chord to E9 which hits on the "and" of beat two.

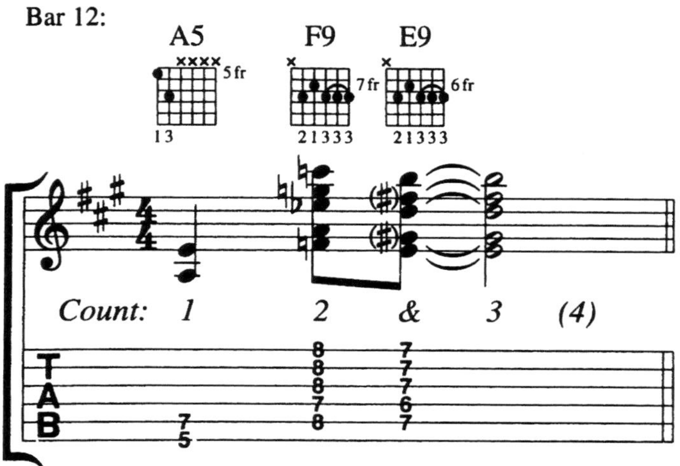

OTHER RHYTHM PATTERNS

Now that the fundamental rhythm pattern has been established, it is important to compliment it with contrasting patterns that can be played simultaneously or separately.

Example 50

This first variation uses an A7 barre chord played with accented "stabs" on "1" and the "and" of 2. Notice there are only two stabs per measure, the rest of the strums are muted string hits that serve as your metronome.

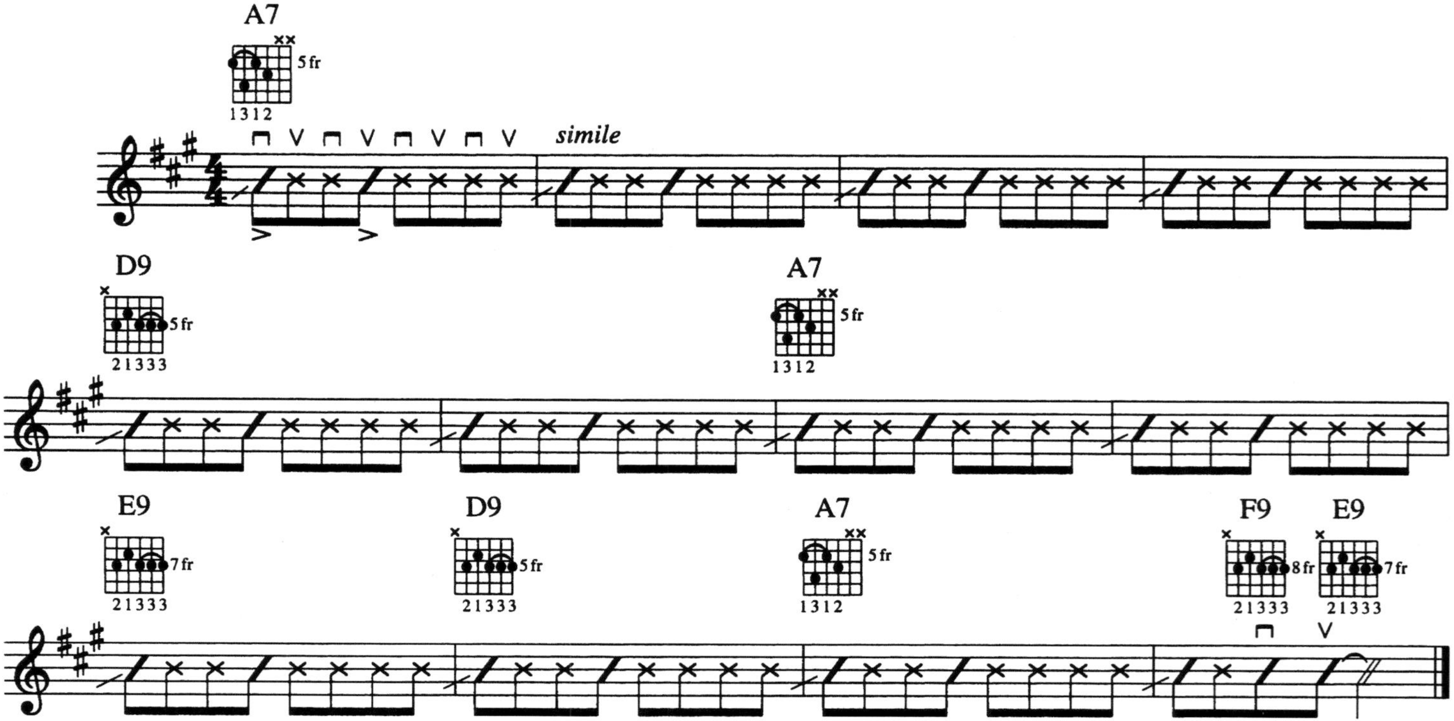

Example 51

This variation involves a hammer-on while other notes are sustained. The 1st finger is barred across the top four strings at the 5th fret, momentarily creating an Am shape. Hammer the 2nd finger onto the 3rd string/6th fret. The shape becomes A major. A small 3rd finger barre at the 7th fret is played before repeating the hammer-on. This idea is then transposed to the IV and V chords.

Example 52

An alternative to hammering is sliding. In this example we slide into the I, IV and V chords from a half-step below.

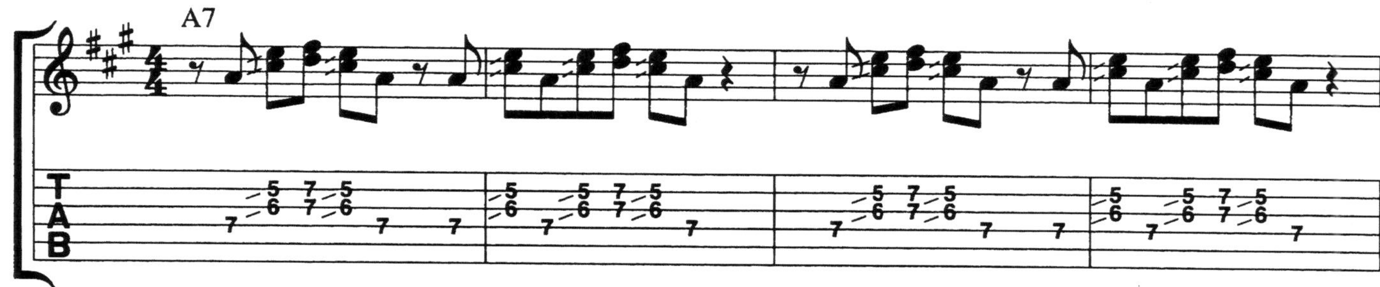

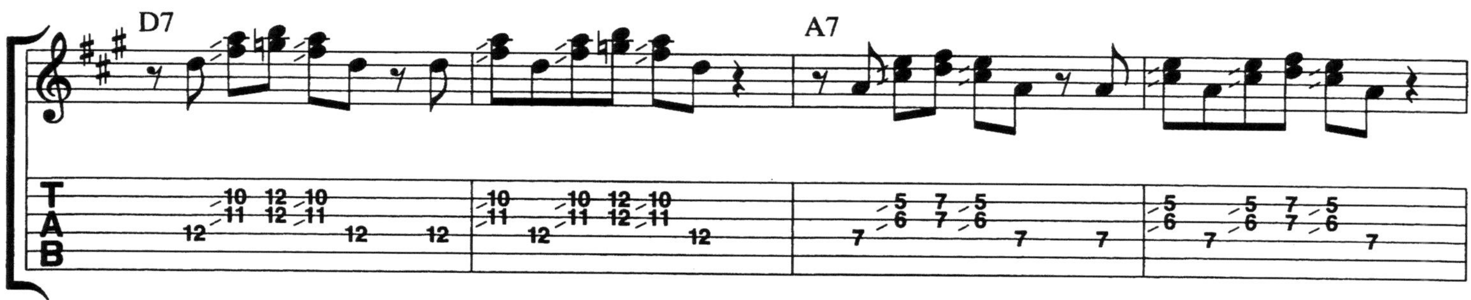

Example 53

This example requires some quick changes of position and fingerings as it goes from 5th position to 7th position and back again. The chord at the 7th position is a two-note voicing for A7 — a useful sound for blues.

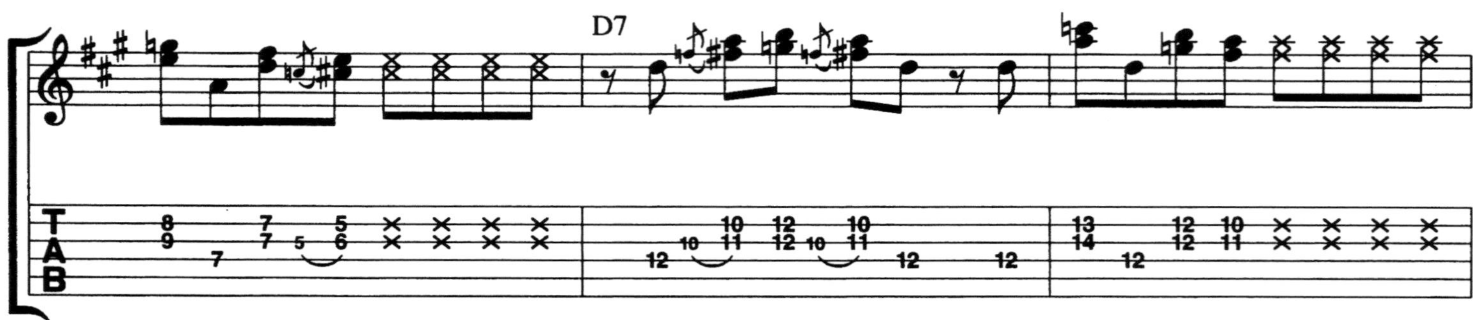

Example 54

With this variation, let's add the first string to the two-note chords of the last example. Notice how adding the high notes gives the chords more melodic interest. This pattern employs the hammer-on and the slide together.

SECTION 7: BLUES SOLOING

The most important sound for blues guitar is the **minor pentatonic scale**. This is a five-note scale derived from the full seven-note minor scale. In the key of A, the minor pentatonic scale is:

A	C	D	E	G
1	♭3	4	5	♭7

These minor pentatonic scales can be fingered across the neck in every position and octave, but we will concentrate on the most common fingerings used by blues guitarists.

Example 55

This is the most common fingering for the minor pentatonic scale. It is shown here in the 5th position (key of A).

The A Minor Pentatonic Scale

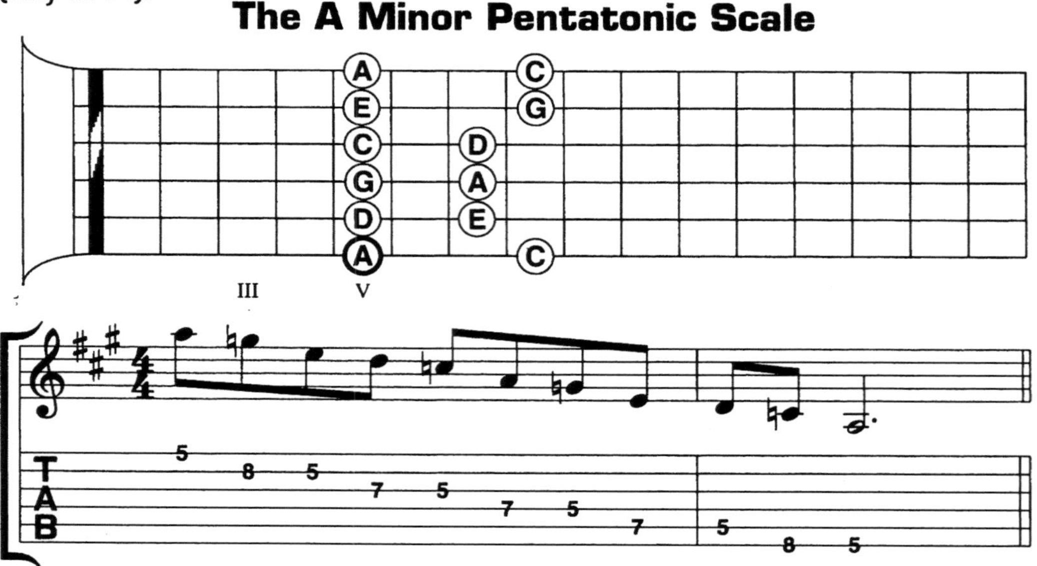

Example 56

Adding the note known as the ♭5 (E♭ in the key of A) makes the minor pentatonic scale even "bluesier". Now we have a six-note scale with this "blue note" added in two places. It is known as the **"blues scale"**.

The A "Blues" Scale

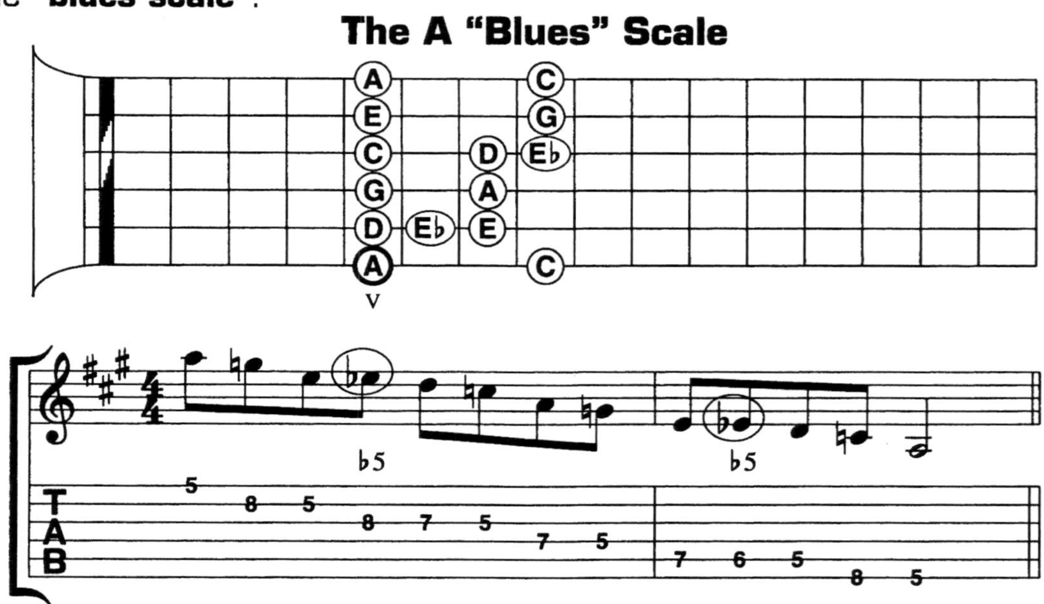

Example 57

Here is a good example of blues phrasing using the ♭5 to add "color" to the minor pentatonic scale. Notice how slurring (hammer-ons, pull-offs and slides) gives the E♭ blue note a "singing" quality.

Example 58

Here is another example that highlights the ♭5 in the blues scale.

Example 59

To get your fingers used to the blues scale pattern, try running up and down this complete 5th position version of the blues scale.

Example 60

Now we will extend the scale fingering. This will give you more room to move around the neck while improvising. These extensions are affectionately known as "boxes" to guitar players. The lower extension (or blues "box") adds a low G and a C which sounds exactly the same as the C you've been playing on the 6th string, 8th fret. The high extension adds an alternate fingering for the E and A and a new high C and D.

Your 1st and 3rd fingers create the "boxes" as you shift in and out of 5th position.

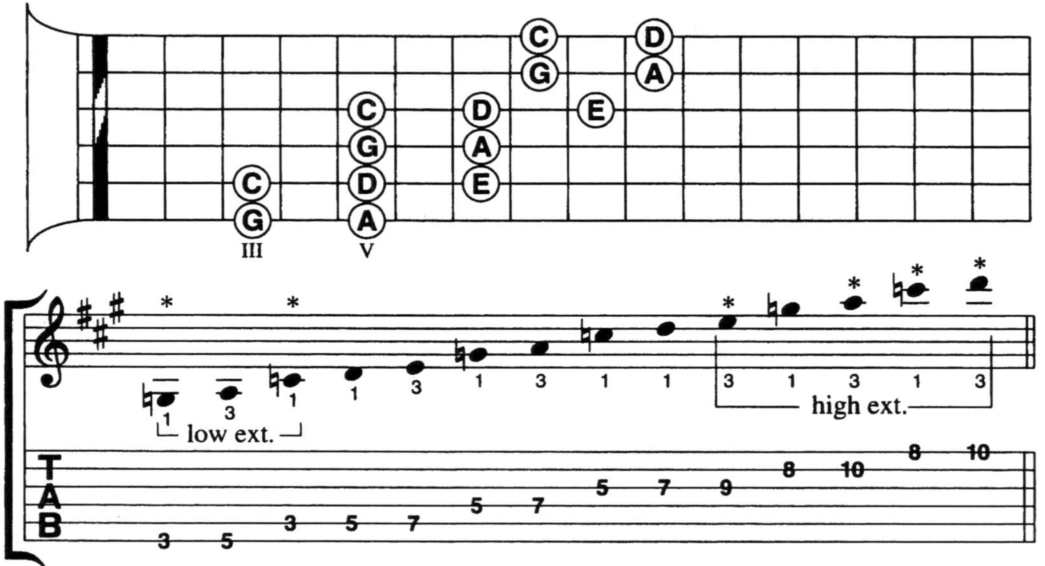

Example 61

The high extension is a hot spot in blues guitar playing. All five notes of the minor pentatonic scale are found here and it's a great place to bend notes. This next example shows some blues phrases with bends on the 1st string.

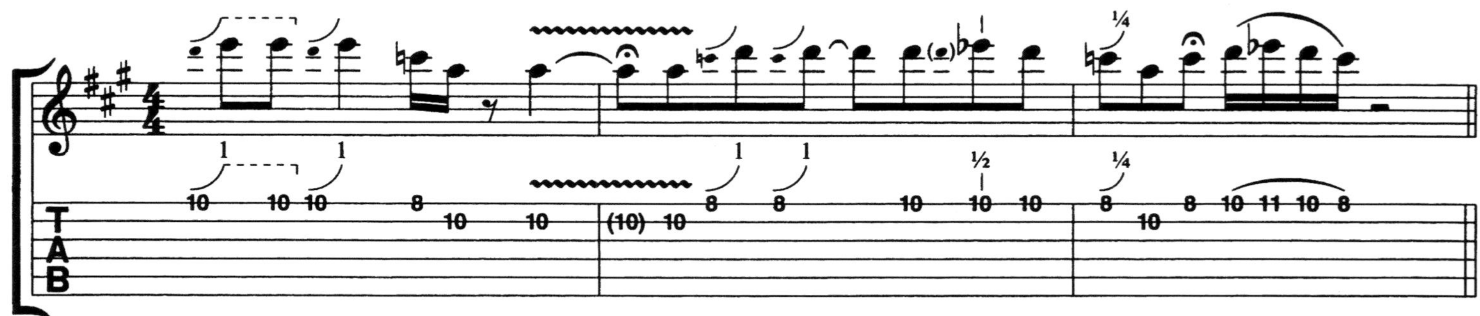

Example 62

Here is a three-octave blues scale pattern. This one again highlights the ♭5.

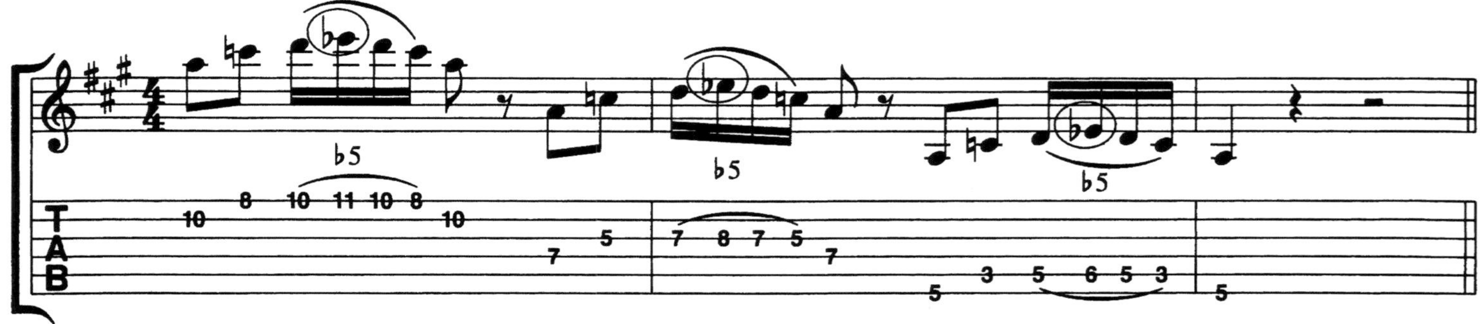

BLUES PHRASING

Everything we have played so far has been built from the same six notes: A C D E♭ E and G. What you do with them in terms of note choice and rhythm is known as **phrasing**. The more you play the guitar as if you were singing, the more musical you will be. When you sing, you tend to use only what is musically important, as opposed to just singing scales. Breathing when you sing is equivalent to resting. Not playing (or resting) when you are soloing can be as important as playing.

Example 63

This short phrase proves that "less is more." Built into this lick is a beginning (the first five notes) a middle, (the rest) and an ending (from E♭ to the last A). The melody of these notes is memorable and easy to sing, while the rhythm feels very natural in the way it fits the shuffle groove.

Example 64

Employing hammer-ons and pull-offs blends, or slurs, the notes together — giving you a more "vocal" sound.

Example 65

Adding slides is another way of imitating the voice. The first slide takes you to "A" on the 10th fret. The second slide replaces the hammer-on from the grace note "D."

Example 66

The last technique we will add is the bend. In this case, a 1/4 step bend is used on the G and C notes. This bend places the pitch between the note your finger is on and the note one half-step above (one fret). Next is a half-step bend from "D" to E♭ (the ♭5).

Example 67

This example illustrates the most common bends in the blues scale. The first is from the ♭7 (G) up to A on the 2nd string. The next bend is from the 4th (D) on the 3rd string. This type of bend is called a "ghost" or "pre-bend". This is when you bend the string to the desired pitch **before** striking it. The next bend is also from D on the 3rd string, but this time up a half-step to E♭.

The A Minor Pentatonic Scale

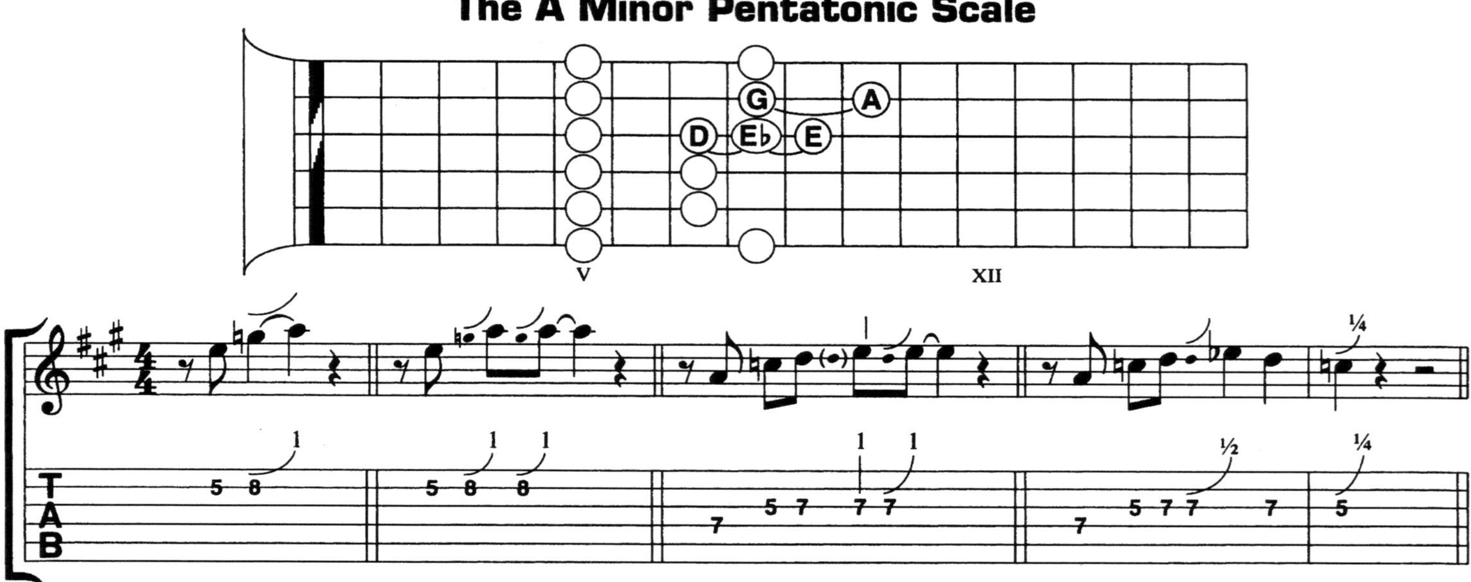

Example 68

Practically every guitar player who plays blues makes use of the 1/4 step bend. It is usually heard with the ♭3rd. This example covers three different octaves of the ♭3 (C) in the key of A.

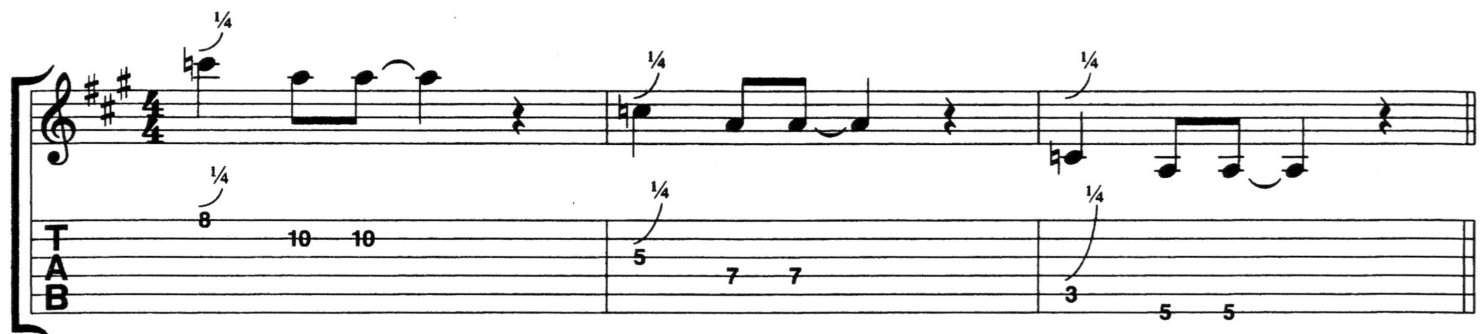

"CALL AND RESPONSE"

Before the proliferation of guitar tab books and instructional videos, blues musicians taught each other simply by listening and copying what they heard. It still remains the best way to learn music because it helps you discover how to listen and interpret what you hear.

Example 69

In this example, I'll play a two-bar phrase—that is the "call." Your "response" will be to try to copy what you hear on the spot. Don't get frustrated if you can't pick up each lick perfectly at first. This takes a lot of practice. The most important thing is to get as close to the "vibe" and the general feeling of a particular phrase. Try this with the video a few times before checking out the transcription below.

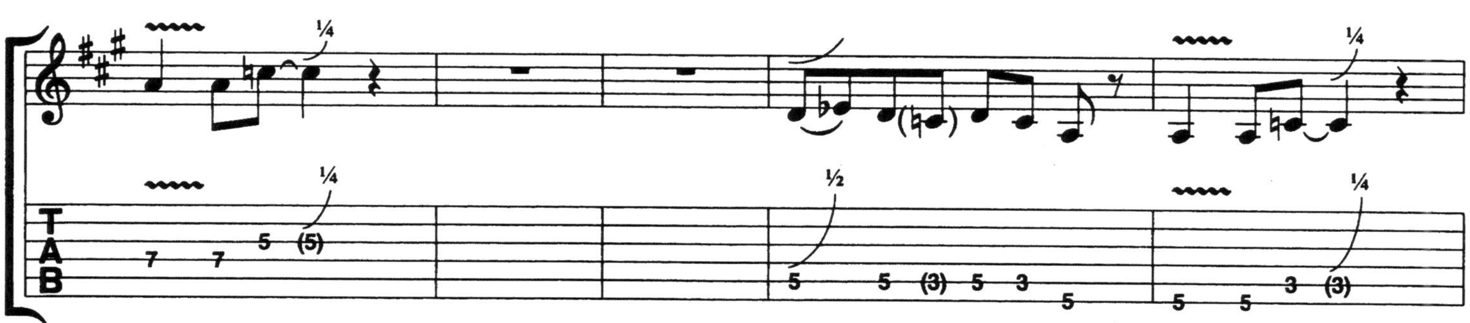

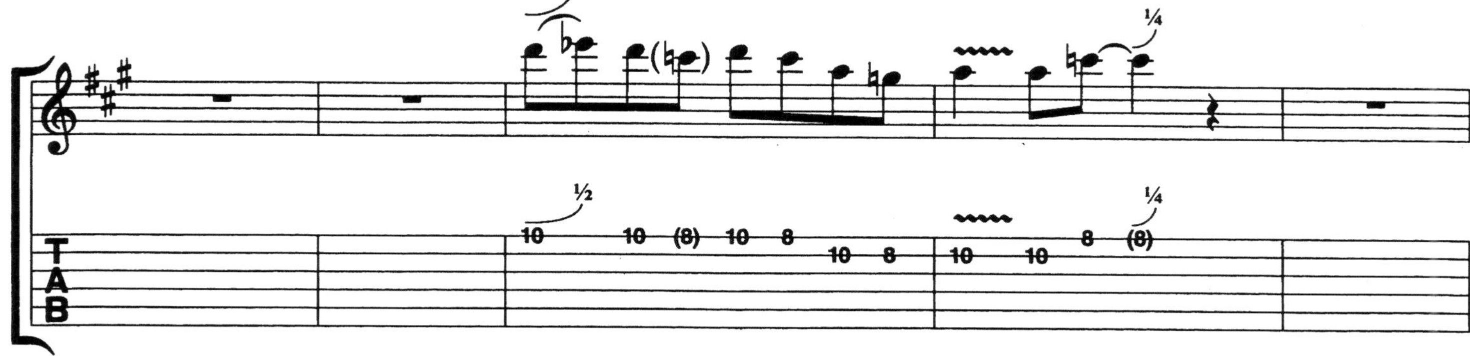

hold
hold
hold
straight ♪'s
grad. bend

SOLOING OVER THE 12-BAR PROGRESSION

The short phrases we have been learning can be "plugged in" to any 12-bar blues solo. As you know, the magic of the blues scale is that you can use it over all three chords in the progression. Here are some approaches for soloing over the 12-bar progression that include call and response, phrasing like a blues singer, and working the turnaround to the V chord at the end of the progression into your solo.

Example 70

You can literally play the same lick over each chord in the blues progression. It is balanced, makes sense and it feels good. Here is a blues scale lick played over the entire progression.

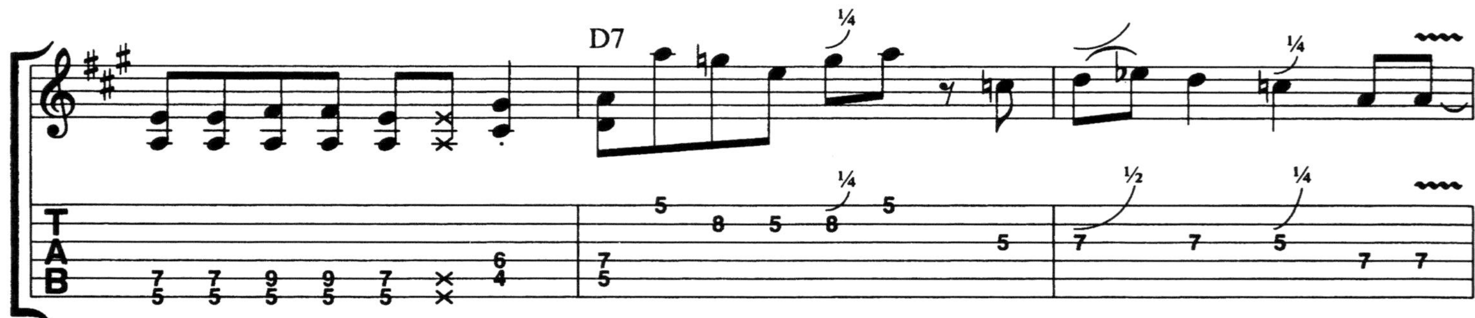

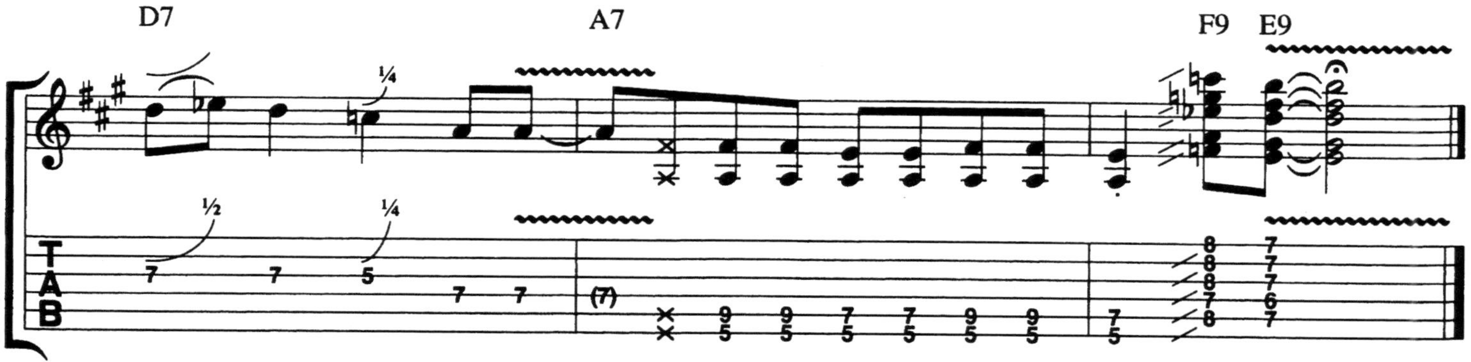

Example 71

Traditionally, blues singers use three phrases in a 12-bar blues: the call over the I chord, the same call again, (perhaps with slight variation) over the IV chord, and then a different, contrasting response over the V chord. This example demonstrates how it can be done with a guitar instead. The first eight bars are the same as the previous example, so only the V chord response (the last four bars) is shown here.

Bars 9 – 12:

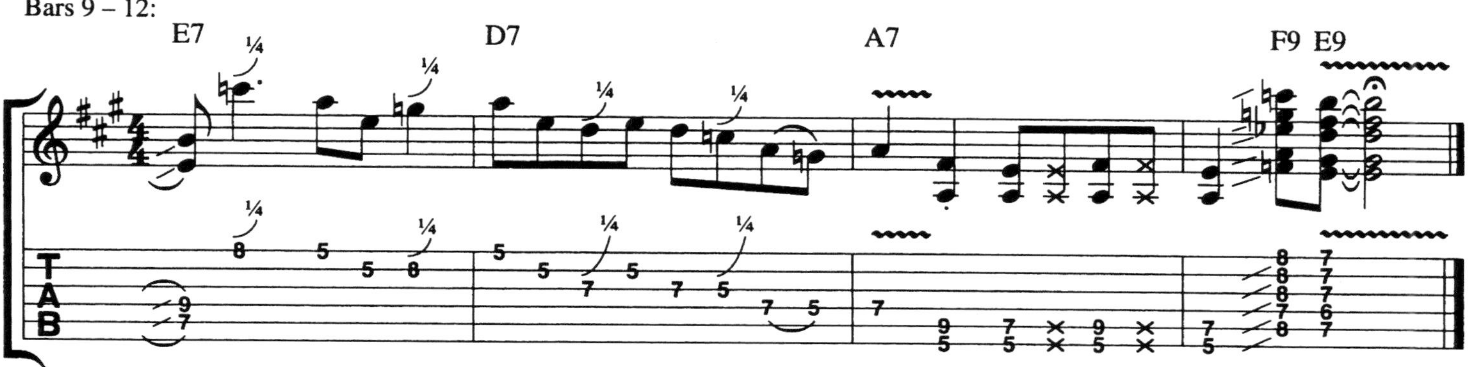

Example 72

A staple of good blues soloing is to acknowledge the V chord turnaround at the end of the progression by working the root of the chord (in this case, E) into your line. When the rhythm section hits the V chord in bar 12, end your phrase with an E note. This turnaround lick uses the 5th string, 7th fret E to end the phrase. Again, I've only indicated the last four bars.

Bars 9 – 12:

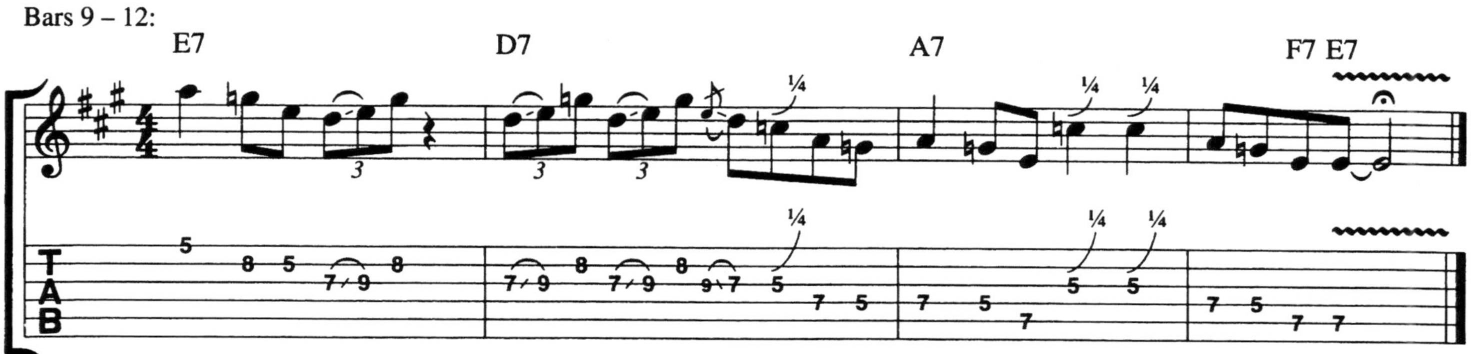

Example 73: Time To Play With The Band

Following is a three-chorus blues solo that demonstrates how to bring the elements we have been working on together into a solid, well paced solo. At the end of the solo we'll start the rhythm section from the top so you can play-along.

About soloing: Think of a solo as a big phrase, it should have a beginning, a middle and an ending. It's a good idea to pace your solo so that not too much happens too soon. Use all the material we have covered and consider taking it up an octave to 17th position, where the blues scale pattern repeats. Remember, it doesn't take a whole lot of positions and notes to play the blues — some of the greatest blues guitarists of all time have used scarcely more than two or three positions.

A7
E7
D7
A7
E7
hold
A7
D7
A7
E7
D7
A7
B♭9 A9

SECTION 8: THE SLOW BLUES

A slow blues can be thought of as a slowed down shuffle. Remember, in a shuffle each quarter note beat is subdivided into a triplet with the first and last note of the triplet being accented.

In a slow blues you feel all three notes of each triplet. Count off the four triplets in the bar as:

1 2 3 4 5 6 7 8 9 10 11 12

Accent the 4th and 10th notes in the bar and those become the "backbeats". This is known as 12/8 meter: 12 beats per measure and an eighth note gets one beat.

The Quick Change: Until now, the 12-bar progression remained on the I chord for the opening four bars. A common variation is the quick change to the IV chord in bar 2. We return to the I chord for bars 3 and 4 and the rest of the progression is unchanged. This is a traditional variation, and is usually talked about before a tune begins.

Example 74

Let's learn a rhythm pattern to help warm up to the quick change. This type of pattern originated with the great T-Bone Walker, the father of electric blues guitar. He was heavily involved with horn sections in his music, and this rhythm part attempts to imitate one. We will now be playing in the key of G. Everything we have been playing in A can easily be shifted down two frets to G. Here are the first four bars of a 12-bar blues in G with the quick change.

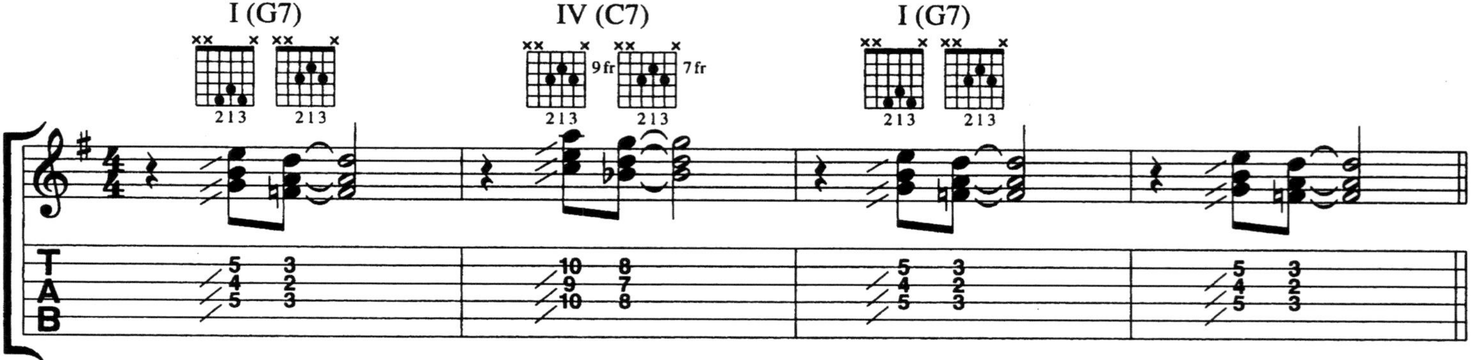

Example 75

The first of the two chord shapes found here is derived from the familiar G major barre form at the 3rd fret. Delete the 6th and 5th strings and that leaves a major chord shape on the top four strings. Raising the 5th (D) of the chord a whole step up to E on the 2nd string gives us a G6 chord. The high G on the 1st string, 3rd fret tends to be optional. Shifting the shape down a whole step makes a G9 chord. The two sounds together are thought of as a substitute for the I chord (G7). When transposed to the IV and V chords, you now have all the substitute chord forms to play a 12-bar blues with. The pattern always begins on the 2nd beat of the measure. Note the familiar turnaround at the end.

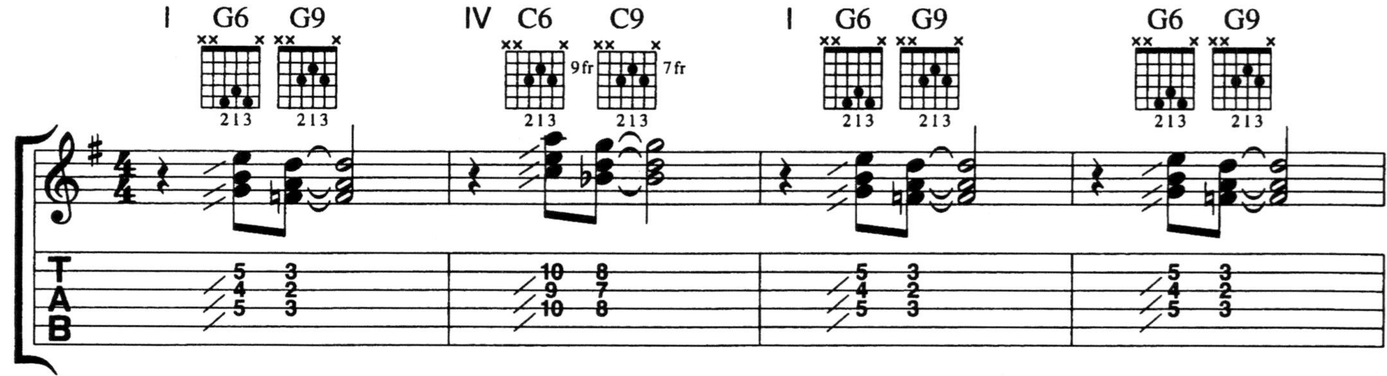

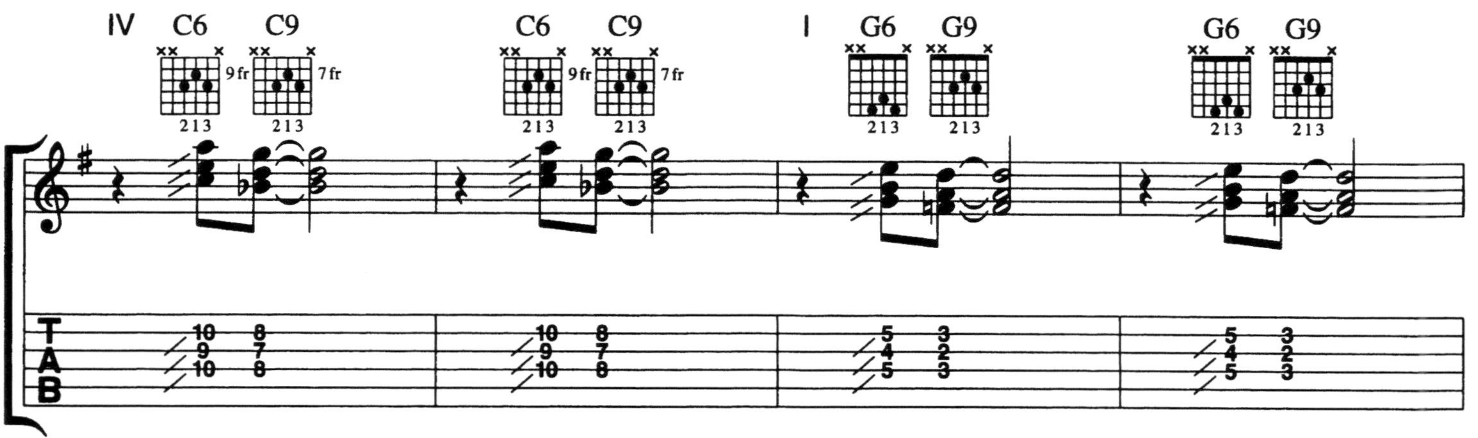

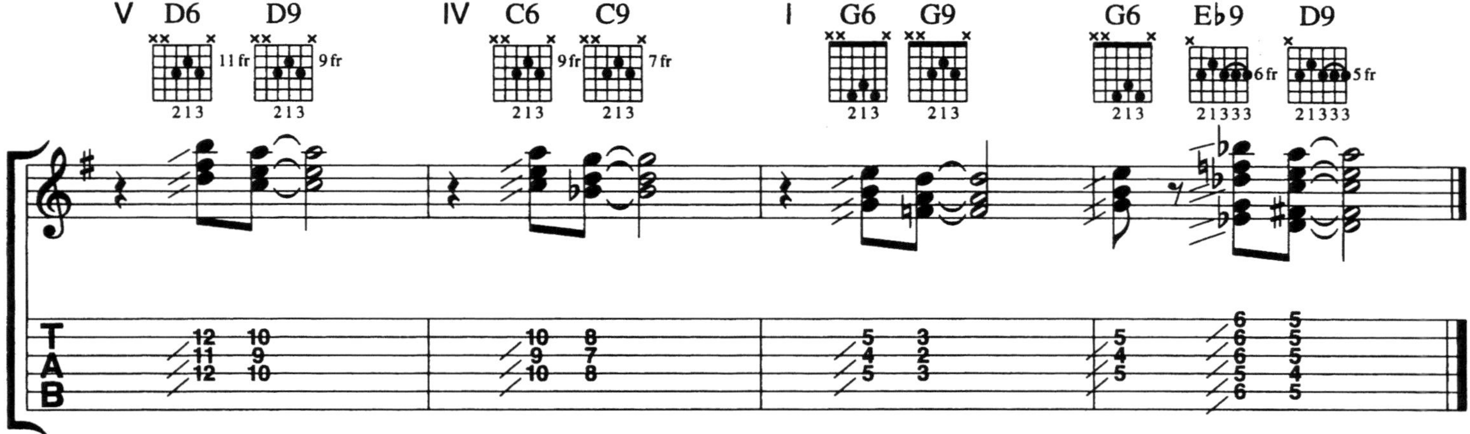

Example 76

There is often more than one place to play a particular chord on the guitar. Instead of moving high up the neck to play the IV and V chords, we can play them on the top three strings. This is a good way to limit your hand movement. Here we simply show the new shapes. Carry on through the entire progression as usual.

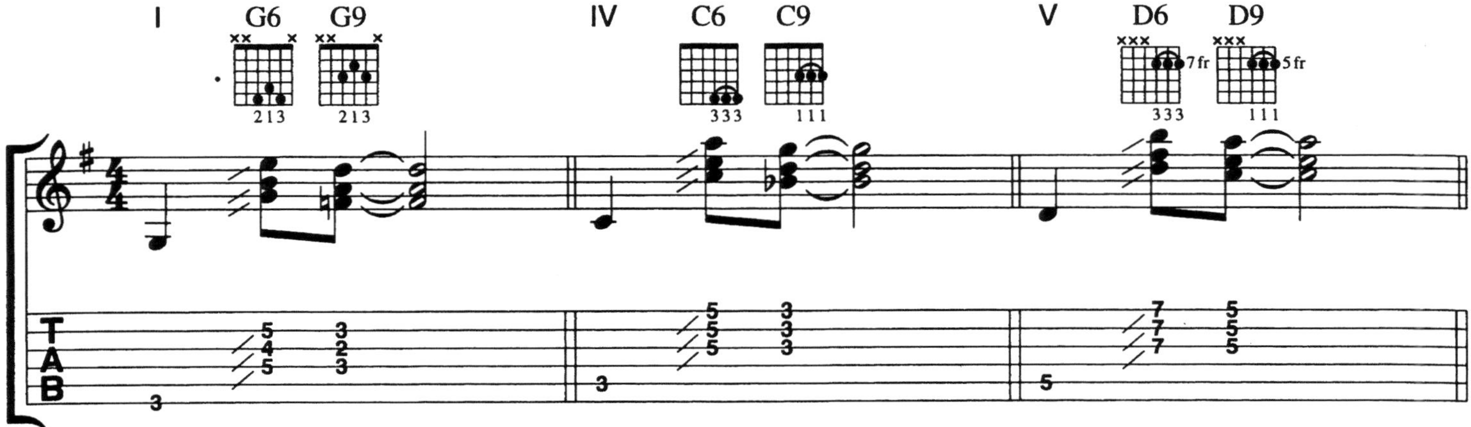

Example 77

Now let's add the optional 1st string G to the G6 chord for another horn section inspired rhythm part. We're also going to use the 9th chord. Notice that all the shapes are approached by sliding from a half-step below. This gives it some "grease".

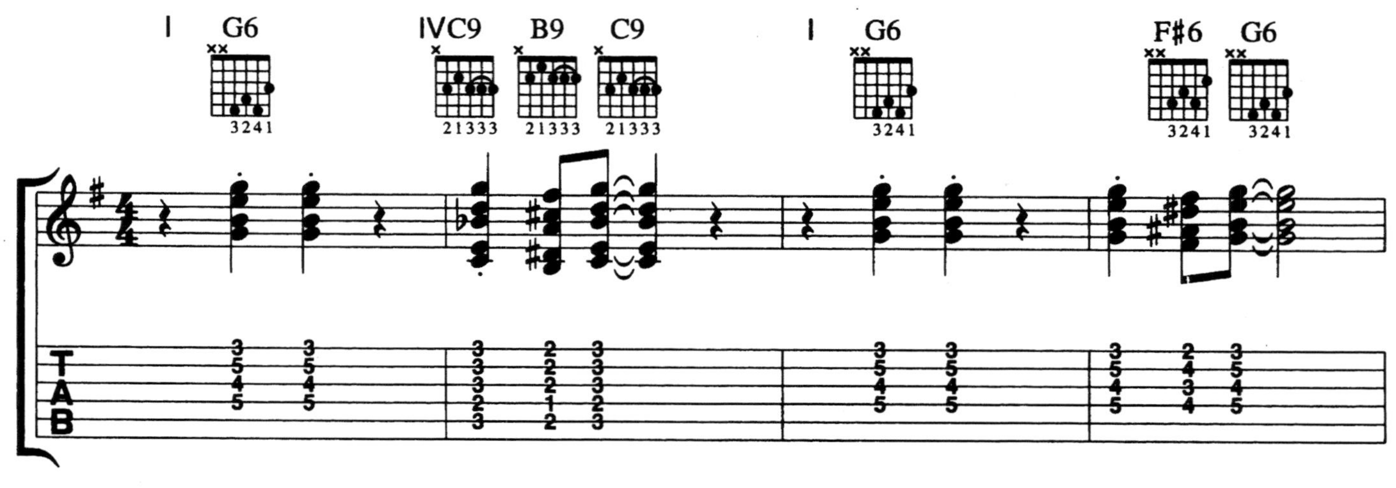

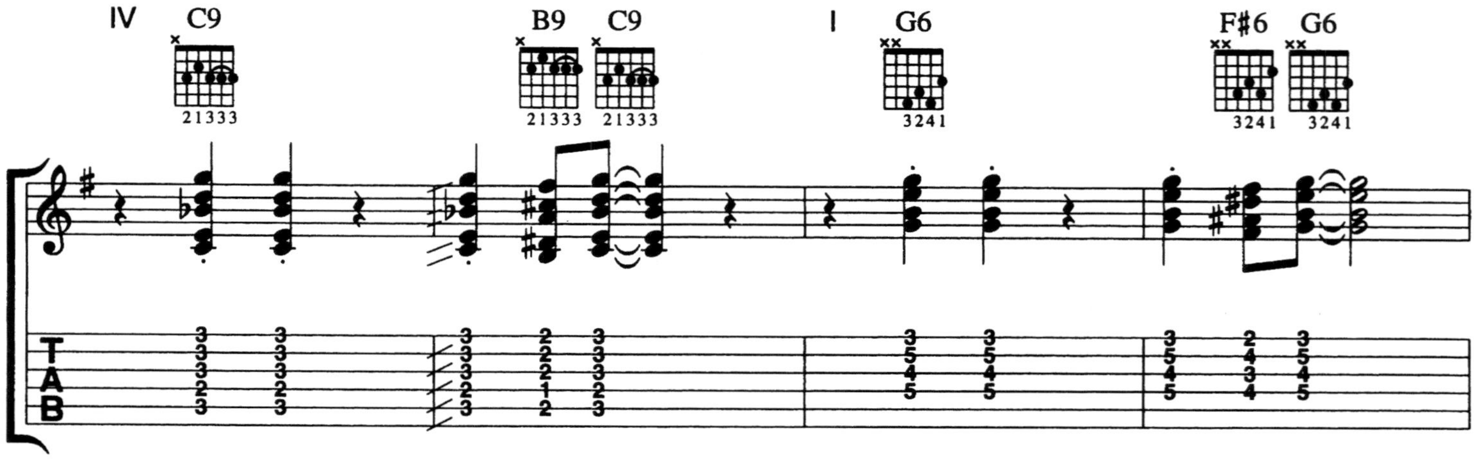

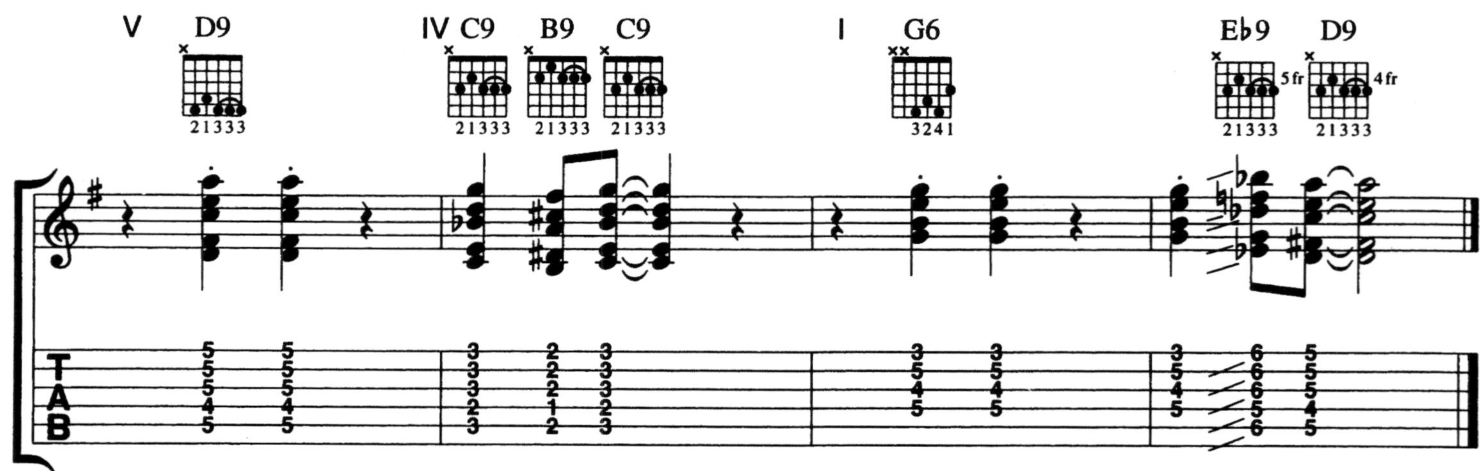

Example 78: Blues Intro

The last four bars of the blues progression can be used as an introduction as shown in this example.

Bars 9 – 12:

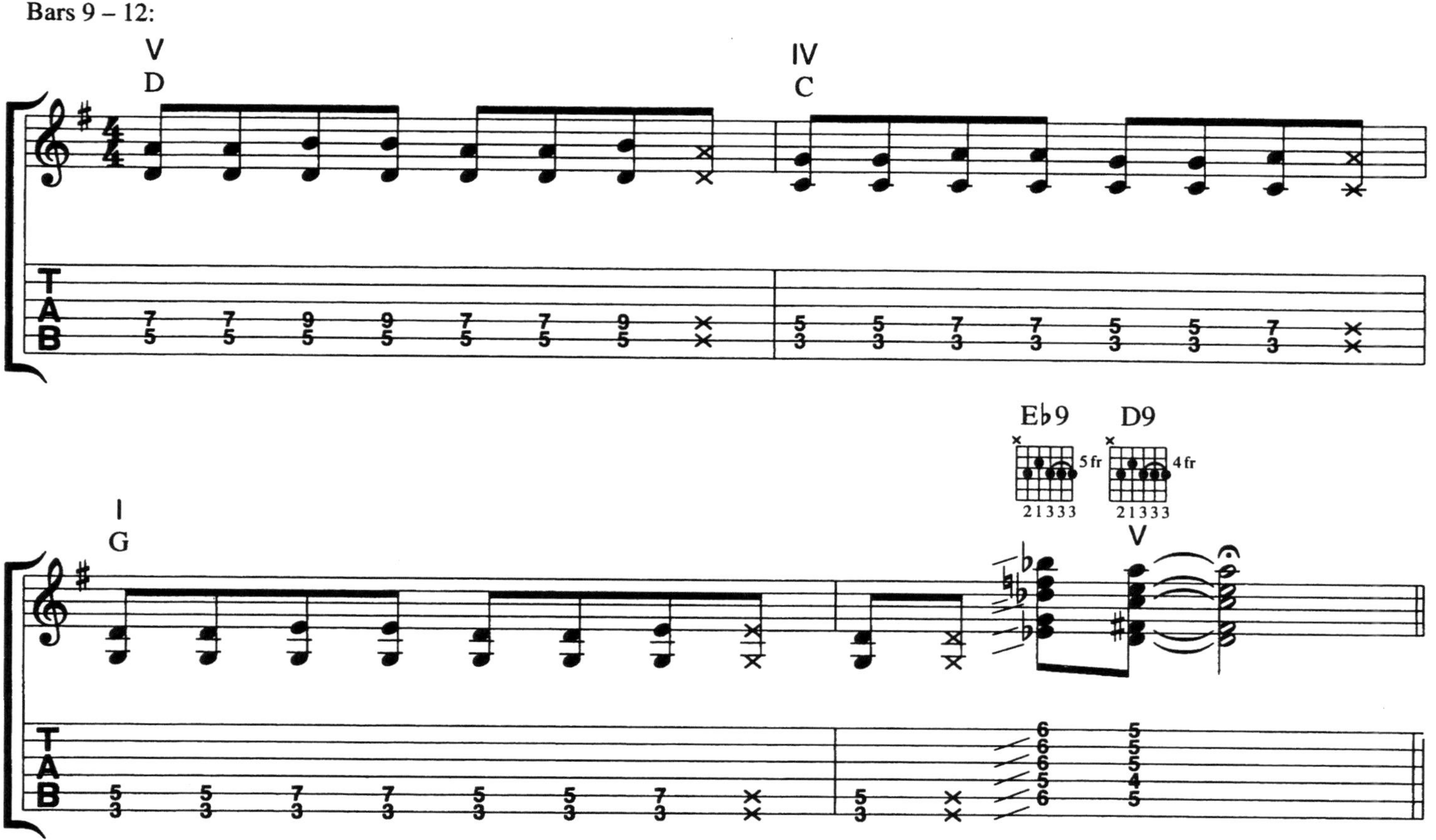

Example 79: Blues Ending

At the end of a song, you'll want to finish on the I chord, in the same rhythmic place (beat two) of the 12th bar that you played the V chord turnaround. The V chord turnaround leads you back to the beginning. Playing the I chord at the end of the phrase sounds final.

Bars 9 – 12:

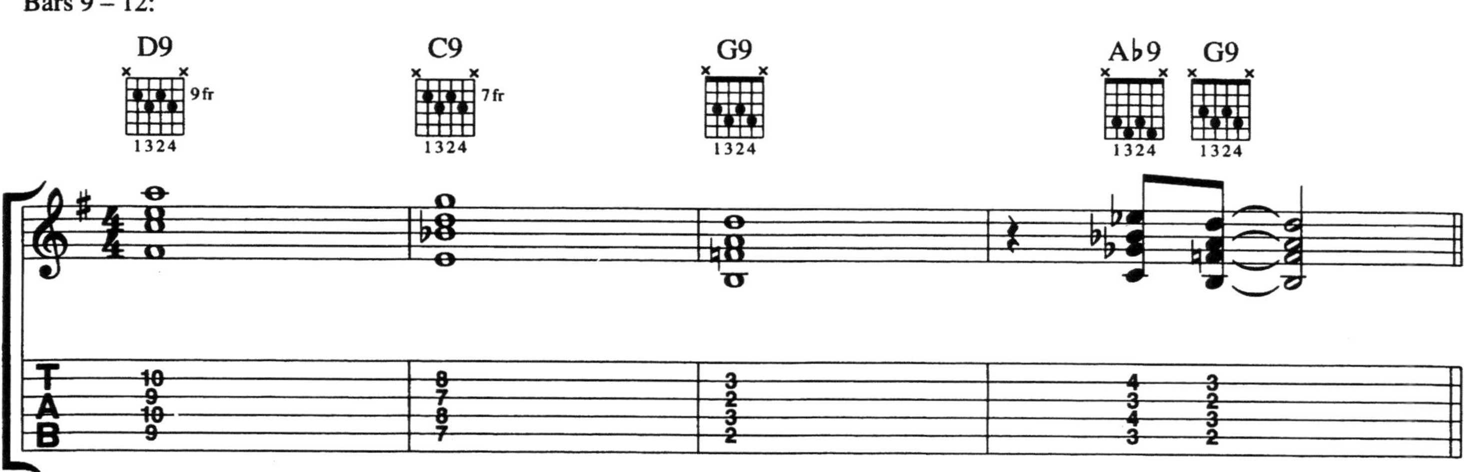

Example 80

This next example uses all of the techniques you've learned so far. It's a 12-bar blues, key of G, with the intro from the V, to a quick change and a stop on I at the end. A space is left for the lead guitar to make a final statement.

G9
D9
T
A
B
5
4
5
3
2
3
5
4
5
5
4
5
3
2
3
12
11
12
10
9
10

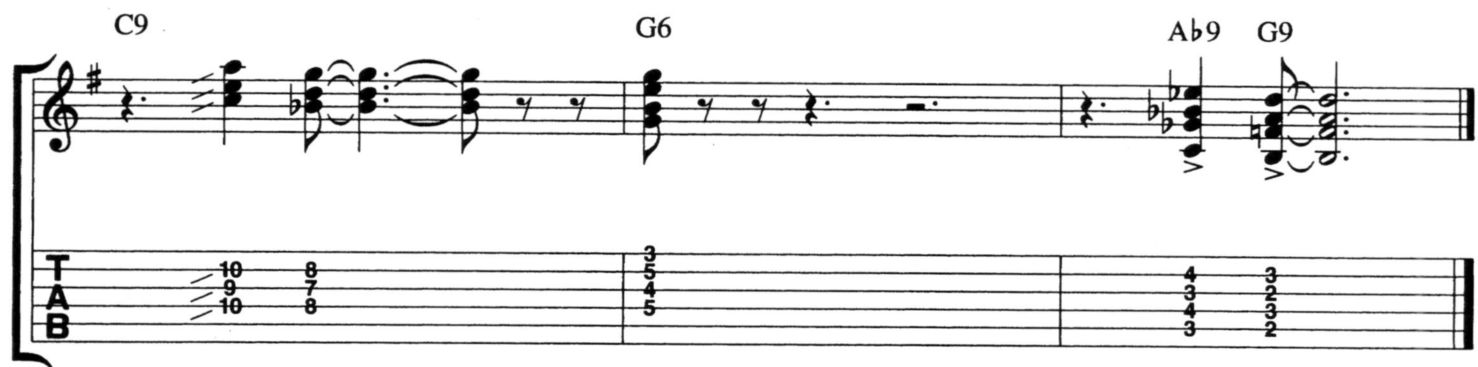
C9
G6
A♭9
G9
T
A
B
10
9
10
8
7
8
3
5
4
5
4
3
4
3
3
2
3
2

SECTION 9: NEW BLUES SCALE POSITIONS

Example 81

Let's quickly review the blues scale positions we learned in the key of A and transpose them to the key of G. The basic fingering for the G blues scale will lie in the 3rd position centering around the G barre chord with the low and high extensions then added. You can also jump up the neck an octave to where these patterns begin again, at the 15th position.

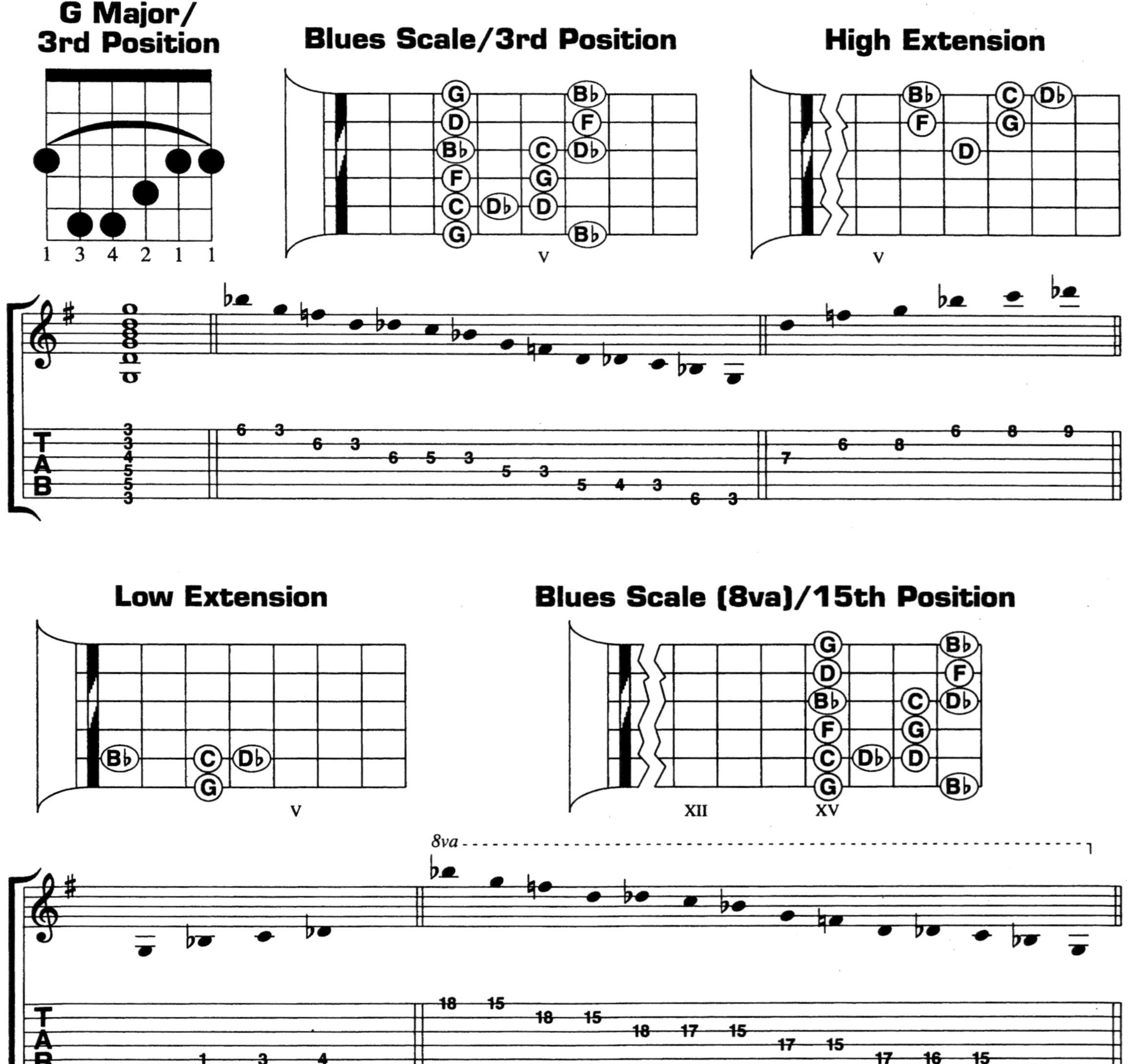

Example 82

It is very important to understand how scales are related to chords. The previous blues scale pattern was based around the G barre chord in 3rd position, this new pattern is centered around the G barre chord in 10th position.

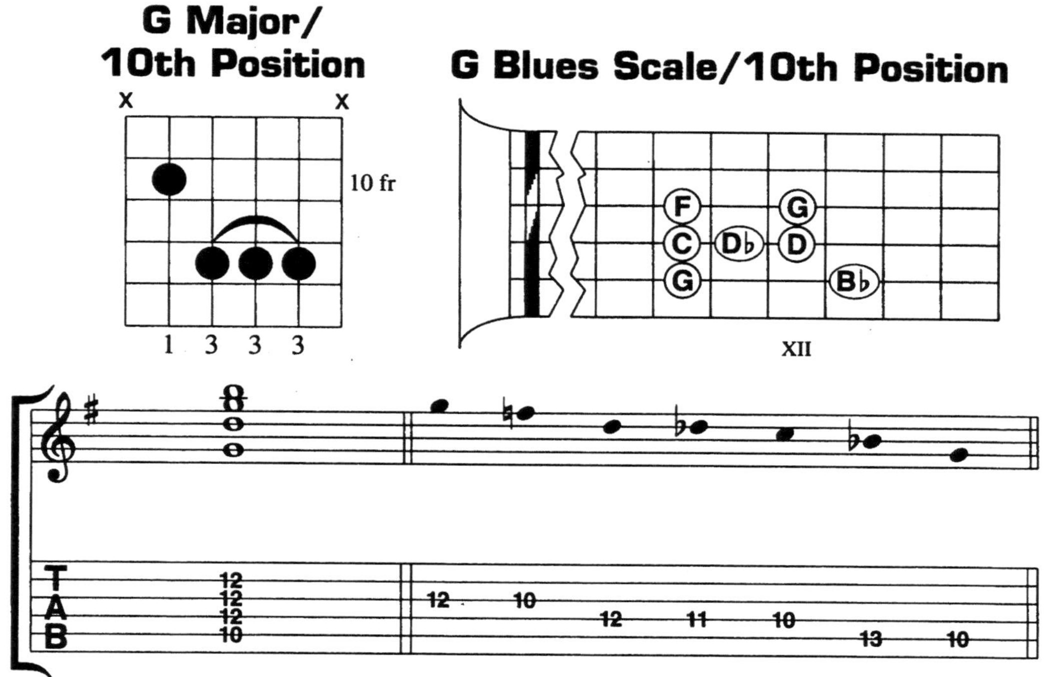

Example 83

Now let's add the remaining notes, including a low extension.

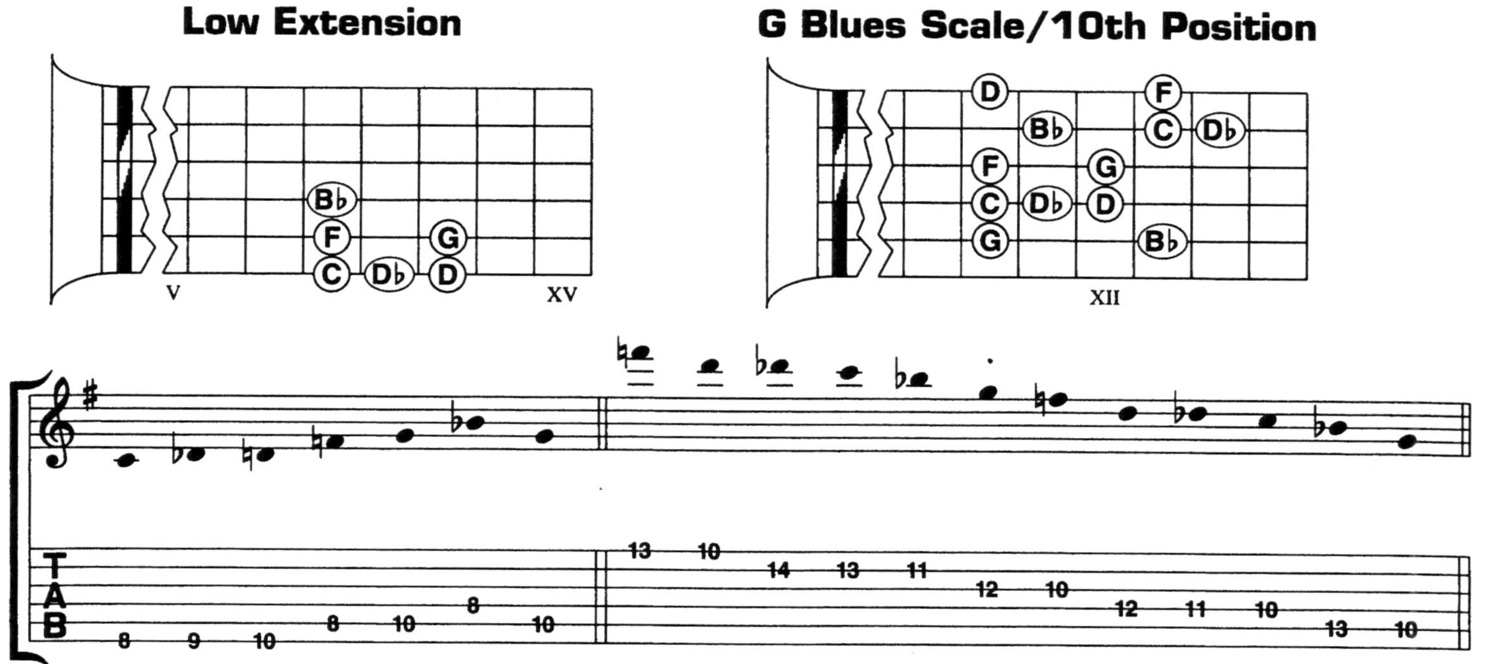

Example 84

The best way to familiarize yourself with this new layout of notes is to take ideas from the known 3rd position area and transpose or "work them out by ear" in 10th position. The fingerings will differ and the transition may be tricky at first, but keep working on it until both neck positions become comfortable. Here are a couple of examples of this method.

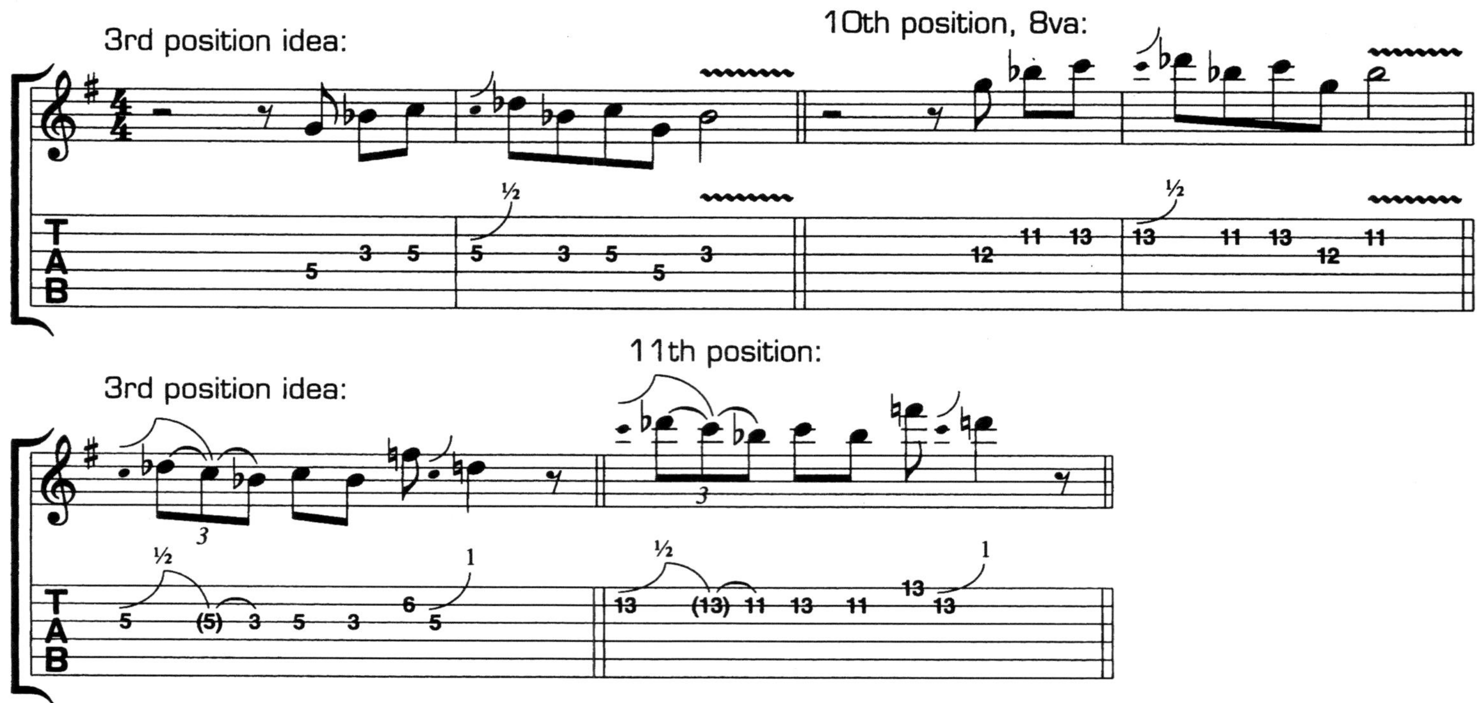

SWEET NOTES

The blues scale is the mainstay of blues. It has a serious, dark character. To add contrast or "sweetness" to it, we are going to bring in some new notes. These notes are new to the scale but not to the chord they are drawn from, G6. In order to sound like your melody matches up with the G6 sound, we will be adding the two notes that stand out the most in the G6 chord, the 3rd (B) and the 6th (E).

Example 85

Here is a classic blues lick that emphasizes the "sweet notes". The 3rd and 6th are circled. A typical blues scale lick follows it so you can compare the sound.

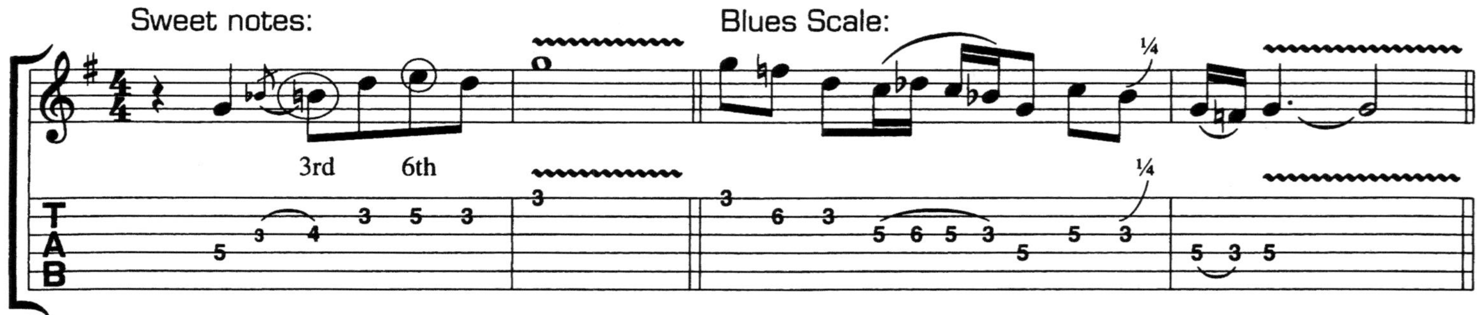

The B.B. King Secret Scale Pattern

Now let's check out an area of the neck that blues great B.B. King has spent so much time with, it is known affectionately by guitar players as "the B.B. box". This is an ideal pattern for soloing because the sweet notes are arranged comfortably under your fingers, while the blues scale notes are never far from reach. Shown here in the key of G, this "box" pattern is two frets higher than the high blues scale extension.

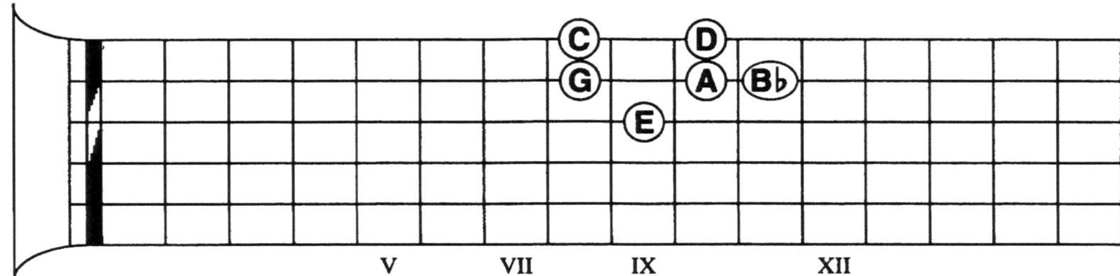

Example 86

In this example, the sweet notes are circled and identified by interval. Pay attention to the fact that these notes are sometimes played as bends — which emphasizes them musically.

Example 87

The mark of an experienced bluesman is the ability to mix the moods of the blues scale and the sweet notes to a balancing point. Experiment by starting with one and answering with the other. Here is an example beginning with the blues scale at the high extension and answering with the "sweet spot" position, two frets higher.

Vibrato

Vibrato is another very integral mark of musicianship for singers and players of any instrument. Vibrato takes more time to develop than many other techniques but it is well worth the time and effort as it is probably the most personal and identifiable part of a guitar player's sound. Whichever string it is applied to, vibrato is nothing more than a repetitive slight bend at varying speeds. The high strings (1st – 3rd) are generally "pushed" upward when vibrato is applied. The low strings are "pulled" downward. On bent notes, the string is allowed to fall back down from the destination pitch towards the fretted note — at varying degrees based on vibrato speed and intensity. Vibrato techniques are extremely difficult to teach and therefore require your utmost attention and concentration. Listen to the vibrato of your favorite guitarists and most importantly, listen to your own.

Example 88

First let's just add vibrato to the note G on the 2nd string, 8th fret. Use your 3rd finger, reinforced by your 1st and 2nd fingers. Pivot your wrist back and forth to repeatedly bend and return the string. The faster you do this the more like a natural vibrato it will sound. Strive for control of the width and speed of the vibrato.

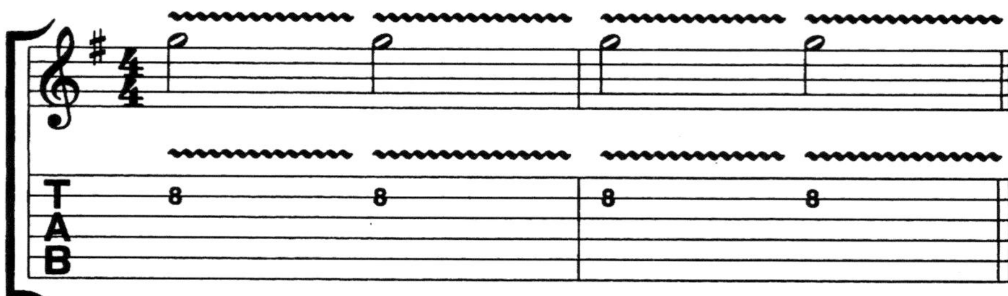

Example 89

Adding vibrato to a bent note is more difficult because as you slightly release the bend from its destination pitch it is essential that you control the return to that pitch accurately — regardless of how wide or fast you choose the vibrato to be.

Dynamics

Experiment with picking notes as softly as possible — at a whisper level. Also try picking with your fingertips instead of the pick for a rounder tone. Then, without using your volume controls, play as loud as you can. Amplification aside, this is your dynamic range — it's all in your hands. Like with vibrato, strive for dynamic control of your instrument at all times.

Example 90

Now we are going to play another call and response over the I chord that brings together all of the blues scale positions and the "sweet notes". Take your time with your response and remember the most important point is to get close to the general "vibe" and shape of the lines. You can always go back to the beginning and try to get closer to playing exactly what you hear.

grad. bend
grad. bend
grad. bend
grad. bend

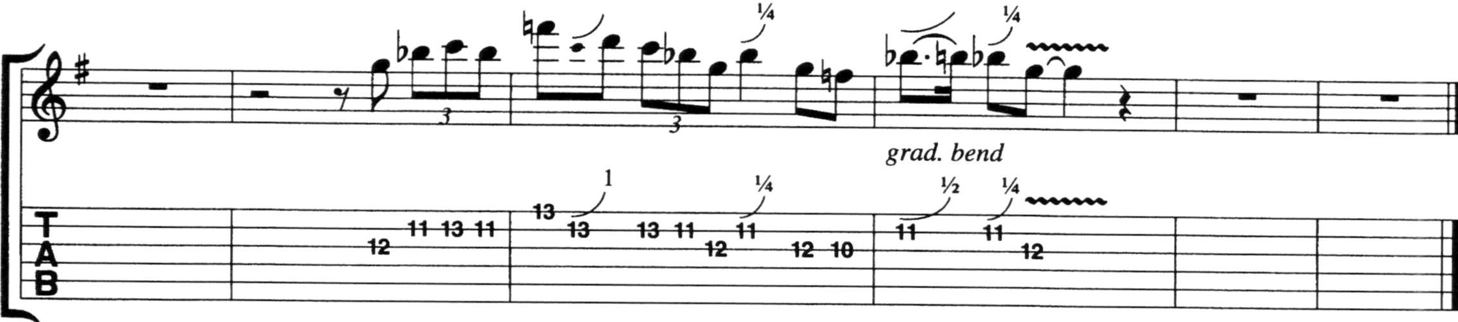

Example 91: Matching Solos To Chords

Compare the G6 and C7 (I and IV) chords shown below. The crucial difference is the change from B♮ to B♭. Otherwise the two remaining notes (G and E) are common to both. The solo lick arpeggiates each chord. Practice going back and forth from the I chord to the IV highlighting the change from B to B♭.

Example 92

Now let's extend this concept to an entire 12-bar blues progression.

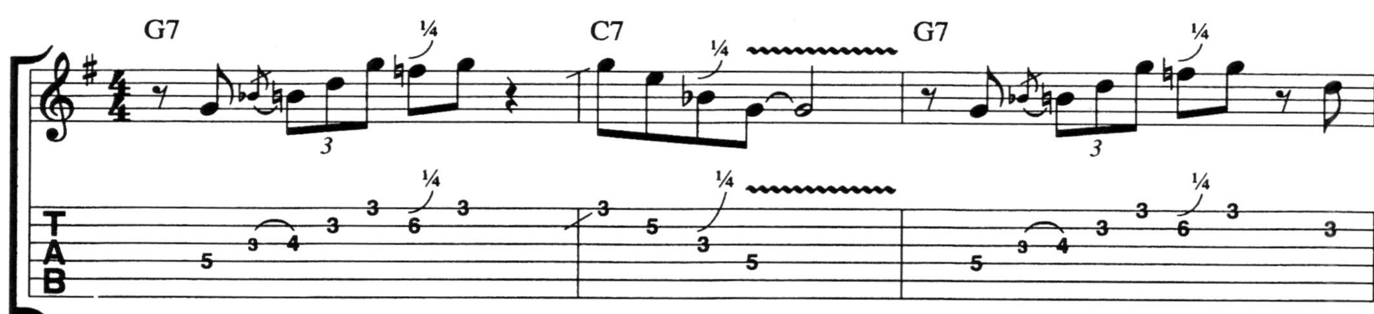

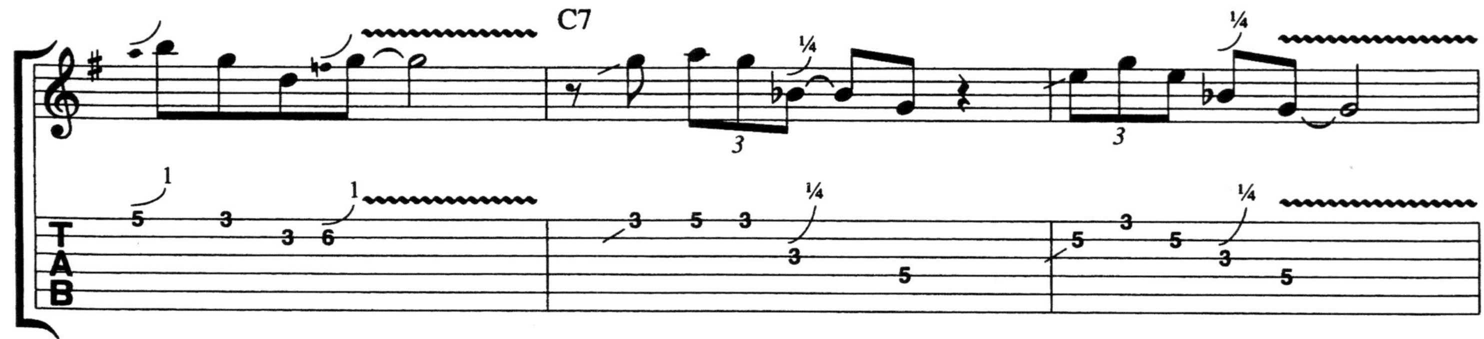

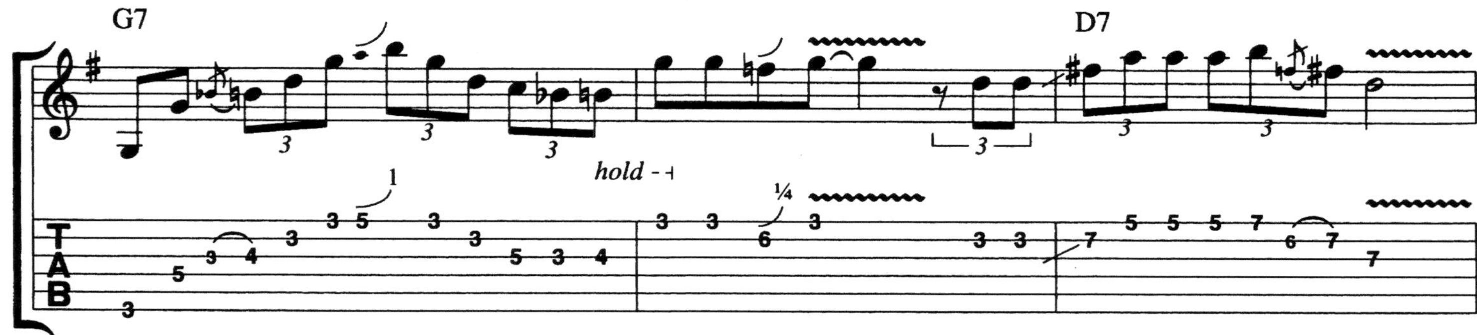

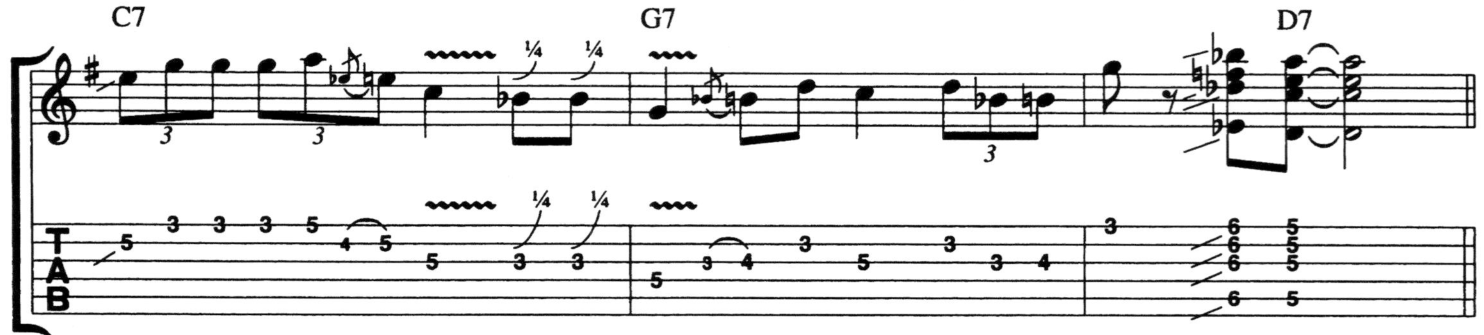

Example 93

Some classic blues licks, like this one from B.B.King, are derived directly from chord shapes. Here, a dominant 7th sound is transposed from the I chord (G7) to the IV (C7) and V (D7) chords.

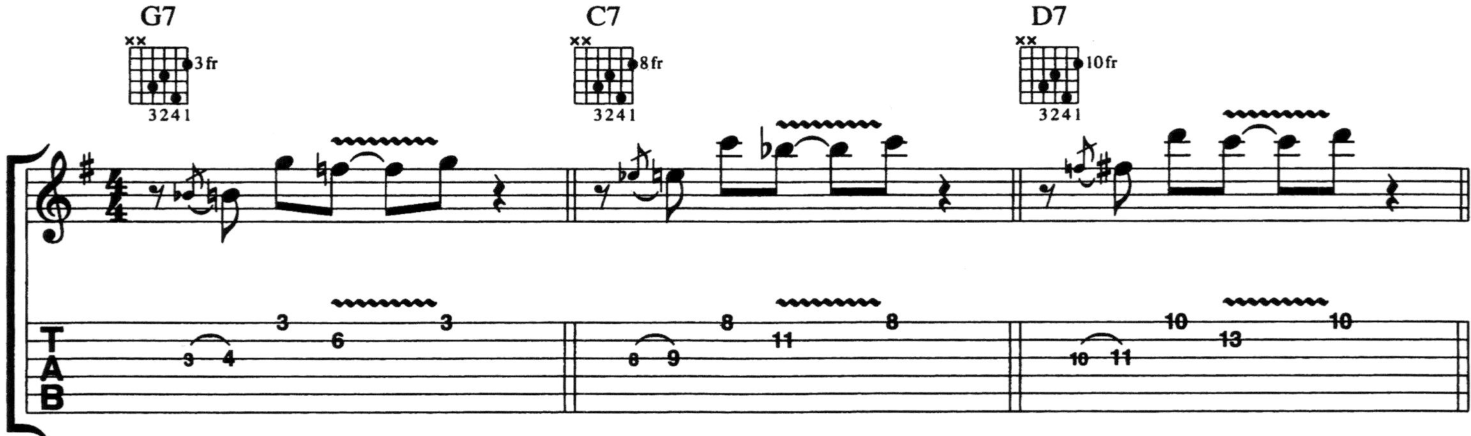

Example 94

Now let's move all of the patterns to the key of C. Try to work in the same types of parts that we used for the keys of G and A. Remember to think of chord shapes as springboards for matching lead lines to. The 8th position, C Blues Scale (C E♭ F F♯ G B♭) is a good "homebase" for all of our fingerings and licks. See below for how the scales and extensions lay out in the key of C.

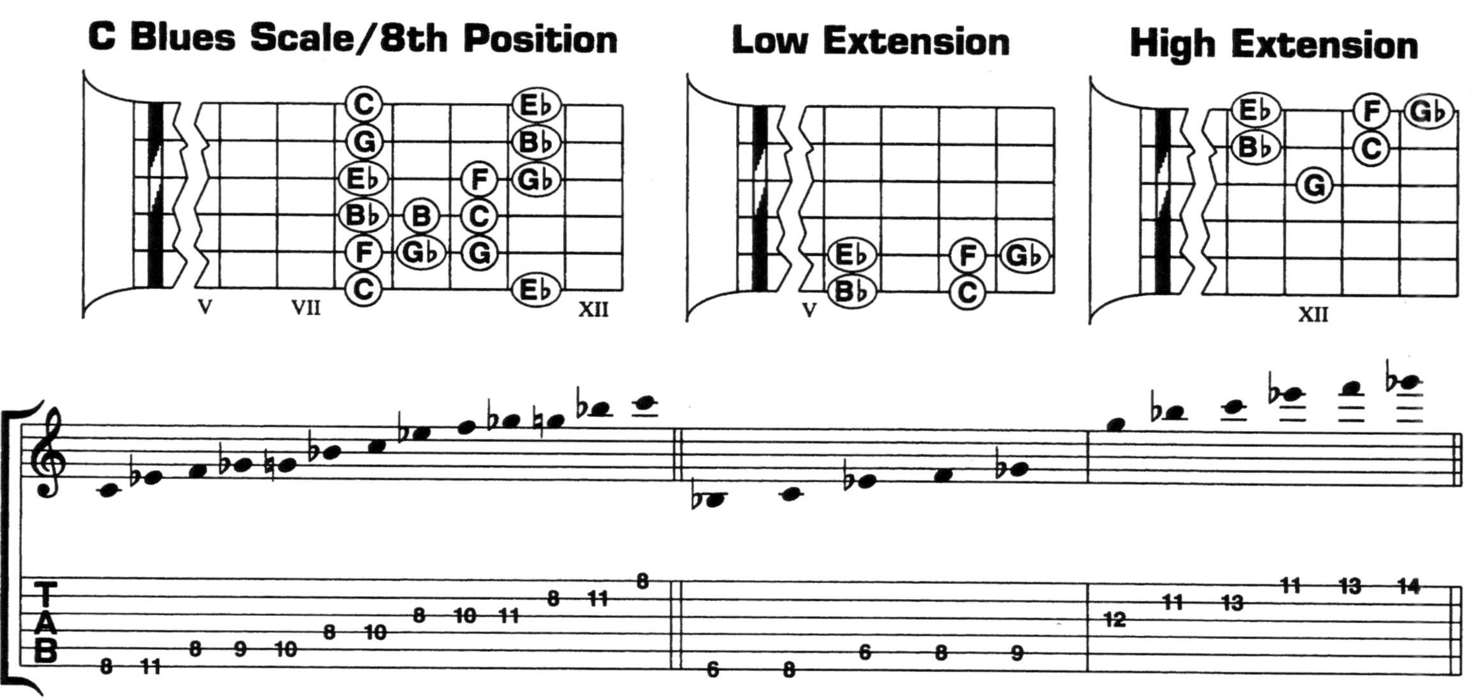

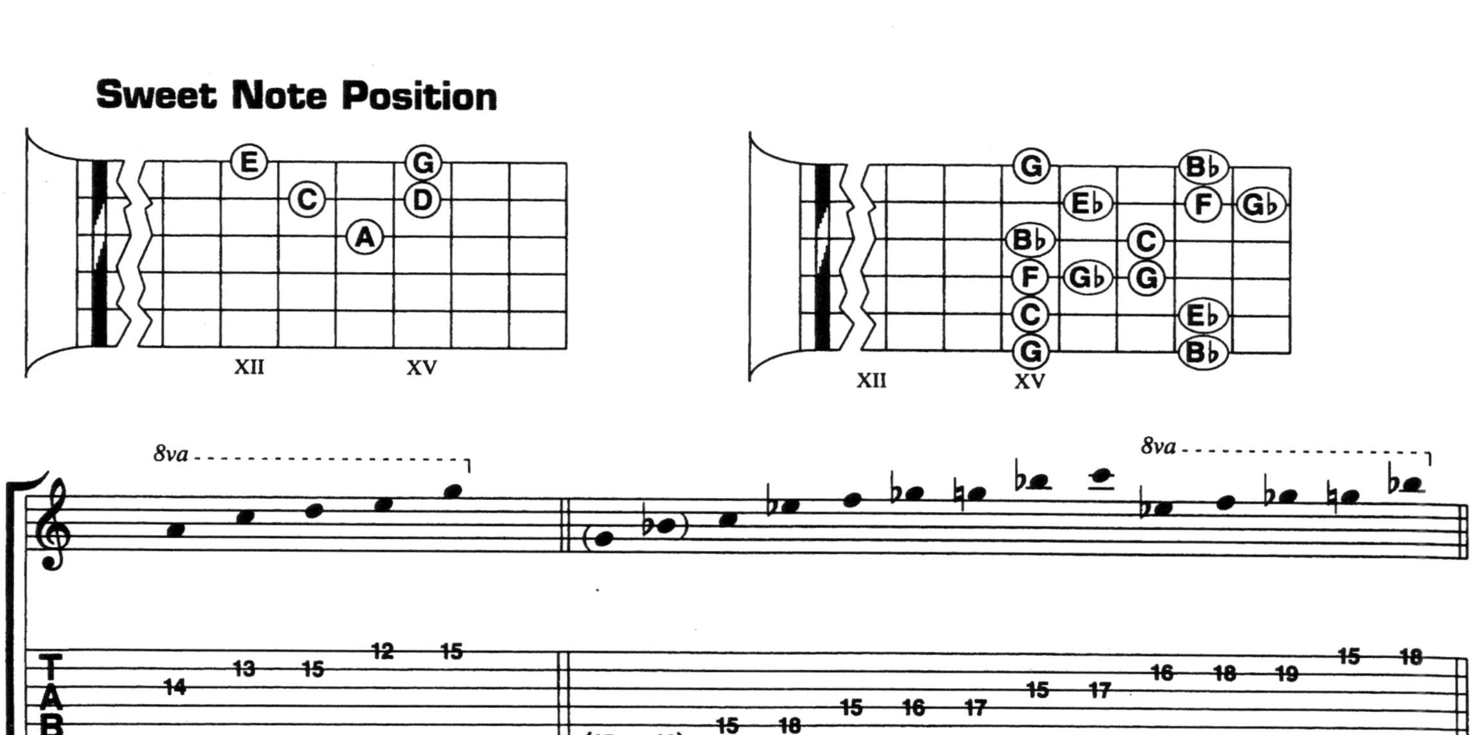

Example 95

In this solo, pay close attention to the excellent balance between the moods of the Blues Scale and the sweet notes, the lengths of short and long phrases and soft to loud dynamic levels.

F7
C7
G7
F7
C7
F7
C7
G7
C7
F7
C7
grad. bend
grad.
bend

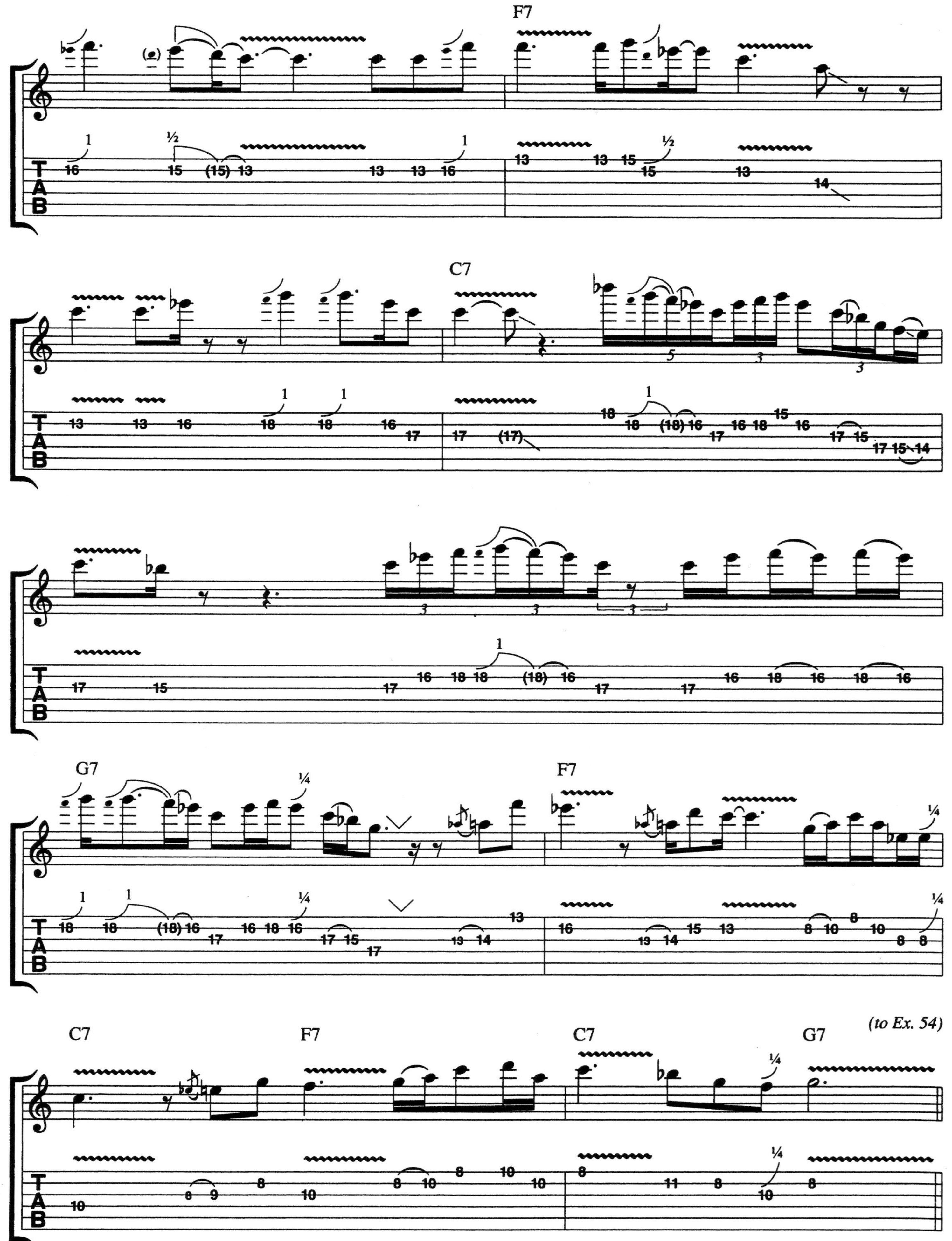
F7
C7
G7
F7
C7
F7
C7
G7
(to Ex. 54)

Example 96

This example is the rhythm guitar part that follows the solo (Example 95). Note how these chord voicings were transposed from other keys and how well-balanced the playing is overall. The mark of an experienced rhythm player is knowing how to become "invisible" by playing the right chords at the right dynamic level consistently through the course of a solo. Always strive for this by listening carefully to the soloist and the rhythm section simultaneously.

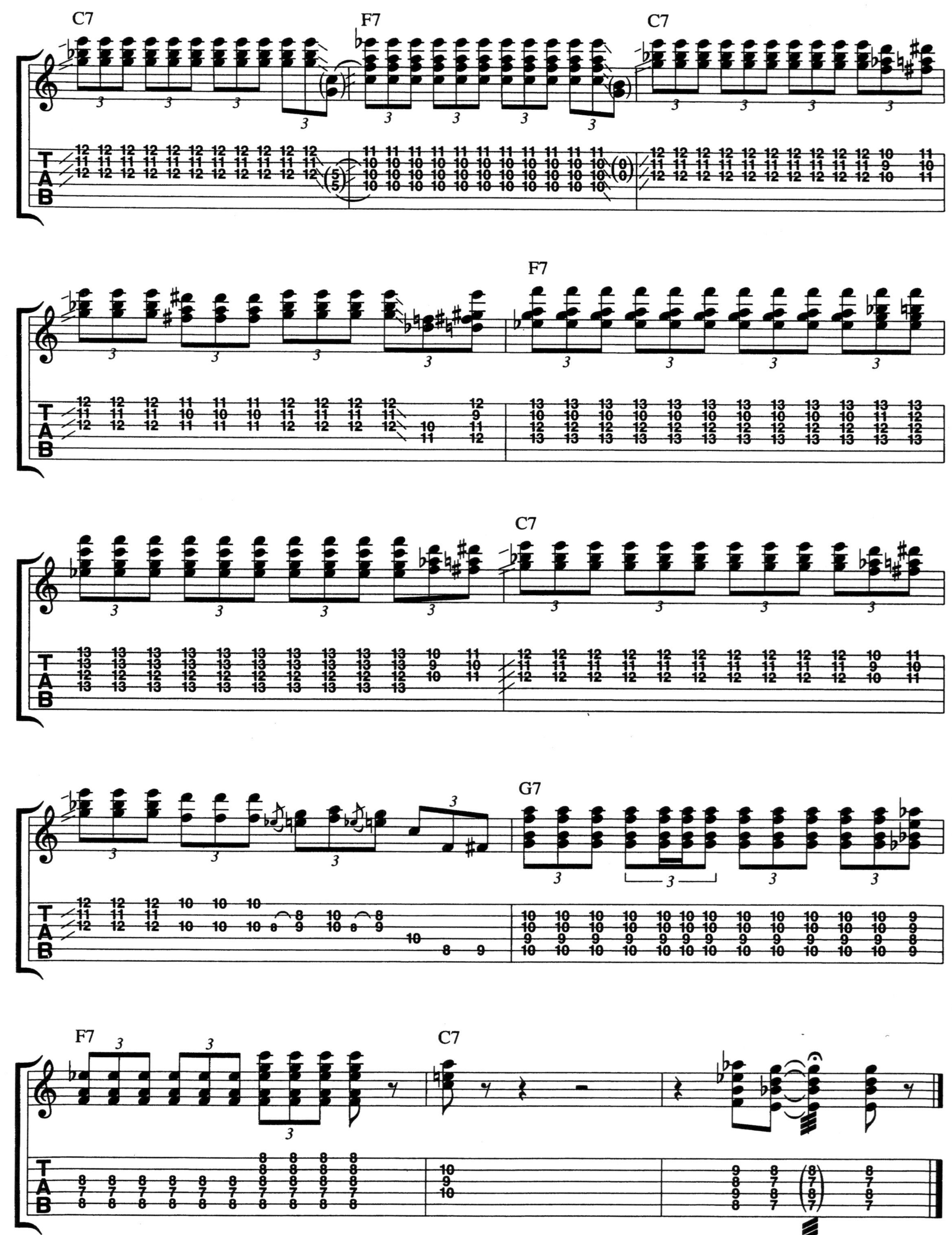
C7
F7
C7
F7
C7
G7
F7
C7

ROCK GUITAR

SECTION 10: POWER CHORDS & RHYTHM PLAYING

Barre Chords

Let's review the movable G and C barre chords. Major chords have three notes; the root, 3rd and 5th. For example:

G: G B D
1 3 5

C: C E G
1 3 5

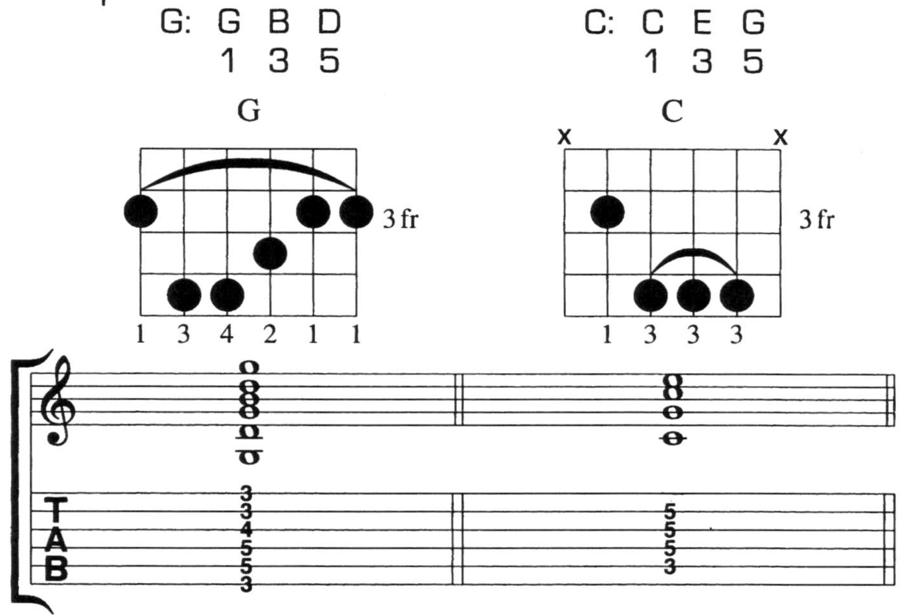

Power Chords

The rock guitarist's main chord is often called the "**power chord**." The symbols for these chords are either '5' or (no 3rd): C5, G5, D5 or C(no3rd), G(no3rd), etc. These are two-note chords containing only the root and 5th:

G5: G D
1 5

C5: C G
1 5

Barre chords and open chords sound great with a clean sound but do not always sound so great when you turn on the distortion. Power chords work perfectly with distortion because they have only two different notes.

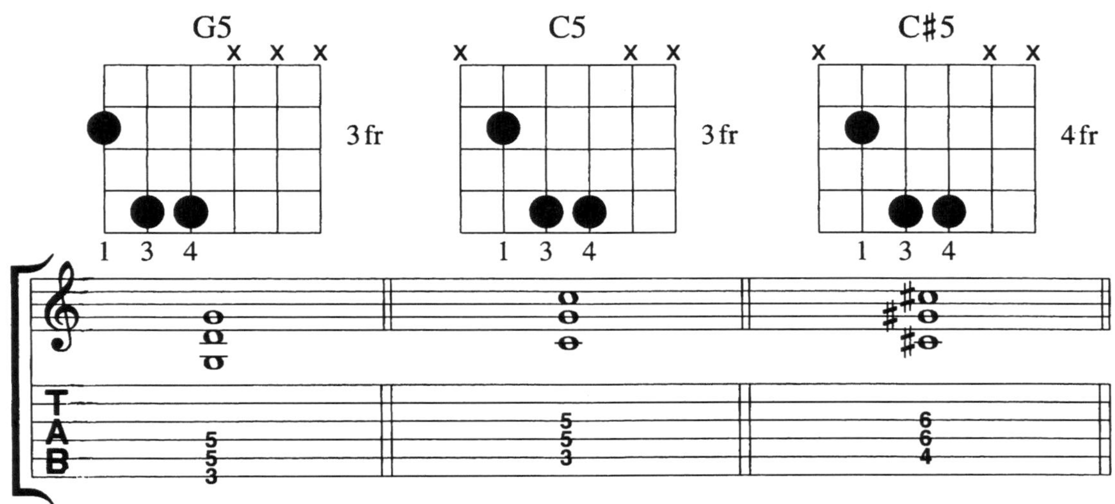

Open Postion Power Chords

It is important to memorize the open power chords. Notice the dead strings on the G5 and the C5 (C5 is not on recording). This is accomplished by allowing the second finger to lightly touch the string while it plays a note on a lower string. This is a valuable technique for cleaning up your distorted sound that will carry over into other areas of your technique.

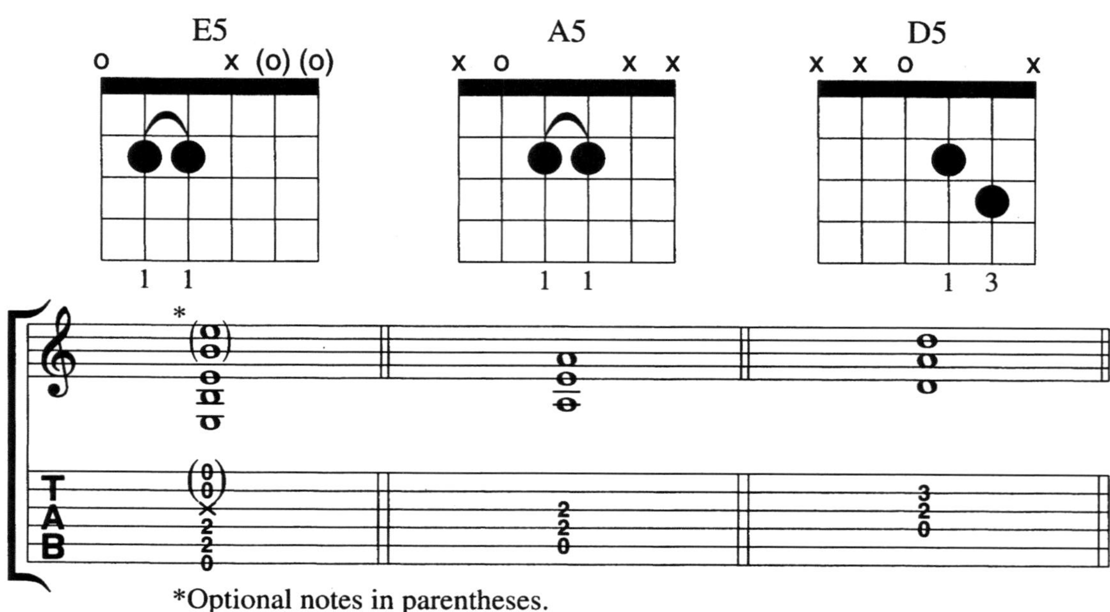

*Optional notes in parentheses.

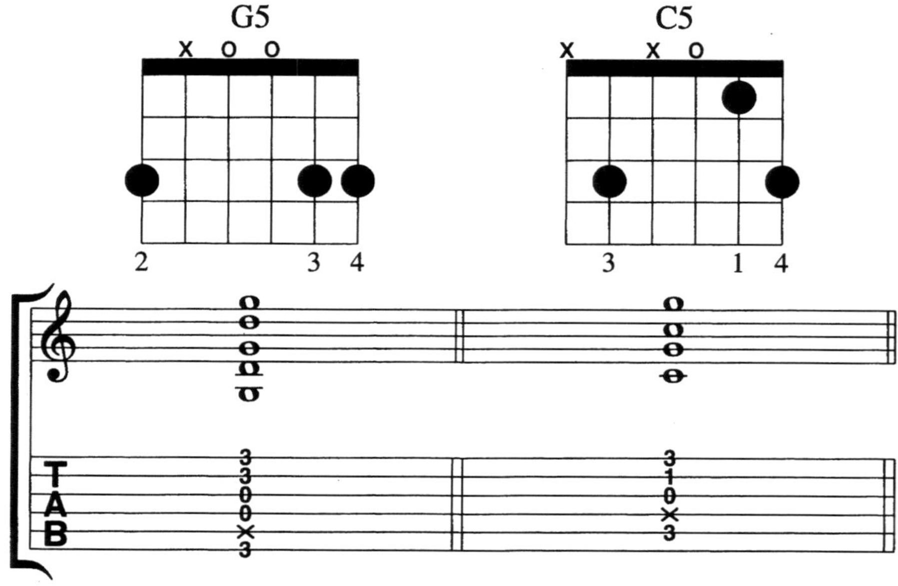

Example 97: Right Hand Rhythm Technique

Palm muting (P.M.) adds variety and control to both a distorted and clean sound. You accomplish this technique by lightly placing the palm of your picking hand on the string either on the bridge or slightly in front of the bridge while striking the notes or chords. Avoid placing your hand too far in front of the bridge or the strings will be too muted. Vary the amount of pressure to create a variety of attacks. The palm mute effect is indicated by the abbreviation: **P.M.**

Using all down strokes for rhythm can add a heavier edge to the sound. Use all down strokes and palm muting for Examples 1 & 2.

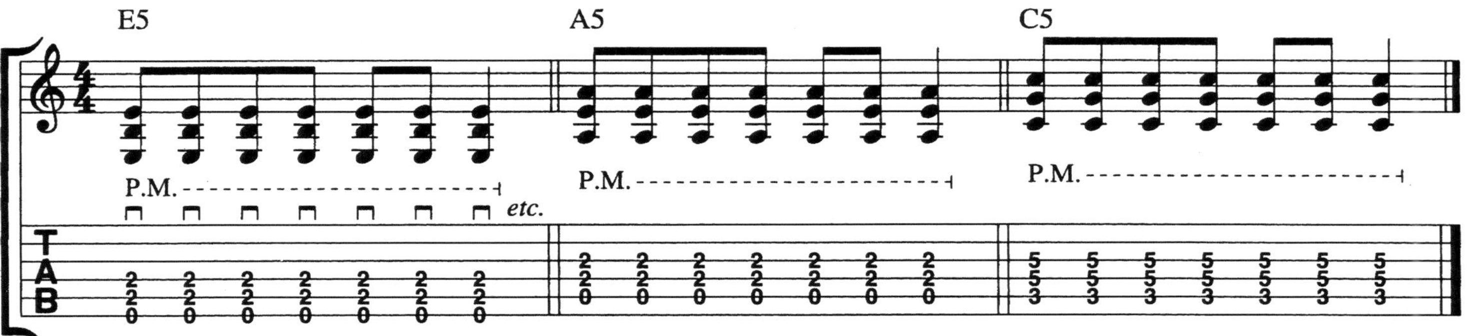

Example 98

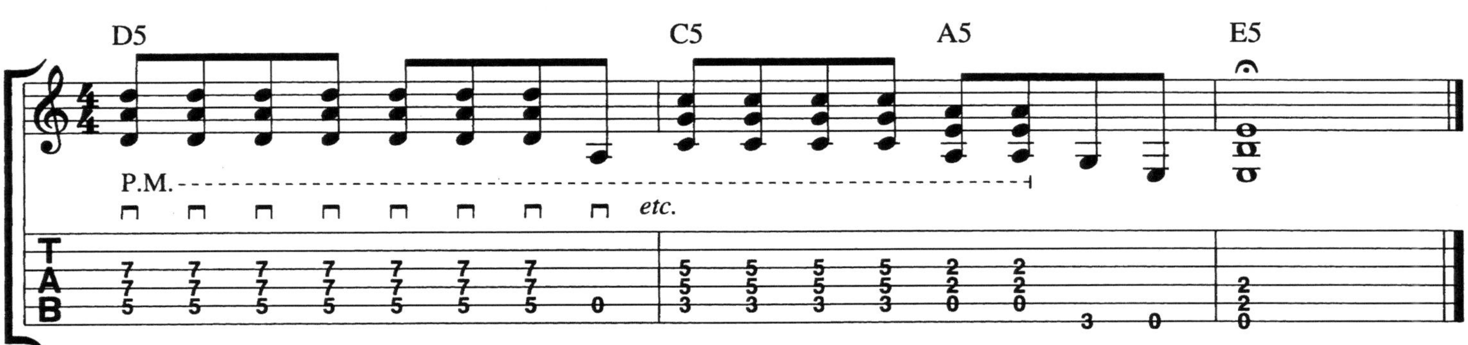

Example 99: Power Chord Test (Play-Along Track 1)

It is very important that you memorize each chord you learn. As an exercise, cover up the tablature and use the chord symbols while playing along with the video. Only refer to the tablature if something doesn't sound right. When you perform with others, you are not likely to have tablature provided. Chord names may be called out to you or you will be given a chord chart.

POWER CHORD TEST

(Play-Along Track 1)

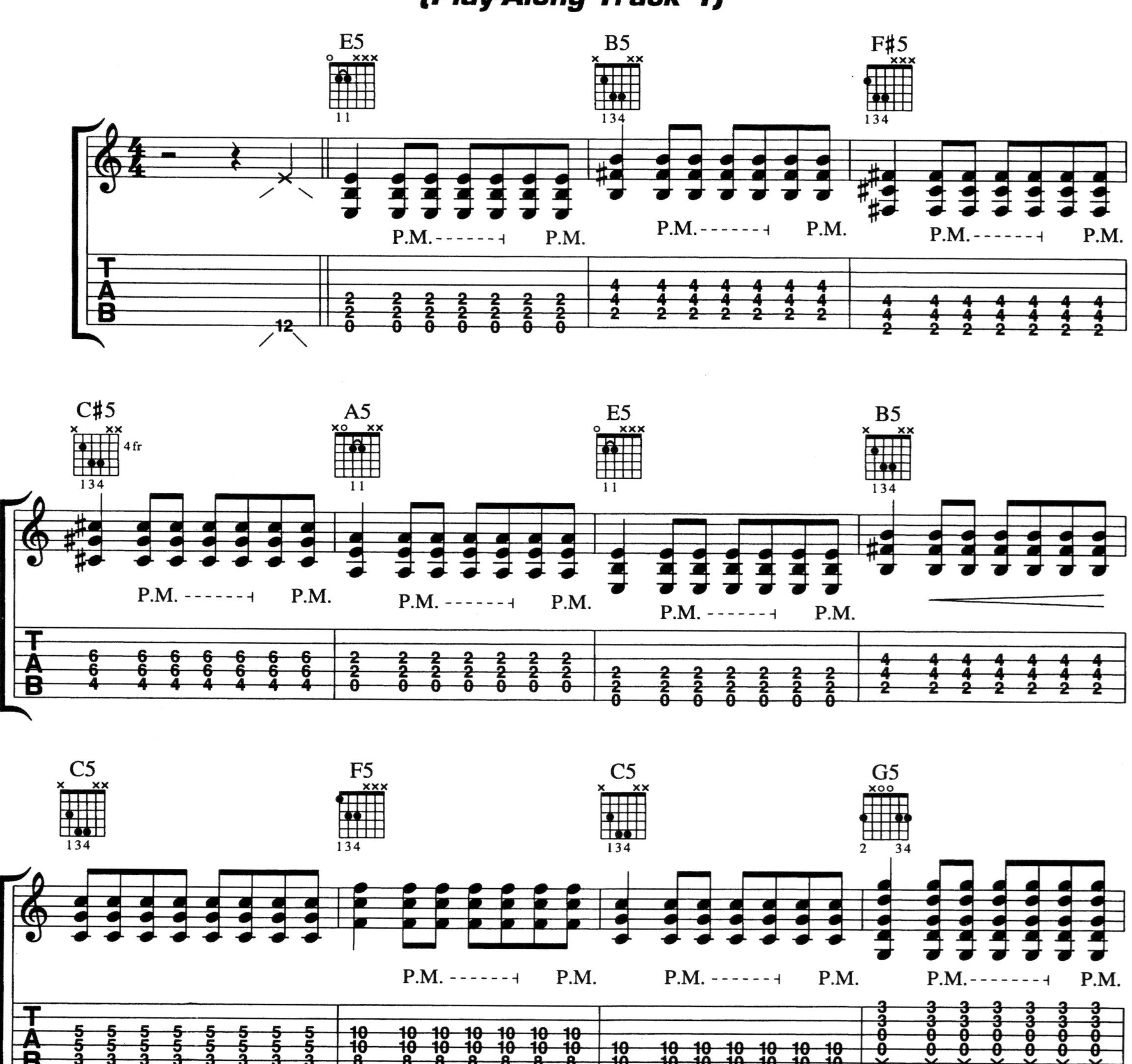

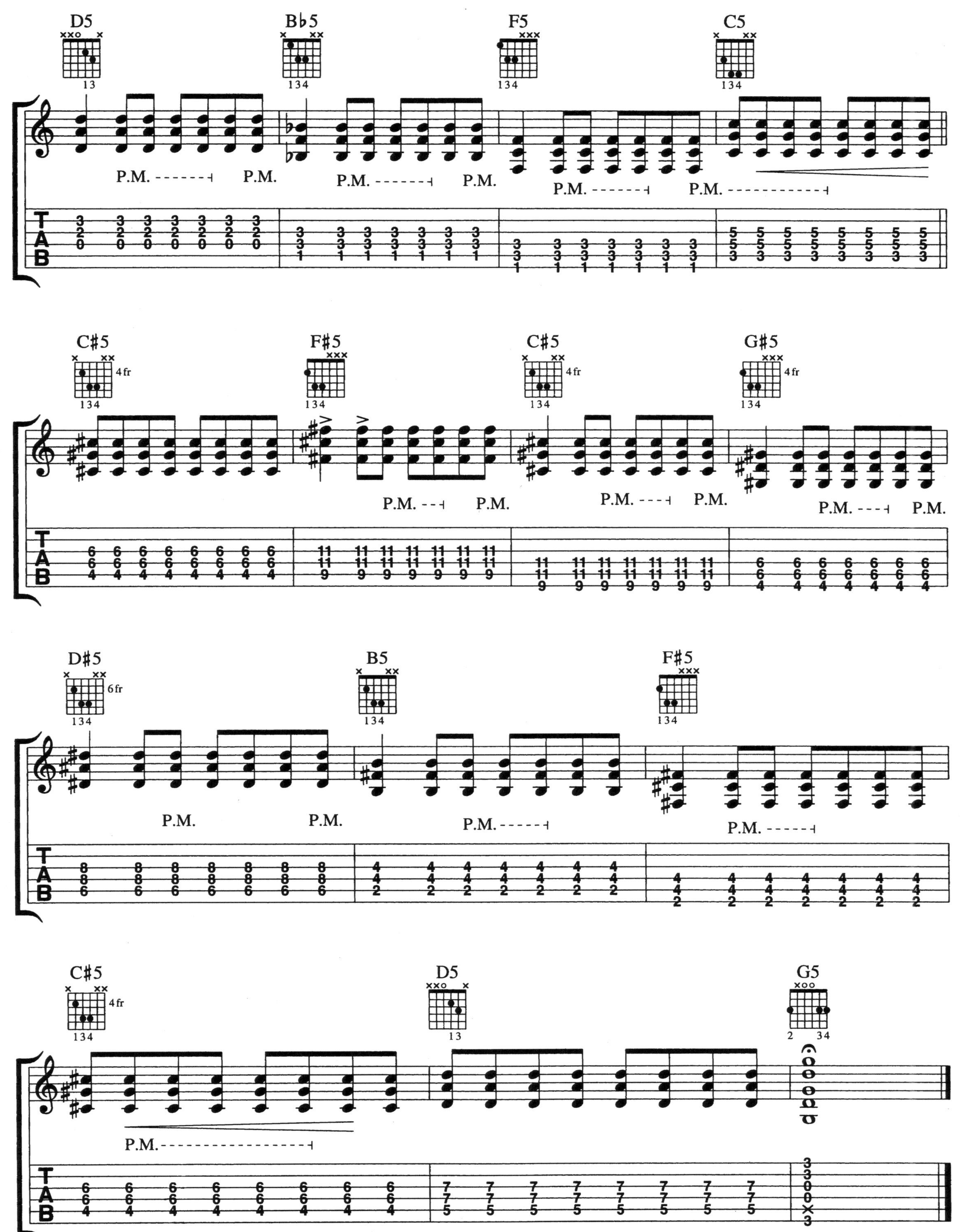
D5
13
B♭5
134
F5
134
C5
134
P.M.
P.M.
P.M.
P.M.
P.M.
P.M.
C♯5
4fr
134
F♯5
134
C♯5
4fr
134
G♯5
4fr
134
P.M.
P.M.
P.M.
P.M.
P.M.
P.M.
D♯5
6fr
134
B5
134
F♯5
134
P.M.
P.M.
P.M.
P.M.
C♯5
4fr
134
D5
13
G5
2 34
P.M.

SECTION 11: MORE CHORDS

The following chords will sound better without distortion. If you do use distortion, palm muting and arpeggiation will reduce the harshness. **Arpeggiation** is playing the chord one note at a time, a useful technique for both rhythm and lead.

The Csus2 Chord

The sus2 chord is an extension of the power chord. As the name states, you add the 2nd note of the scale to the chord. The 2nd note of a C scale is D. Depending on how the notes of these chords are arranged, you can also call them add2, add9, or (9) chords.

The 'Sus4' Chord

The suspended chord (sus), also known as the sus4 chord, replaces the 3rd with a 4th resulting in a chord consisting of a root, 4th and 5th.

Csus:	C	F	G	Dsus:	D	G	A	B♭sus:	B♭	E♭	F	Gsus:	G	C	D
	1	4	5		1	4	5		1	4	5		1	4	5

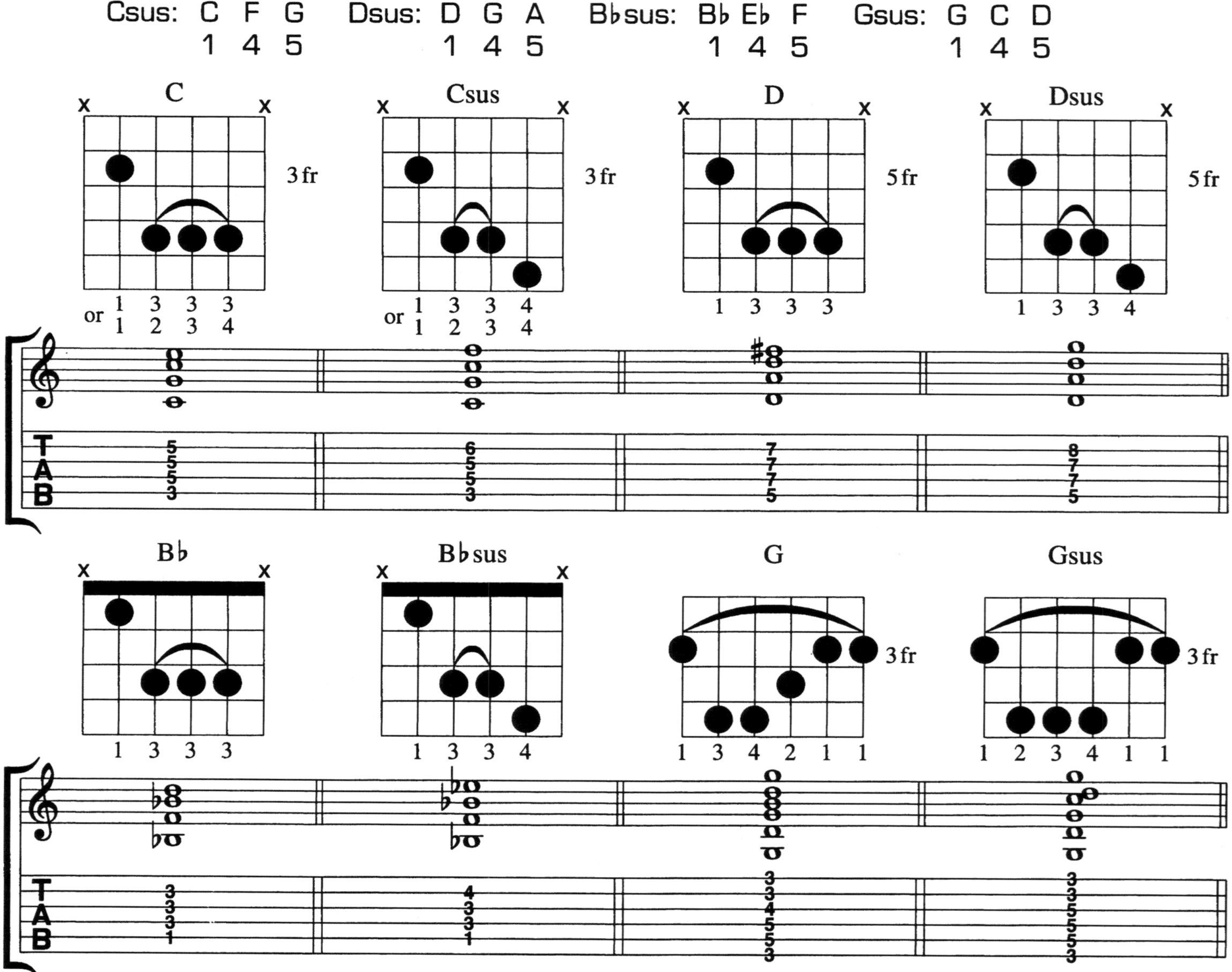

Example 100: Power Jam (Play-Along Track 2)

The best way to master any technique or skill is to apply it to music. If you can't find existing musical examples, write your own. This progression is designed to help you practice all of the chords that you have learned so far: sus2, sus4 and movable and open position power chords.

POWER JAM

(Play-Along Track 2)

A5 G5 A5
Dsus
D
A5 G5 A5
Dsus
D
A5 G5 A5
Dsus
D
Fsus2
C5
P.M.
D5
G5
A5
P.M.
D5
G5
A5
P.M.
D5
G5
A5
P.M.
E5
G5
*D.C.
TAB

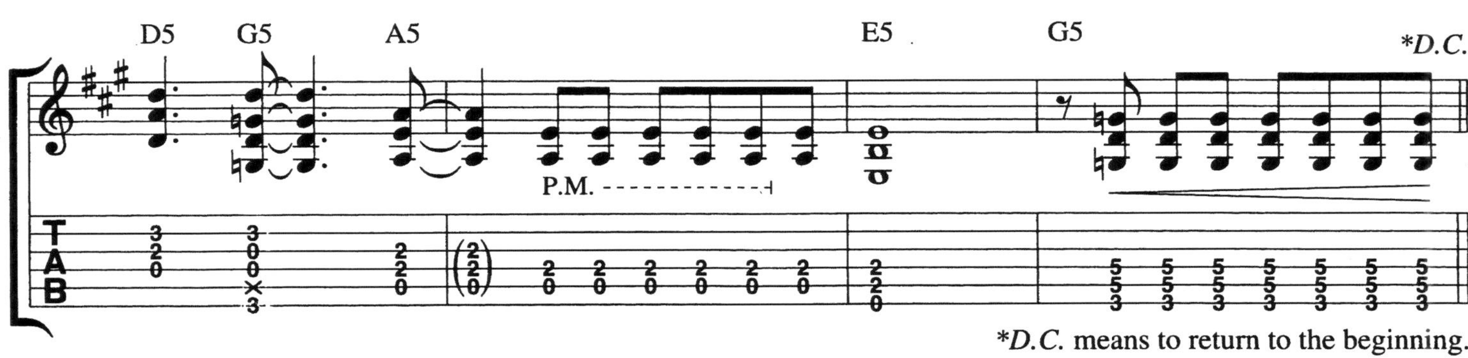

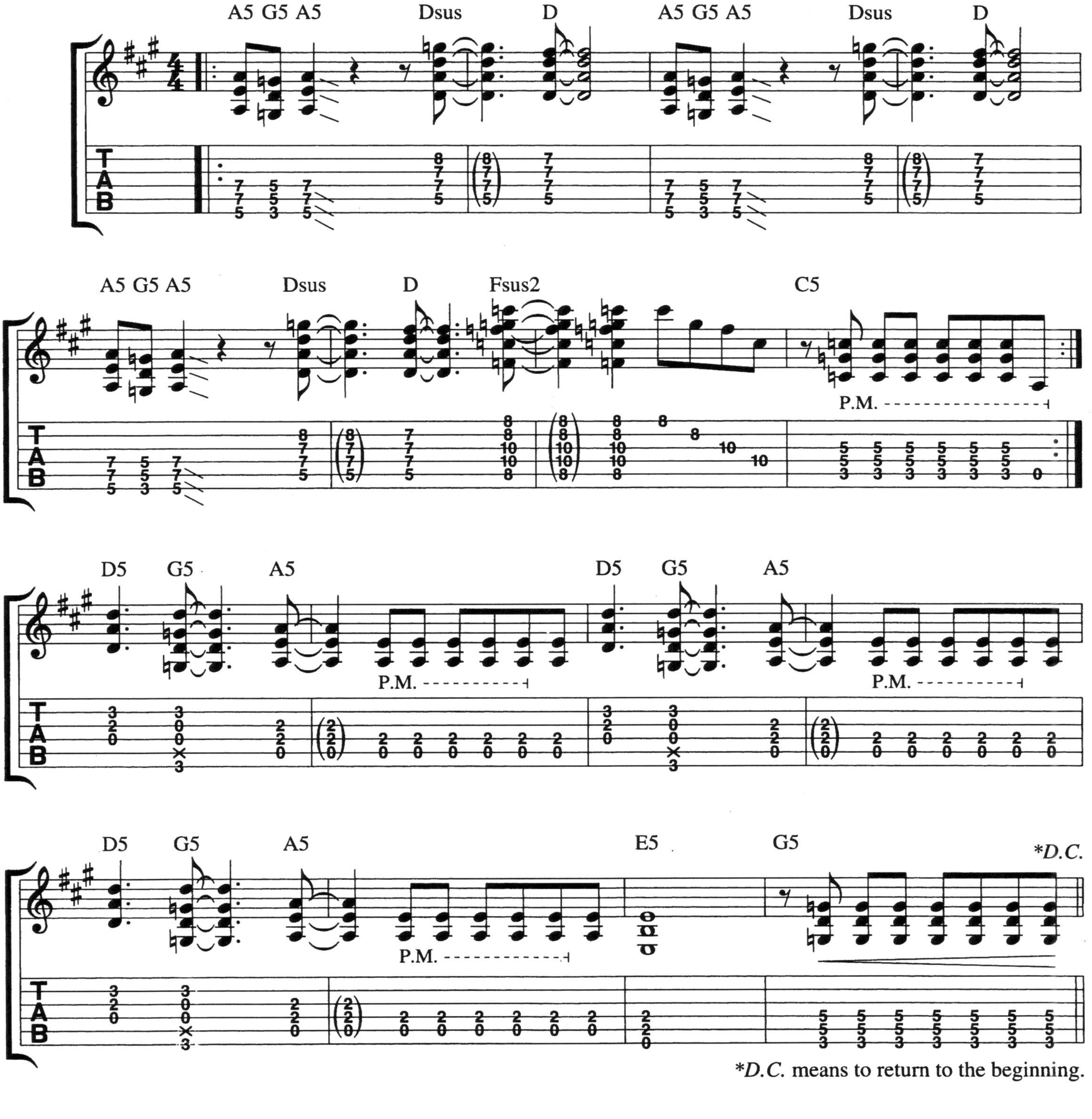

*D.C. means to return to the beginning.

SECTION 12: ROCK LICKS

Example 101: The Minor Pentatonic Scale

The most common rock scale is the minor pentatonic. This scale is a five-tone scale that implies a minor harmony. The lowest note of the following fingering is the root of the scale. Since this root is on A this scale is called the A minor pentatonic. Since the root is played with the first finger on the E string (sixth string), it is called the 1E fingering.

The A Minor Pentatonic Scale 1E Fingering

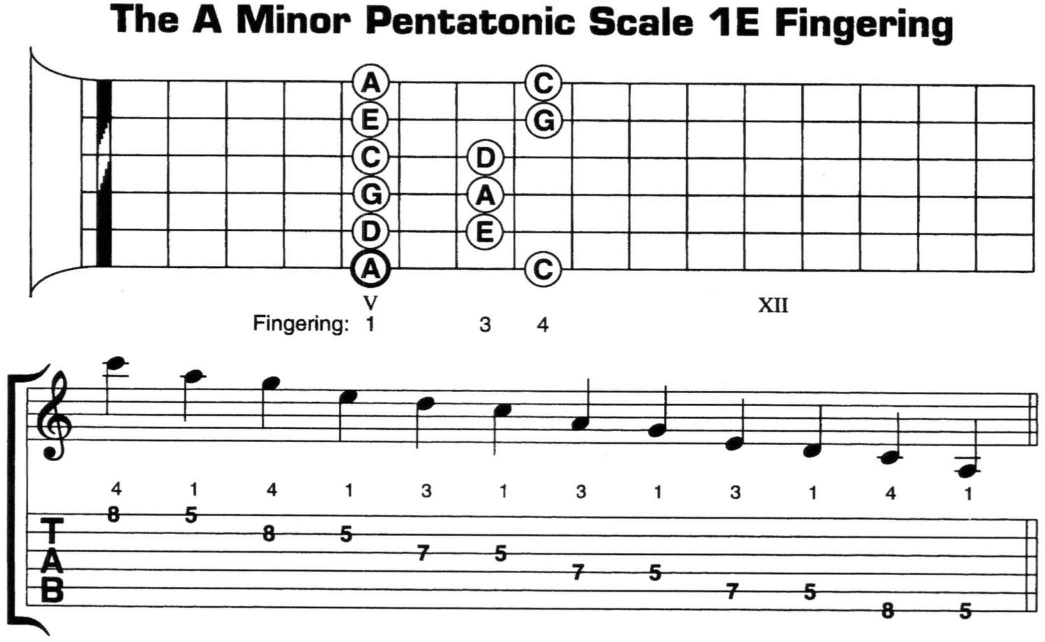

Example 102: Changing Key

Like barre chords, scale fingerings are movable. If for example, you play the 1E pentatonic fingering two frets higher you would have a B minor pentatonic scale. Take some time to play and memorize all of the remaining keys while making sure that you pay close attention to what note the root is.

The B Minor Pentatonic Scale 1E Fingering

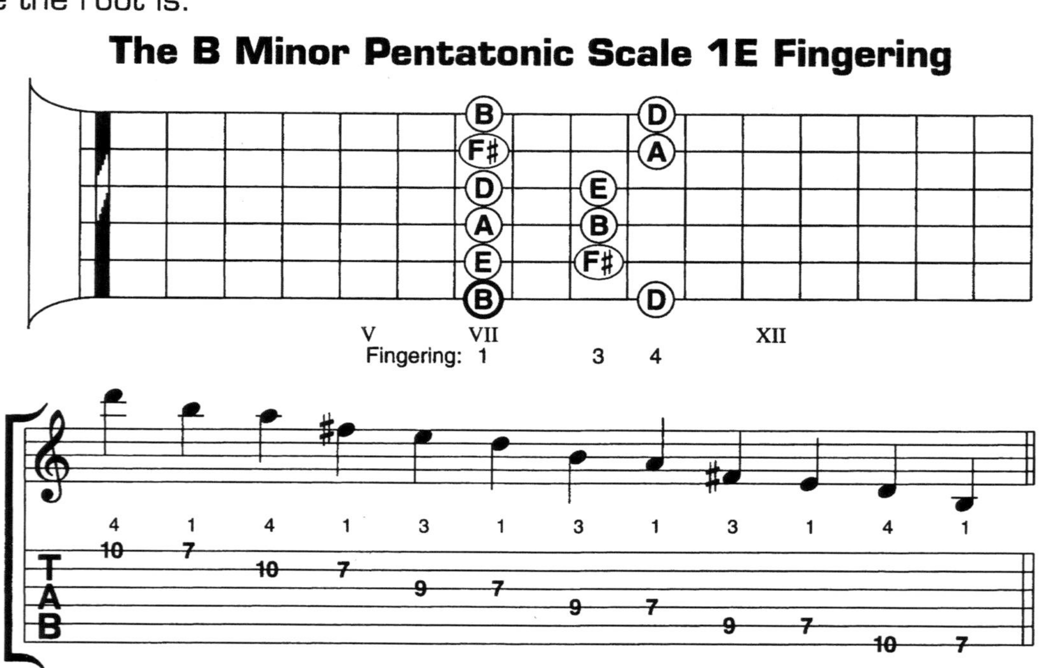

BENDING

The techinque of stretching the string to a higher note is called **bending**. It is very important that you make every attempt to bend the note all the way to the proper pitch; you can't be sharp or flat, you have to be right on target. Having good, accurate bends is essential for any lead guitarist. Let's review the things to remember when bending:

- Use as many fingers as possible. If you're bending with your fourth finger, make sure the other three are right behind it. If you're bending with your third finger, support it with the first and second finger. If you're bending with your second finger, support it with your first finger. The first finger is on its own.

- When bending upward, some people wrap their thumb over the top of the neck for support.

- Make sure you are bending accurately to pitch by comparing the bent note to a fretted note.

Example 103: Bending Lick

Remember to use as many fingers as available for strength and support. If, like the first note of this lick, you bend a note with your 3rd finger, use your 1st and 2nd fingers to help support the bend.

This lick starts off with a bend from the D on the 3rd string, 7th fret to the E which, if the note is bent correctly, will sound like the 9th fret of the same string. So that your ear knows how far you have to bend, strike an E first, bend the D until it sounds correct, then check yourself by playing the E again. You might find it easier to check the bent note against the E on the 5th fret of the 2nd string since that is the E that follows the bend in the lick.

Example 104: Bending Exercise

Here's an exercise that will help you improve your bending precision. Using bends only, play through a C major scale on the 3rd string. You will probably recognize the do, re, mi, fa, sol, la, ti, do characteristic of the major scale. There are two places that you have a short bend (half step): between the E and F and between the B and C. Be careful to avoid bending too far.

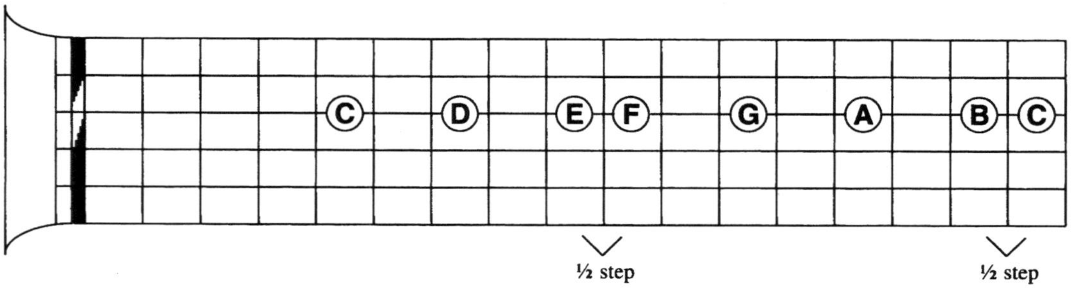

C D E F G A B C

½ step ½ step

Example 105: Minor Pentatonic Bends

In the minor pentatonic scale some notes seem to be bent more often than others. While this does not mean that you have any hard and fast rules about which notes are bent, you should use the following chart to organize your bending ideas.

This diagram illustrates the three most commonly bent notes in the minor pentatonic scale.

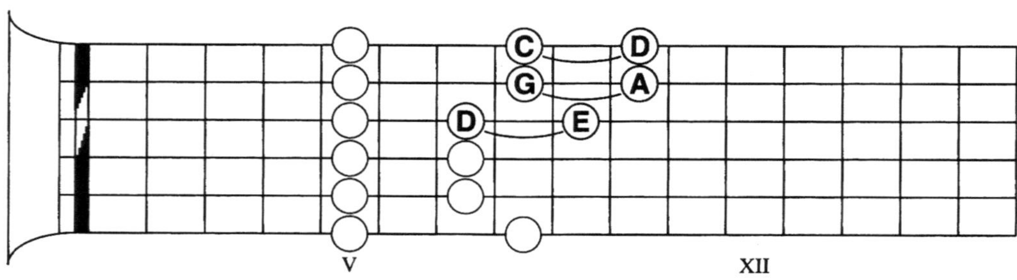

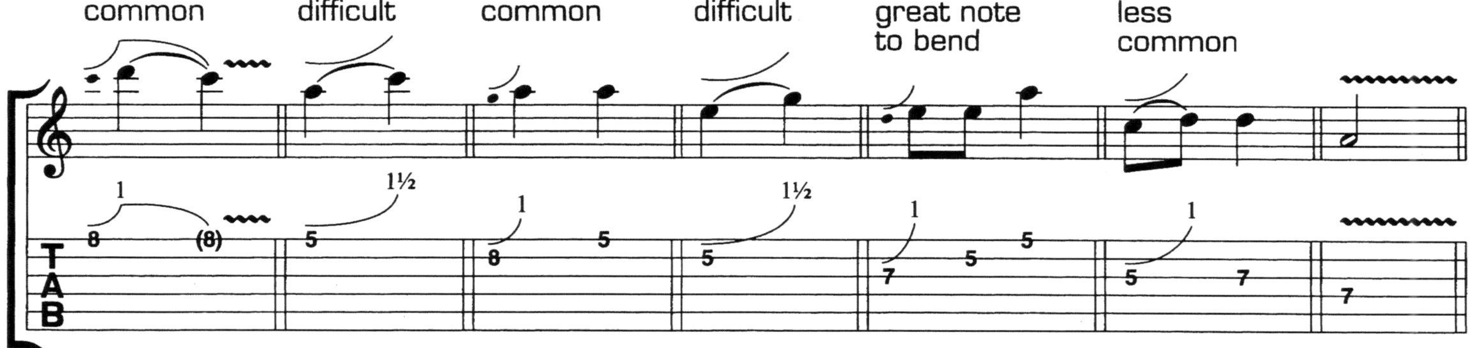

Vibrato:

As the word implies, you can describe vibrato as "vibrating" the notes you play. You can also think of it as a series of tiny bends that make the notes you play have more feeling and emotion. This is a technique often used to make an instrument sound more like a singer's voice. Vibrato is quite often the most identifiable characteristic of a guitar player's style.

The most important aspect of vibrato is eveness, both in distance and in rhythm. How far you bend the string is something that your ear will establish but you have to make sure you bend the string the same distance each time. Sometimes you might prefer a wider vibrato and other times you won't; there is nothing wrong with this as long as your vibrato is always even.

There are many types of vibrato but most rock players use **wrist vibrato**. This is accomplished by bending and releasing the string while making sure that the movement is centered at the wrist.

Some Points to remember:

- Like bending, remember to use as many fingers as available to reinforce the finger that is holding the note.
- Rest the neck of the guitar on the spot where the first finger joins your hand. Use this part of your hand as a fulcrum point. Pivot the wrist back and forth and repeatedly pull the string down (towards the floor) and return. You can also execute a vibrato by pushing upward.
- To move more freely, some people completely release their thumb from the neck.
- Begin with a very slow, wide vibrato and then adjust it according to taste.

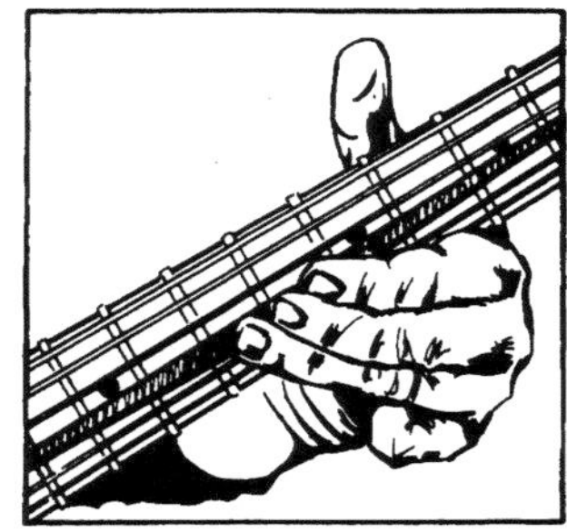

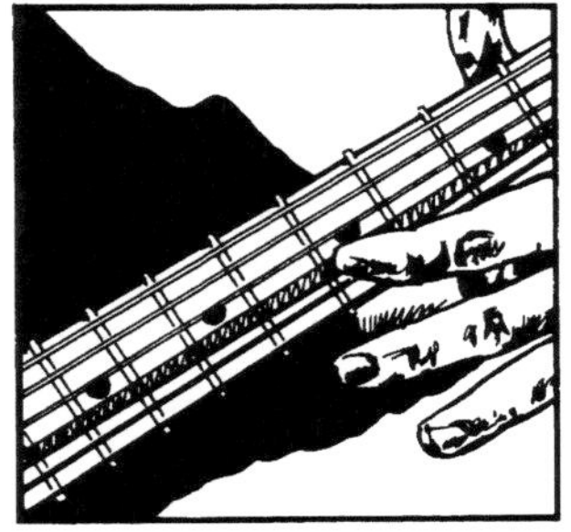

Example 106: Sequence Lick With Pull-offs

This next lick starts off with a **sequence**. A sequence is an arrangement of notes that repeat.

There are a lot of **pull-offs** in this lick which will help you build up speed sooner. To play a pull-off, place your fingers on the first *two* notes of the lick. Strike the first note and then pull your 4th finger across the string as if you're trying to pluck the string with your fourth finger. Make sure that your first finger does not come off of its note. When you pull the fourth finger off the string, you will be exposing the note that your first finger was holding. This way you only pick one note for every two notes you play.

In addition to the convenience, pull-offs add more style to the lick. Try the same lick with and without the pull-offs to get an idea of how much the sound and feel is affected by the inclusion and exclusion of these slurs. Apply this same type of comparison with the remaining licks in the book.

Example 107: Double-Stop Lick

A **double-stop** means playing two notes at the same time. Chuck Berry made this sound popular and now it's a staple riff of almost every guitarist.

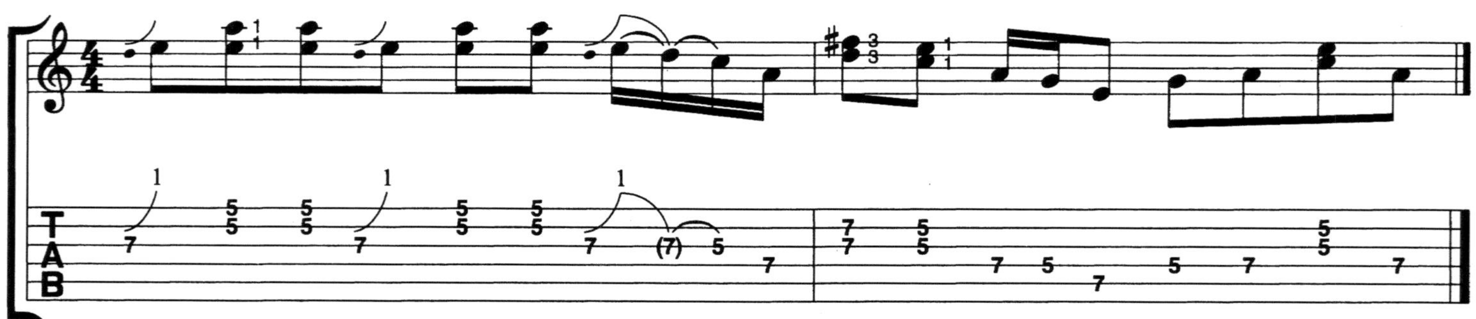

Example 108: Extended fingerings

You can extend the range of the minor pentatonic scale by shifting from one position to another. You will be playing the same notes as before but locating them on different parts of the neck. Not only does this extend the range of the scale but it allows you more options for fingering. The different fingerings can make licks that are difficult, even unplayable in one position, easier to play by re-arranging the fingerings. For example, you can not execute a true pull-off between notes that are on different strings. The best solution is to find a fingering that places the notes you need on the same string.

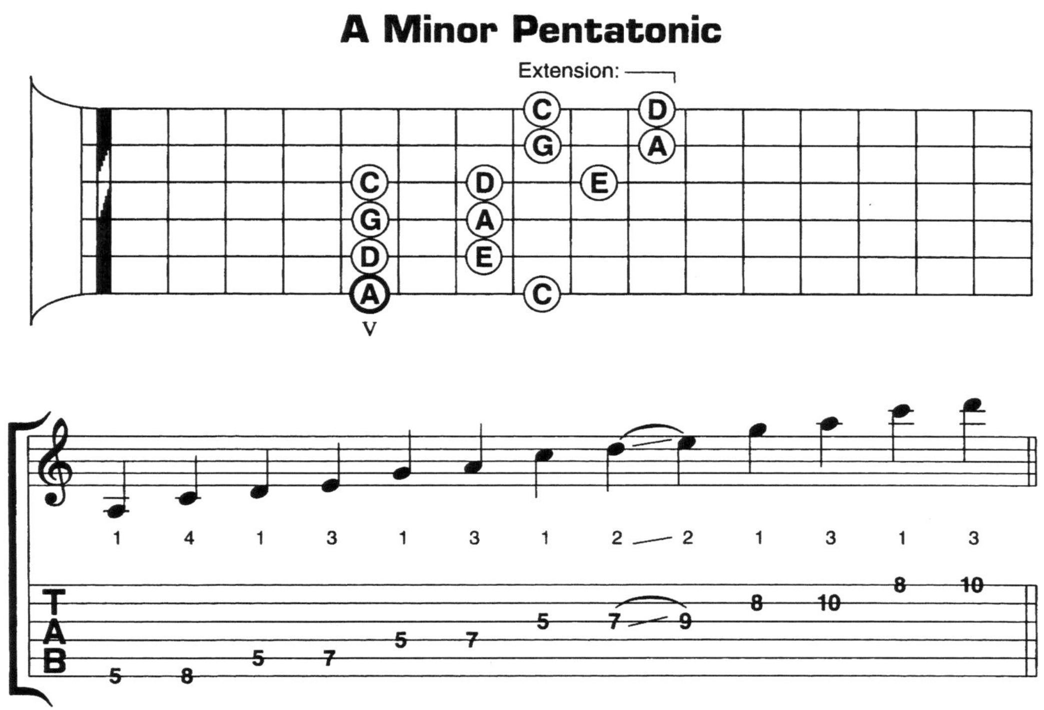

Example 109: Extended fingering lick

The following lick is based on the extended fingering.

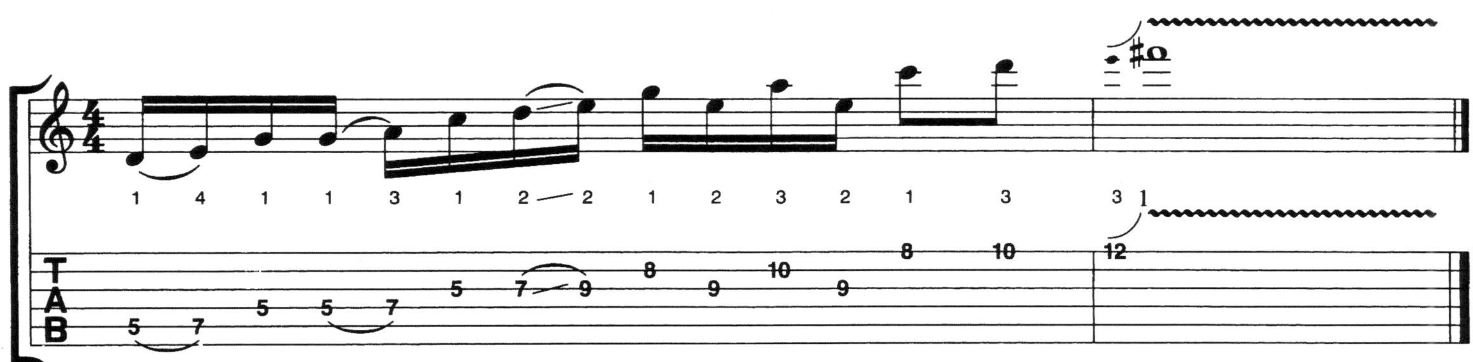

Octaves

The extended fingering contains the same notes as the box fingering but on different strings and different octaves. It is important that you eventually learn all of the different locations for each note.

The following diagram shows all of the possible locations for the note A. The important thing that you should notice is the distance between each of the notes. These distances create visual shapes that are easy to memorize. It is much easier to get around the fingerboard if you memorize the following, movable octave *shapes* and then apply them to the remaining eleven notes:

Octave Diagram

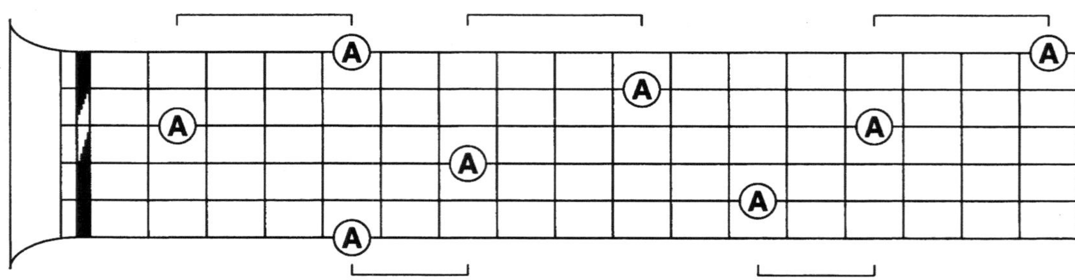

Octave Shapes

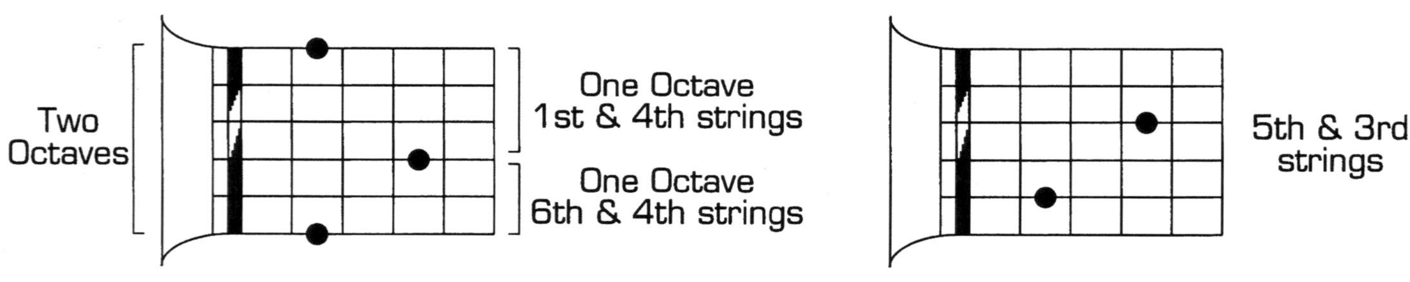

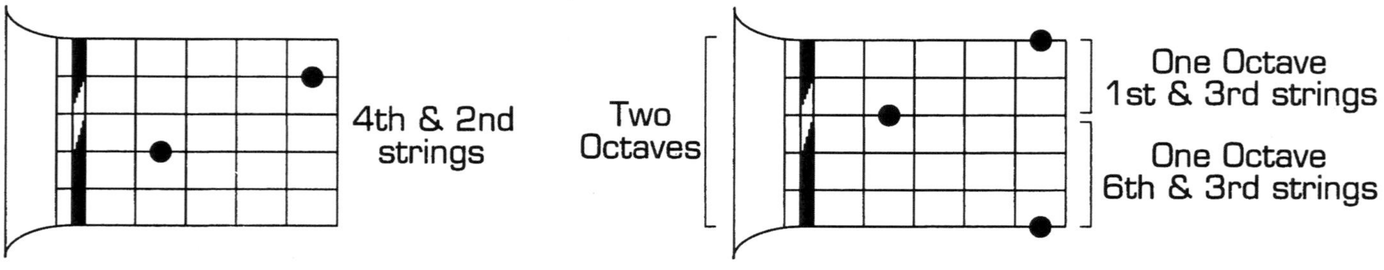

Example 110: New Scale Fingering

When you play a scale within a four or five fret range you are playing a box position. The following fingering is a box position for the A minor pentatonic scale on the twelfth fret. This time the root of the scale is under the first finger on the lowest note on the 5th string. This fingering is sometimes called the 1A fingering because you are playing the lowest root with the 1st finger on the A string.

A Minor Pentatonic 1A Fingering

Example 111

The following example is based on the 1A fingering. Notice some previously discussed devices: bending, double-stops and a pull-off. The second measure introduces a hammer-on which is the opposite of the pull-off. You play a lower note on one string and add a higher note on the same string by "hammering" your finger down on to the fret. You do not have to hit the higher note very hard but you do have to move quickly to keep the string vibrating. If you move too slow you will kill the vibration of the string.

When playing the bend combined with the double-stop, you have to be very careful to bend only the note on the second string. Your 4th finger should hold the note on the 1st string without bending it.

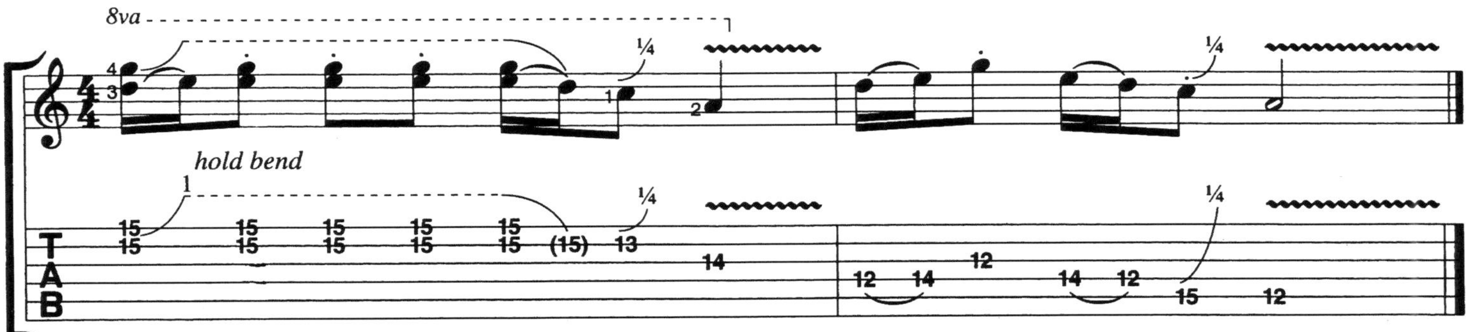

Example 112: Picking Exercise

As you learn more and more licks you will find that some are more demanding than others. What you need to do is work on some exercises to get your two hands working together.

Use the following repetitive picking exercise to help build your picking accuracy. Make sure you play each note separately and do not go too fast. Concentrate on making sure you constantly alternate between down-strokes (⊓) and up-strokes (v). Practice each of the measures separately before you combine them.

Example 113: Left Hand Hammer

This lick is another repetitive pattern that combines bending with pull-offs. There is a new technique involving a hammer-on to the 8th fret of the second string which is called the **left hand hammer**. Unlike most hammer-ons, this one is landing on a string that isn't already ringing.

Example 114: New Sequence Pattern

Here is a sequence exercise. As with all of the other exercises, this works well as a soloing idea.

Example 115: Driving Rock Jam (Play-Along Track 3)

After taking in all of this new information, it would be a great idea to try it all out by jamming with friends or play-along tracks, including the tracks on the recording.

After the solo is over, it is your turn to solo. The progression is in the key of A so it will be easy for you to apply any of the licks and scales that have been covered up to this point.

Try experimenting with mixing ideas from different parts of the neck. For example, try starting something in the A minor pentatonic, 5th position (1E fingering):

Example 115A

"And then move on up to the minor pentatonic in the 12 position" (1A fingering):

Example 115B

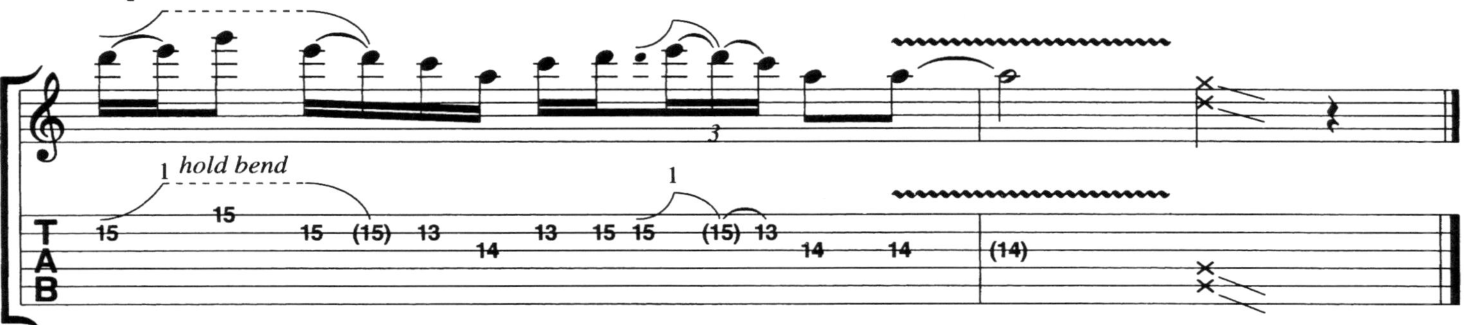

Example 115C: Play-Along

The solo has been transcribed note for note to provide you with more ideas. Make sure that you try to identify the scales and the fingering and that you listen carefully to how the harmony affects whatever idea you learn. You will probably recognize that the progression is the same as the one you learned in Example 4. Accompany the solo using that example.

DRIVING ROCK JAM

(Play-Along Track 3)

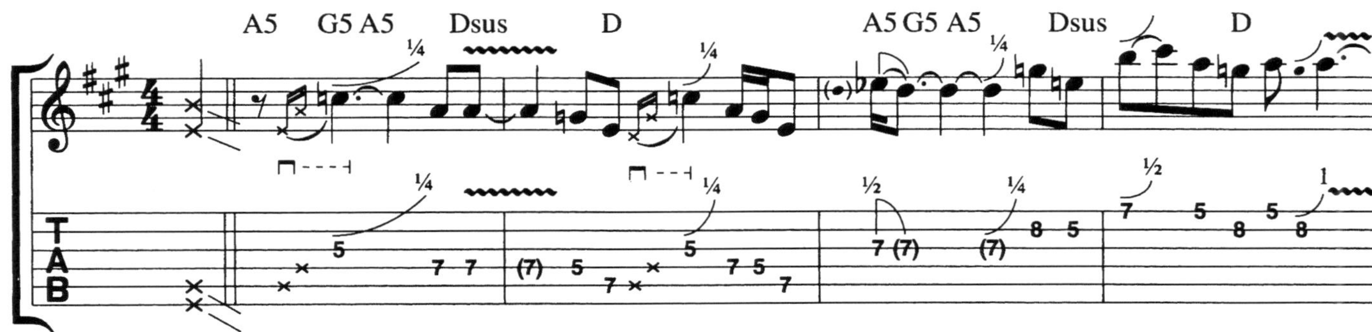

A5 G5 A5
Dsus
D
Fsus2
C
harm.
A5 G5 A5
Dsus
D
A5 G5 A5
Dsus
gradual bend
hold bend
D
A5 G5 A5
hold bend
Dsus
hold bend
D
Fsus2
8va
(8va)
C5
D5
G5
A5
D5
G5
A5

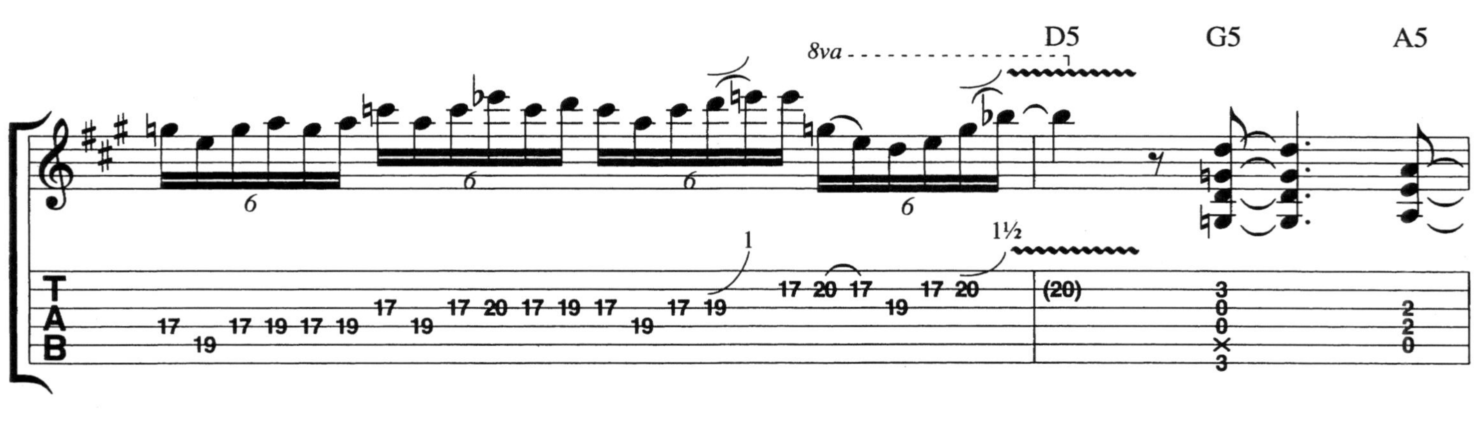

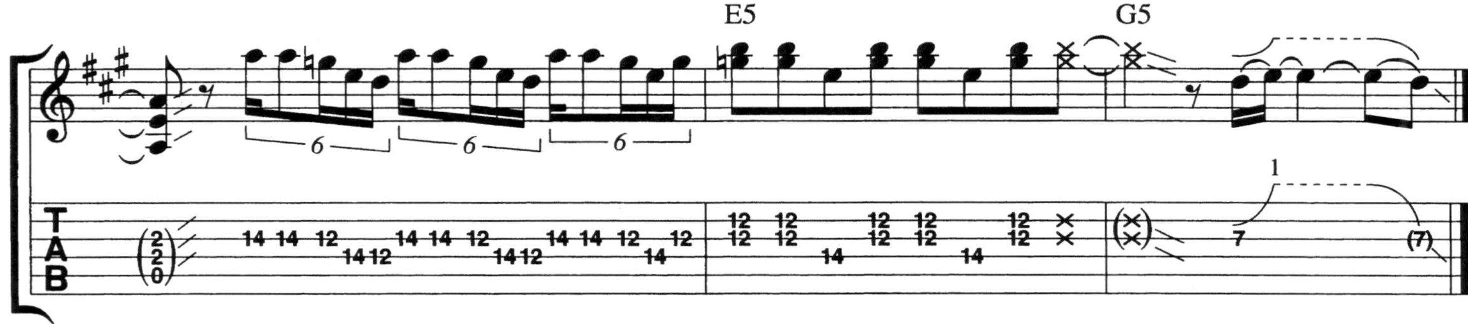

Driving Rock Jam Progression

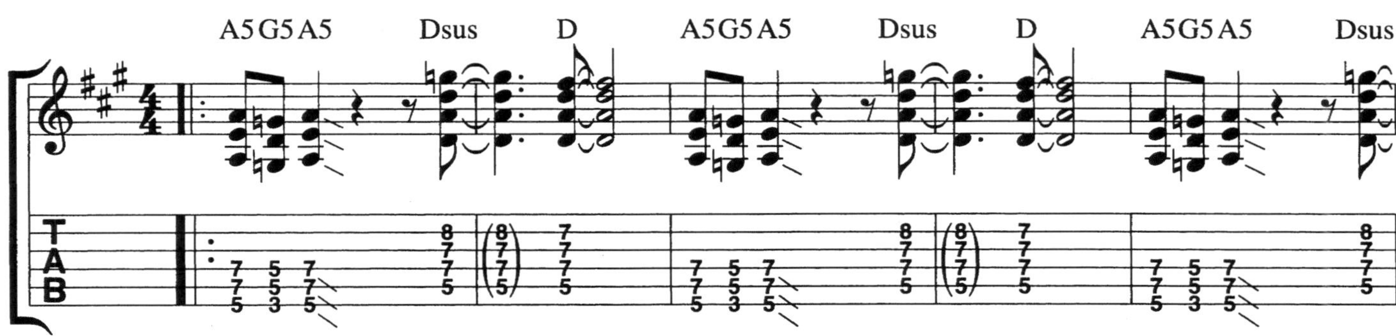

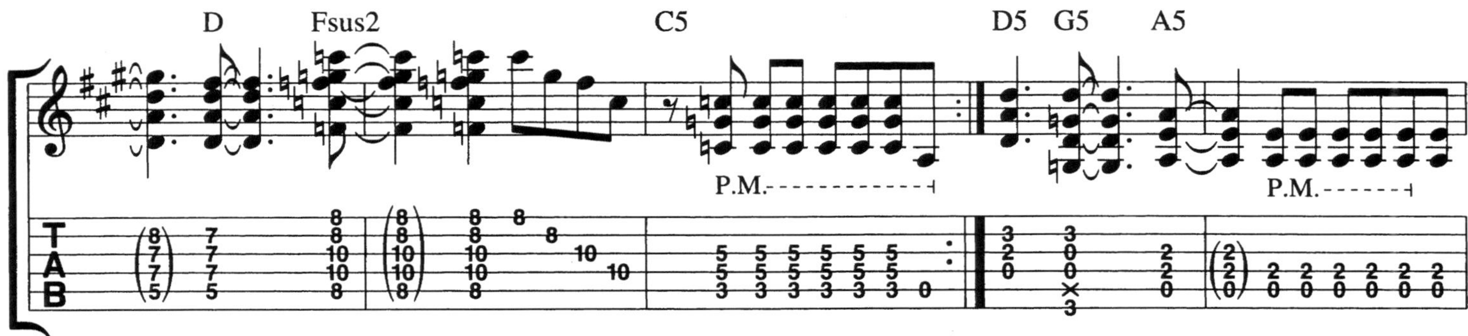

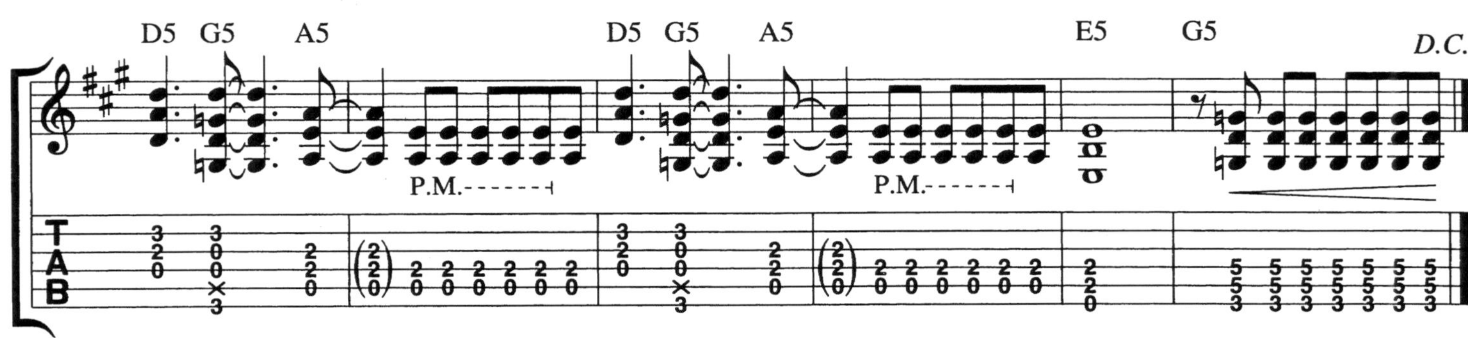

SECTION 13: DOMINANT 7 AND MINOR 7 CHORDS

Example 116: Funk Groove

The following example is a rhythm figure demonstrating a funky groove using thicker harmonies than the previous rhythms covered in this book. Again, notice that with distortion you risk the sound becoming cluttered if you are not careful.

Dominant 7 chords

Let's review dominant 7th chords. These chords are abundant in blues, funk, rock, metal, alternative, country and southern rock. Dominant 7 chords have a root, 3rd, 5th and 7th.

G7:	G	B	D	F
	1	3	5	♭7

C7:	C	E	G	B♭
	1	3	5	♭7

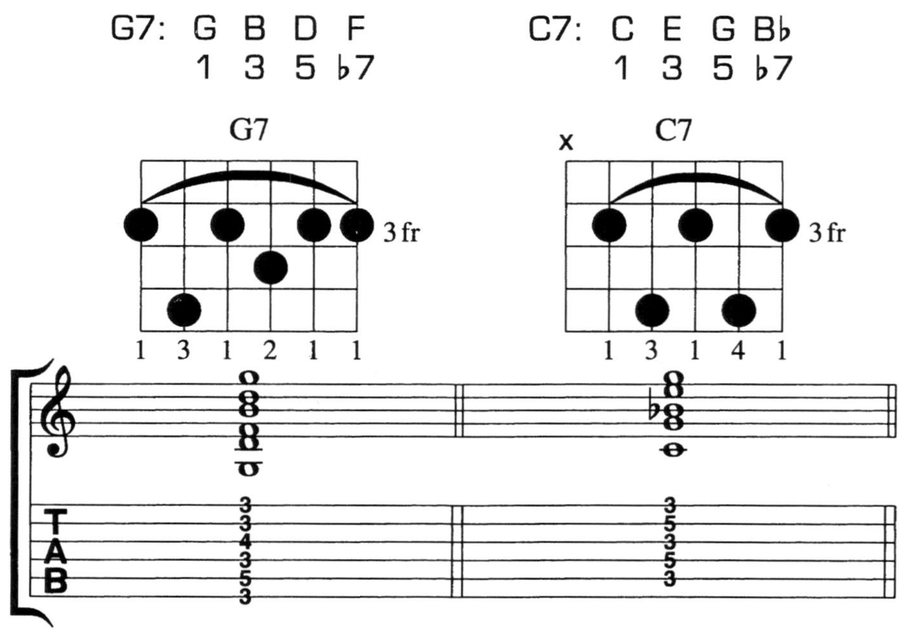

Minor 7 chords

Compare the previous dominant fingerings to these minor 7th voicings. Minor 7 chords have a root, ♭3rd, 5th and ♭7th.

Gm7: G B♭ D F
1 ♭3 5 ♭7

Cm7: C E♭ G B♭
1 ♭3 5 ♭7

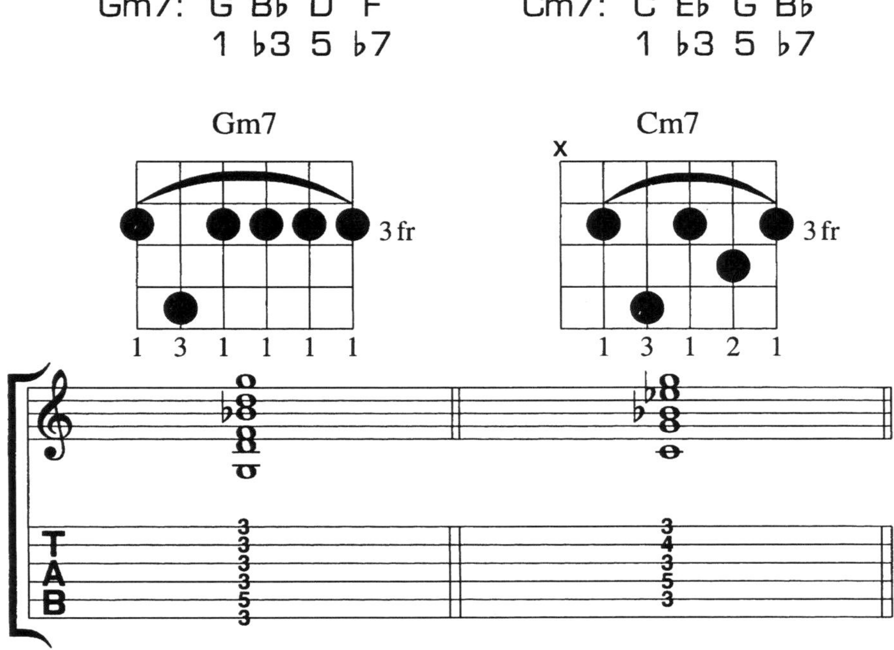

"Emptied Out" Fingerings

Both the dominant and minor 7th chords have a harmonically rich sound; too rich for distortion except in special circumstances. As stated before, you can reduce the "muddy" distortion by reducing the number of notes in the chords. The 5th is an expendable note. With your distorted sound, compare the following fingerings, which omit the 5th, with the previous examples.

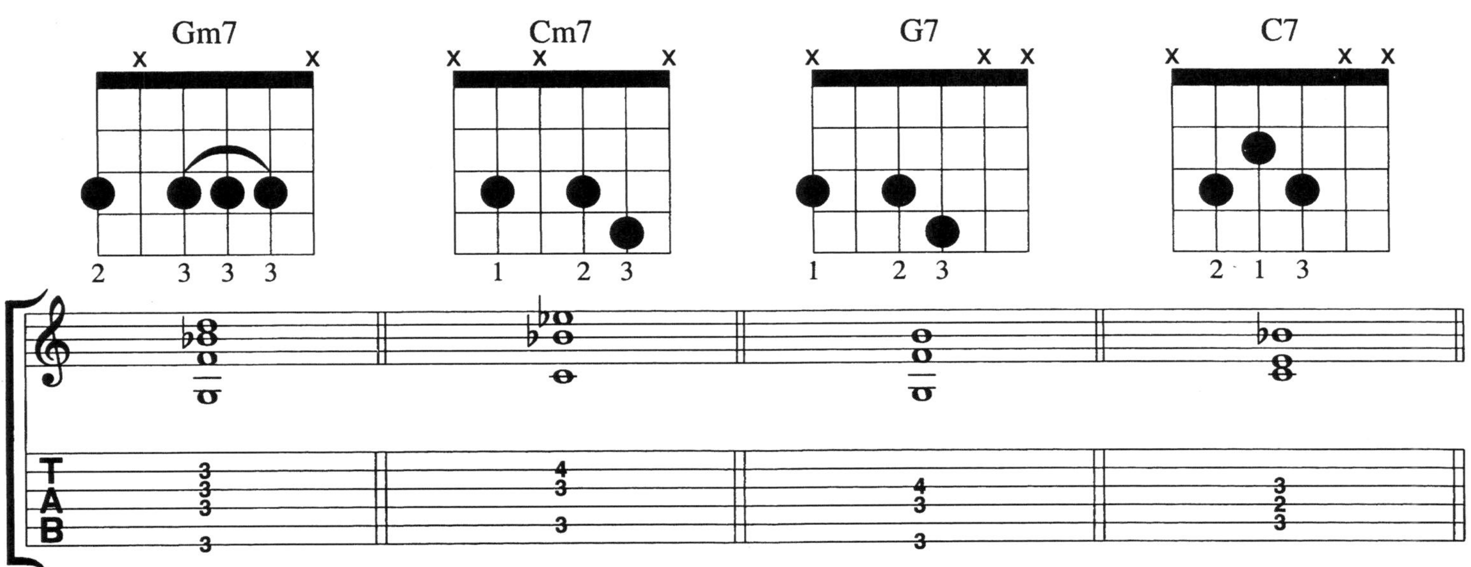

Example 117

Play the full voicing using the clean sound and switch to the "emptied out" version using the distortion.

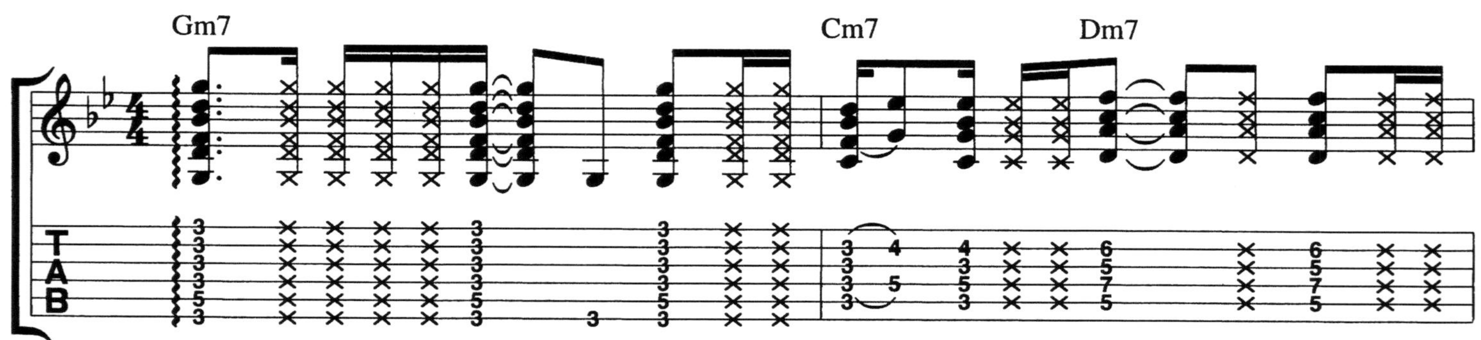

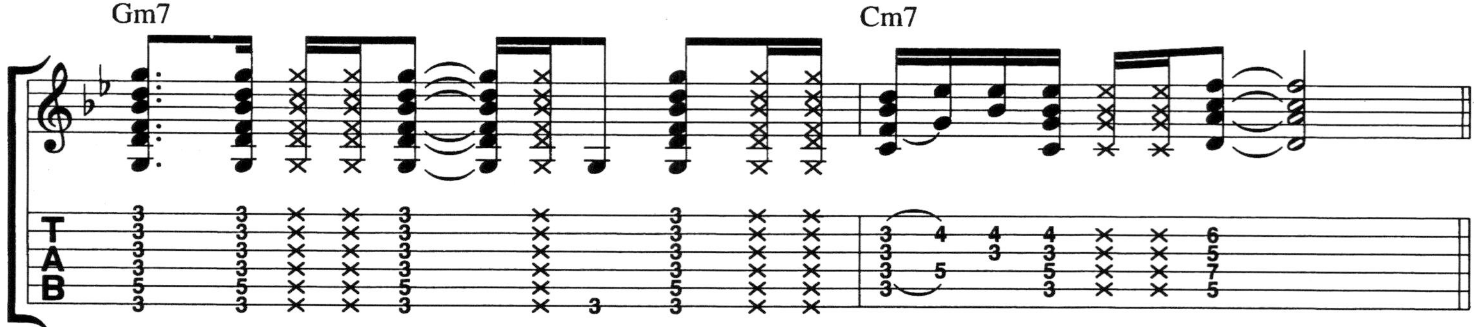

Now add distortion.

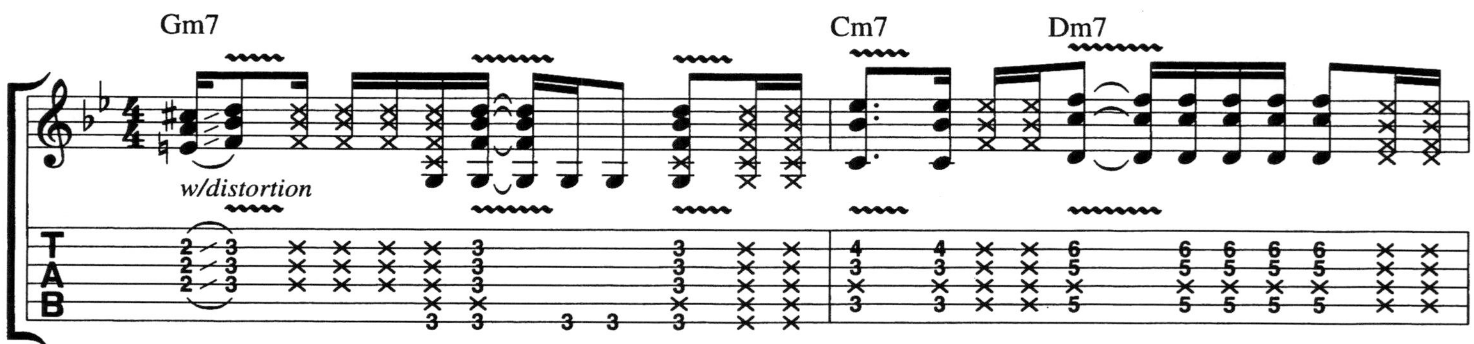

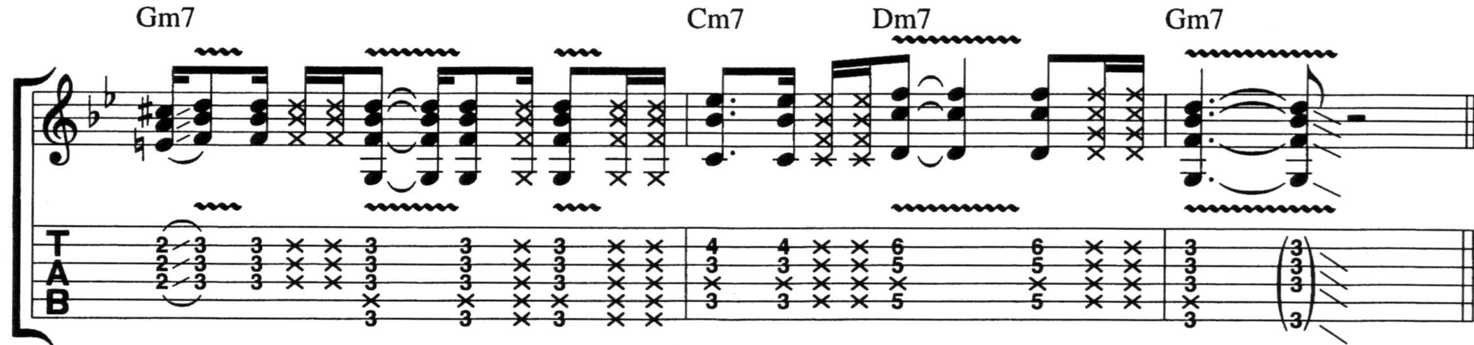

Example 118: Minor Funk Jam (Play-Along Track 4)

The following progression contains examples of "emptied out" voicings of minor 7 and dominant 7 chords and examples of add2 chords.

MINOR FUNK JAM

(Play-Along Track 4)

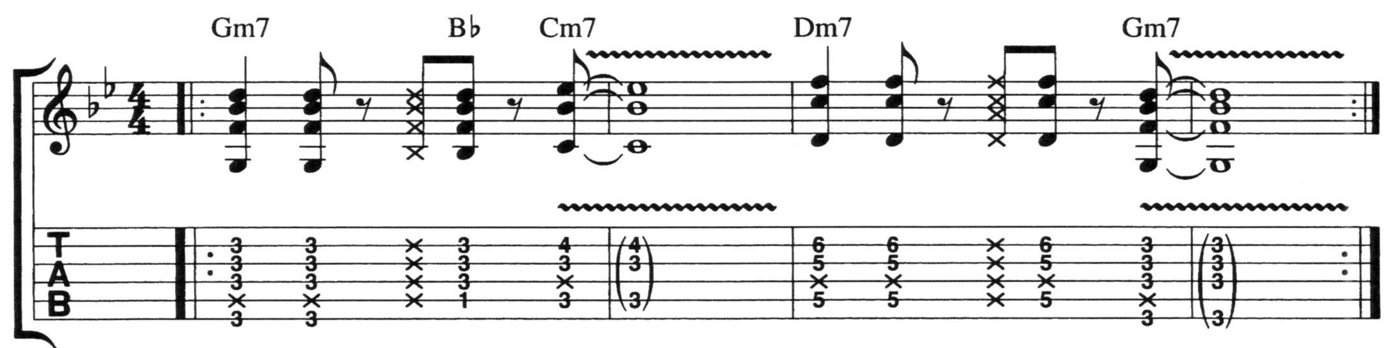

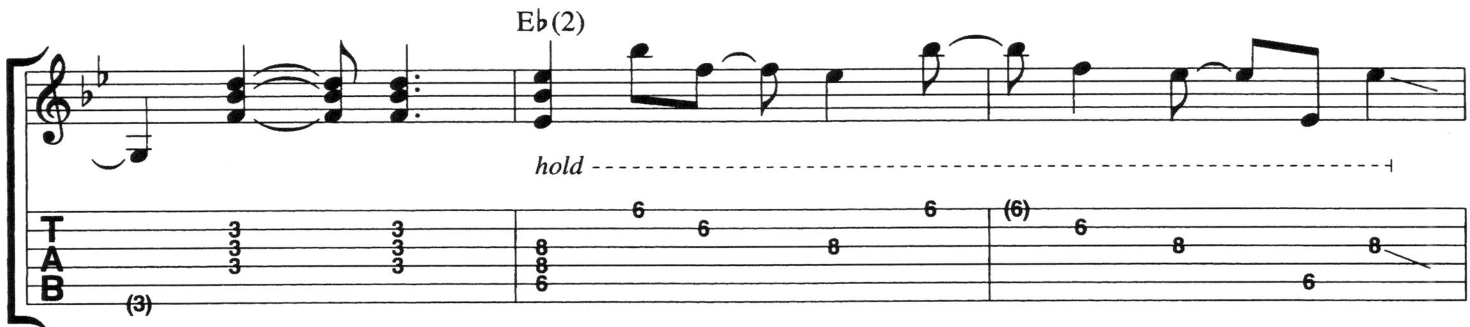

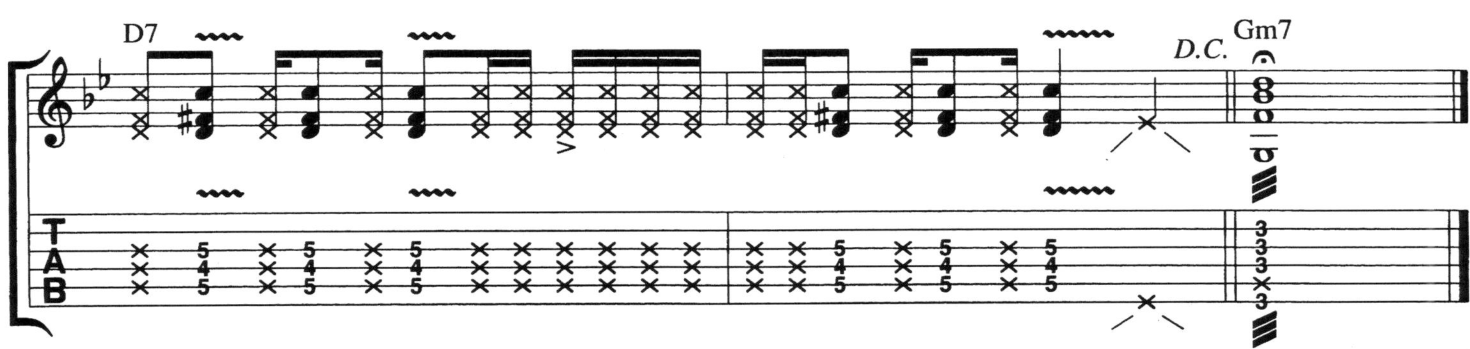

Example 119: Mixing Single Lines With Chords

Let's take the next step, as far as rhythm guitar goes, and approach the chords a bit differently. Instead of just strumming through them, break them up. Hit the lowest note first, stop it, and then hit the upper part. Practice this pattern slowly to make sure that there's separation between the low and high notes. Mute the low note while leaving the upper notes unmuted for better separation.

Example 119A

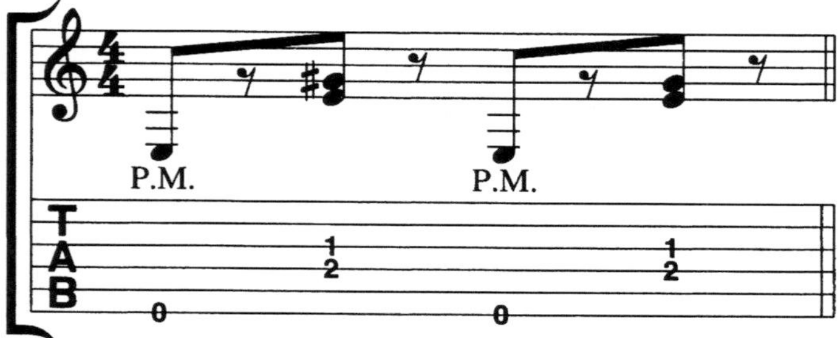

Example 119B

Example 119C

Example 120: Pedal Tone Progression

Try putting different chords together with the open E. The open E is called a pedal tone. While pedaling on the E, experiment with different chords using your ear to determine which ones you like.

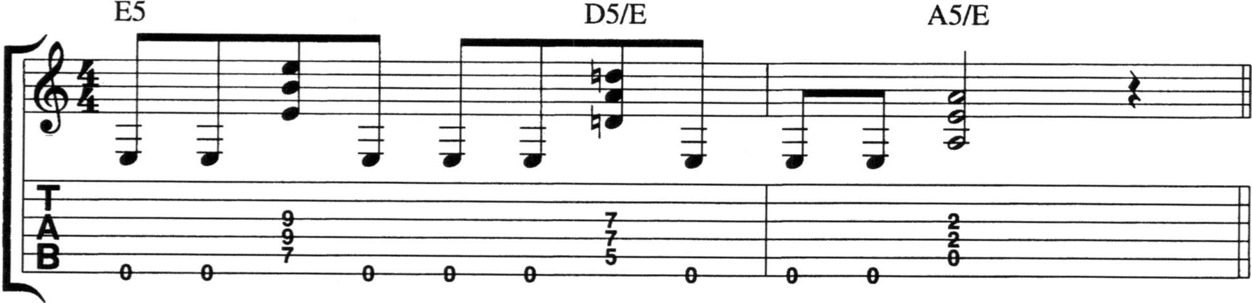

Example 121: Pedal to the Metal (Play-Along Track 5)

The following progression provides examples of pedaling and demonstrates single line accompaniment. Notice the usage of "emptied out" fingerings for the minor 7 and dominant 7 chords.

SECTION 14: PICKING TECHNIQUES

Example 122

For most people, the hardest thing to master about picking technique is getting the two hands to work together. It's kind of easy to go fast, but to be accurate about it with both hands is another thing. The following exercises are designed to syncronize your hands. Your goal is to make each note sound separated and clear. The worst thing you can do is go for speed right away. Play each note slowly, firmly and clearly with strict alternate picking. Also move each exercise to different strings and positions.

Example 122A

Example 122B

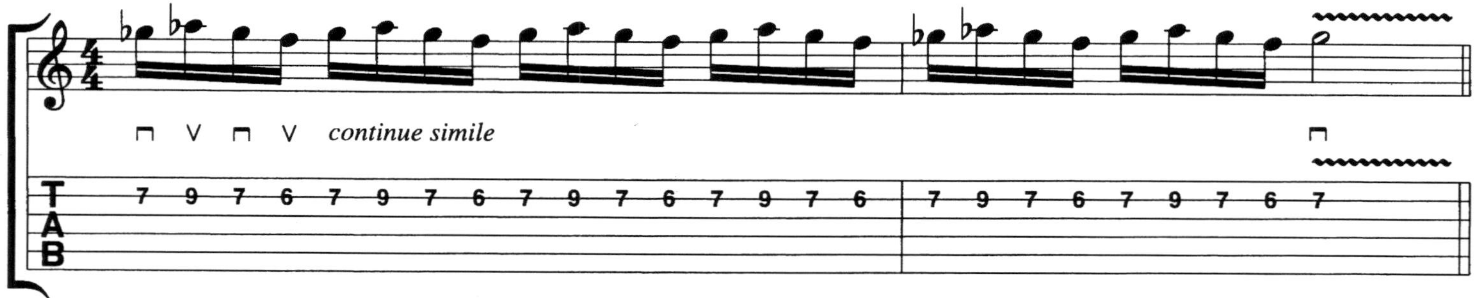

Example 122C

Example 123: String Switching

Examples 123A–123C focus on string switching. String switching is often a challenge for the right hand, especially if you are using alternate picking.

Example 123A

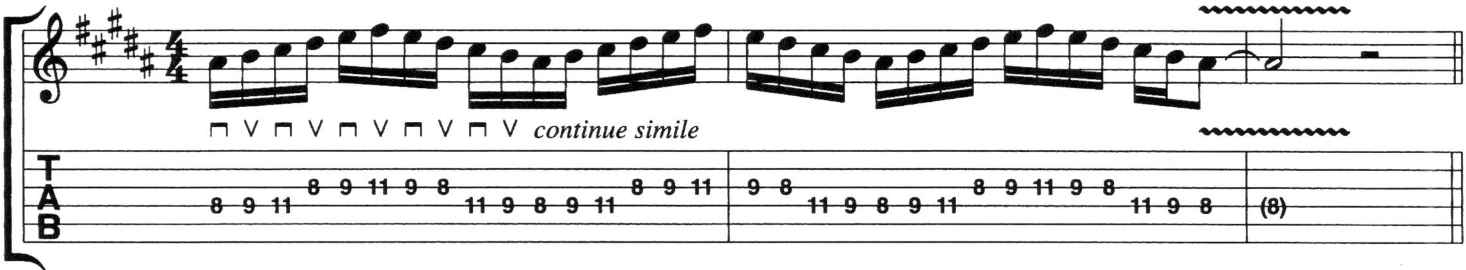

Example 123B

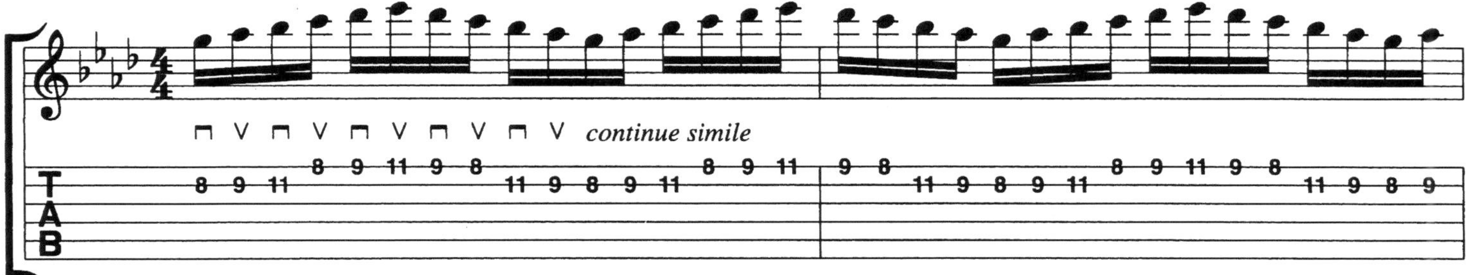

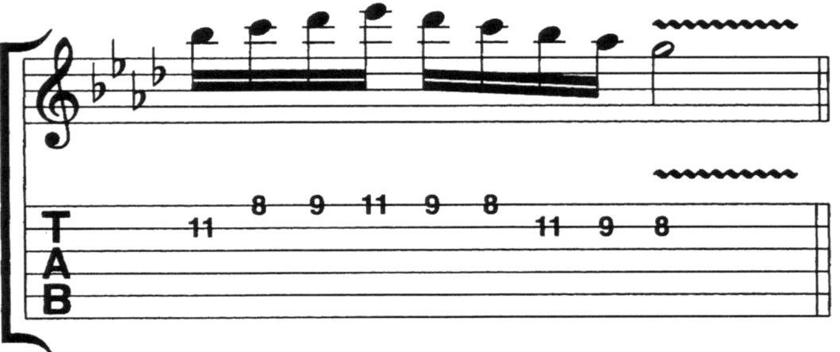

Example 123C

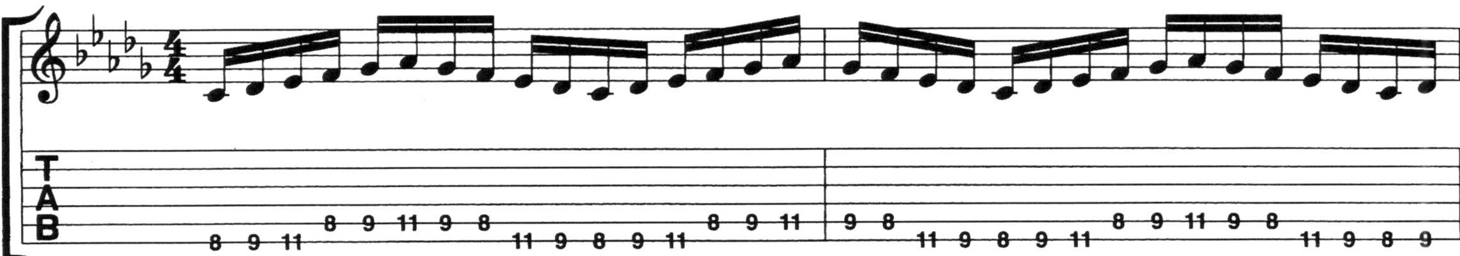

Example 124: Hammer-ons and Pull-offs

Now add hammer-ons and pull-offs while maintaining a separated and clear sound. A hammer-on is the opposite of a pull-off: play the first note with your pick, sound the next note by hammering your second finger onto the string without striking it.

Example 124A

Example 124B

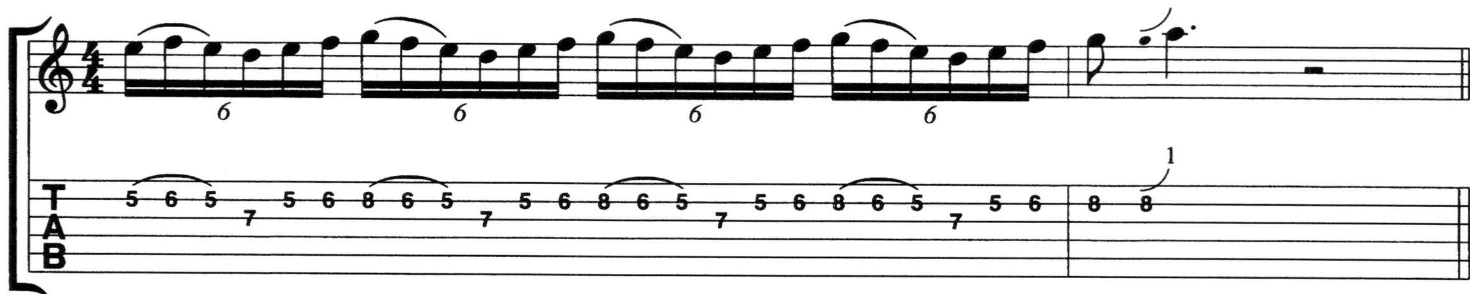

Example 124C

By combining Examples 124A and 124B, you have a lick that works really well for soloing.

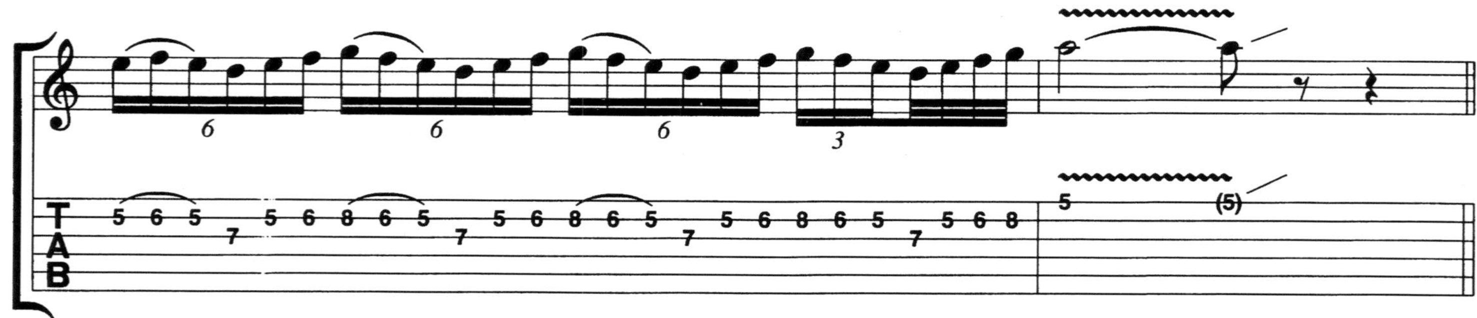

SECTION 15: MAJOR PENTATONIC SCALES

Up to now, all of our licks have come from the minor pentatonic scale; in this case the B minor pentatonic. But B minor is not the only name for this scale, it's also called the D major pentatonic scale. Every minor scale has a relative major and vice versa. The easiest way to remember the difference is that on the sixth string, the note under your first finger is the minor root and the fourth finger is on the major root.

The D Major Pentatonic Scale 4E Fingering

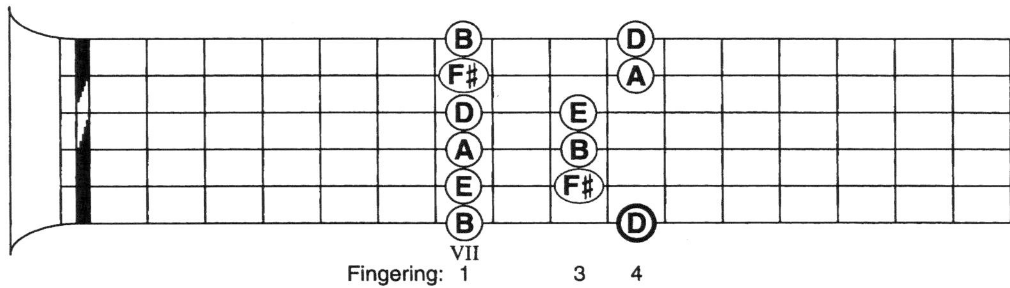

Songs are basically in a major key or a minor key. If you play a song that's in D major then you need a scale that works for D major.

What defines a scale in a major key? Setting aside complicated theoretical explanations, the basic rule to remember is that if the "home" chord is a major chord then you are most likely in a major key. The home chord is usually the chord that starts and finishes the progression.

Example 125: Major Jam (Play-Along Track 6)

Most of the minor pentatonic licks that you've learned so far can work as relative major pentatonic, but you should resolve on the root. Notice the following progression starts and ends on a D chord. As a result, D major pentatonic would be a good choice. Notice how the D note connects the scale to the chord.

MAJOR JAM

(Play-Along Track 6)

D
A
hold bend
hold bend
G
D
A
D
G

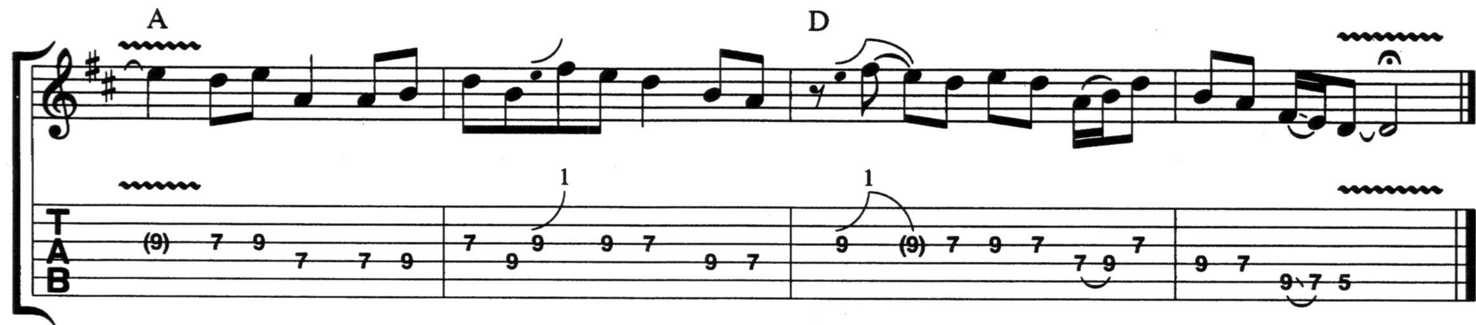

"Now try your own solo, using the D major pentatonic scale, over the following progression."

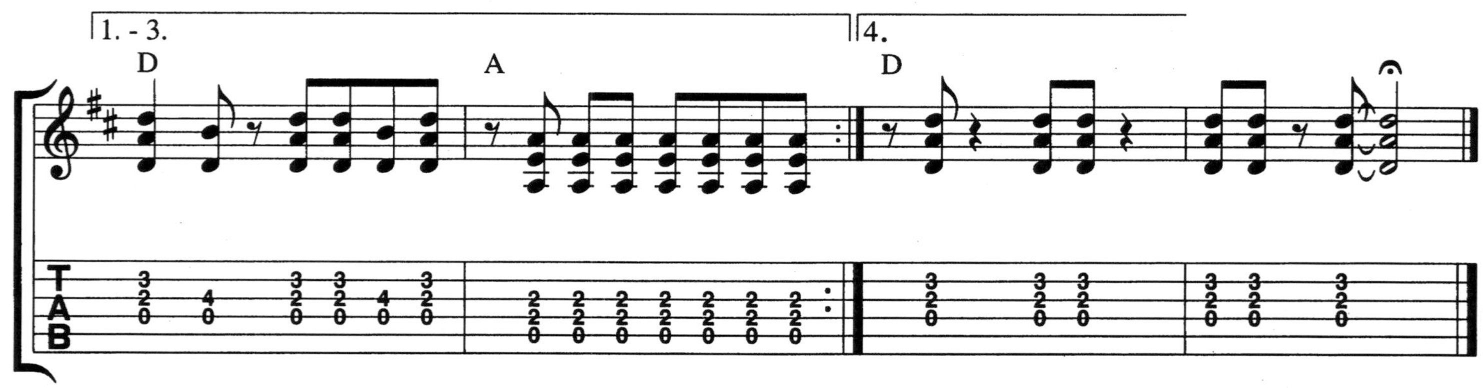

SECTION 16: DIATONIC SCALES

Diatonic scales are seven-note scales; two more than the pentatonic, and they are the basis of almost all the music we listen to.

Example 126: A Minor Scale

This is the diatonic A minor scale, which is usually called A minor, A natural minor or A pure minor. A great way to learn the A minor scale is to take the A minor pentatonic scale and add a 2nd (B) and a 6th (F).

A minor:	A	B	C	D	E	F	G	A
	1	2	♭3	4	5	♭6	♭7	1

A minor pentatonic:	A	C	D	E	G	A
	1	♭3	4	5	♭7	1

The A minor scale is relative to the C major scale; they have the same notes but start on different roots.

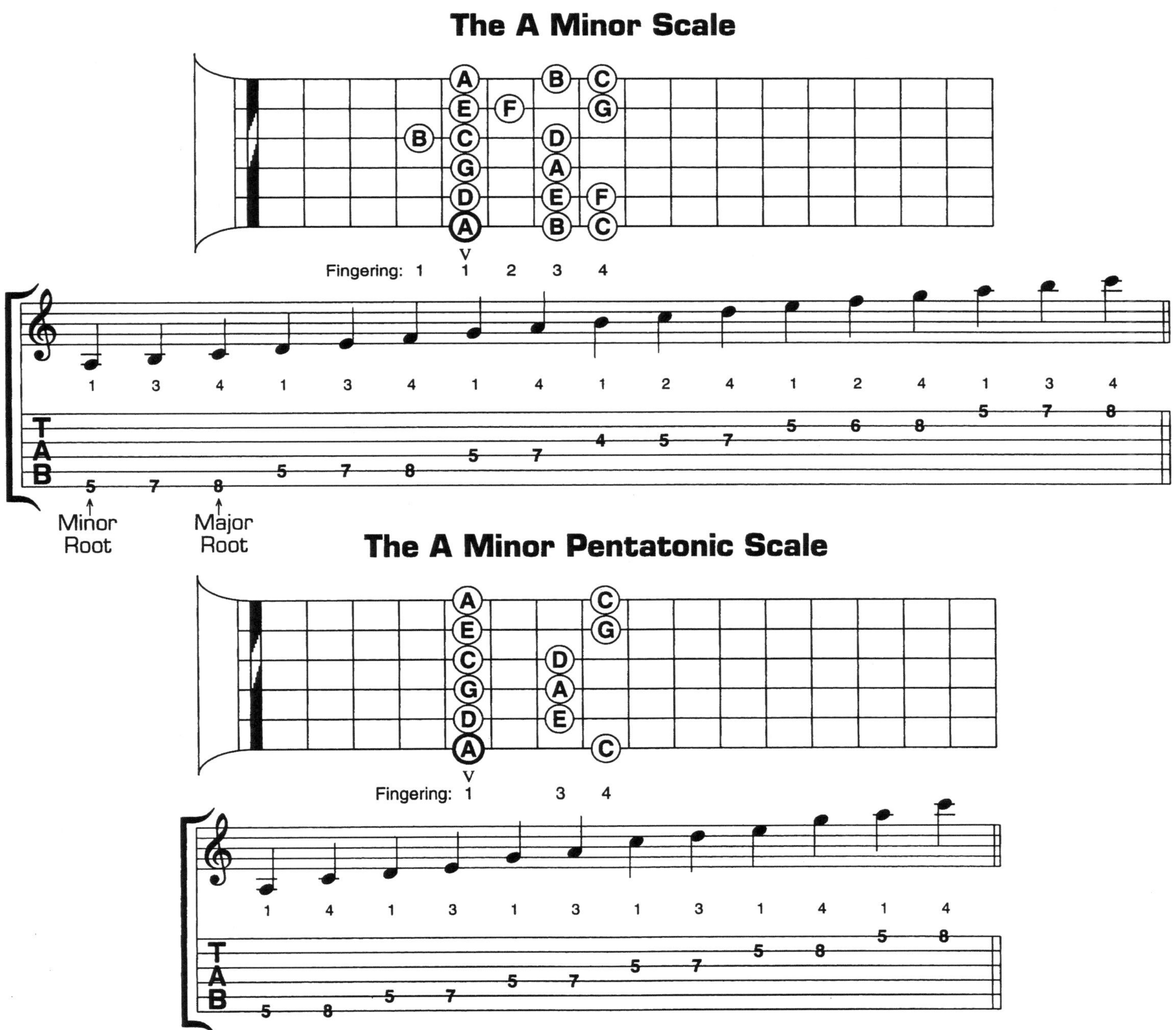

Example 127: Minor Jam (Play-Along Track 7)

The following solo uses the complete A minor scale, notice the inclusion of the B and F and their effect.

MINOR JAM

(Play-Along Track 7)

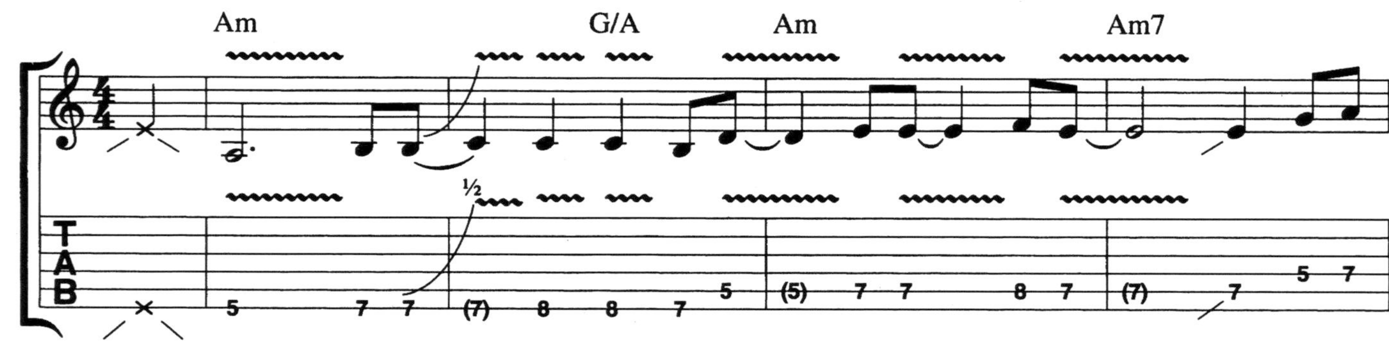

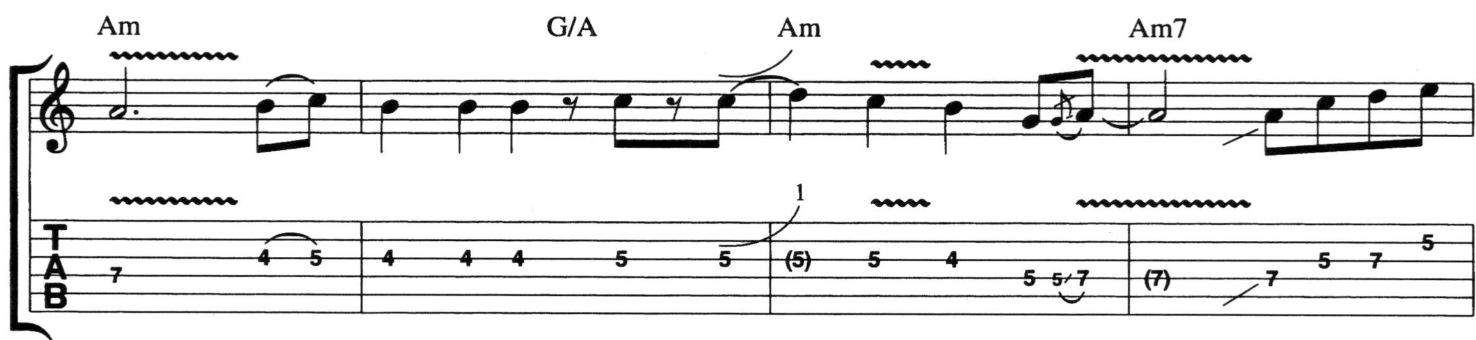

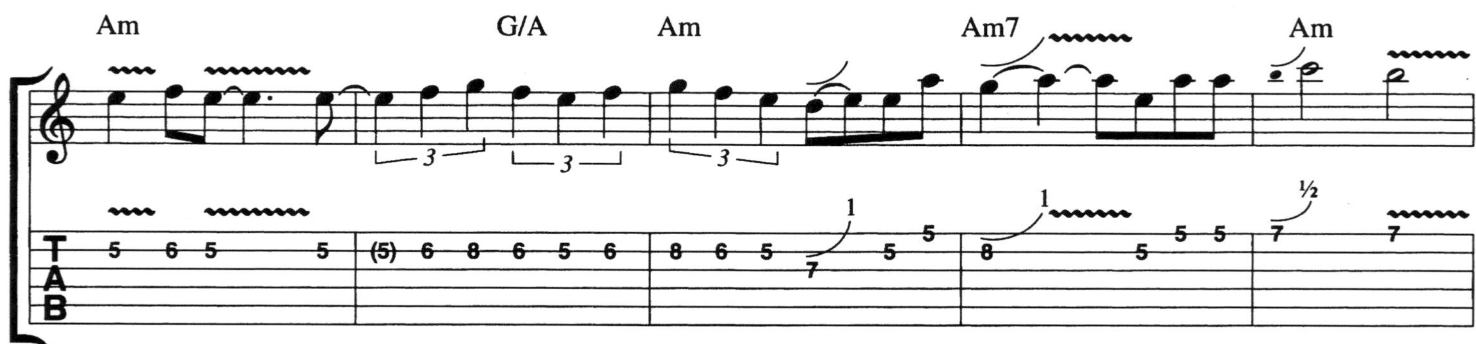

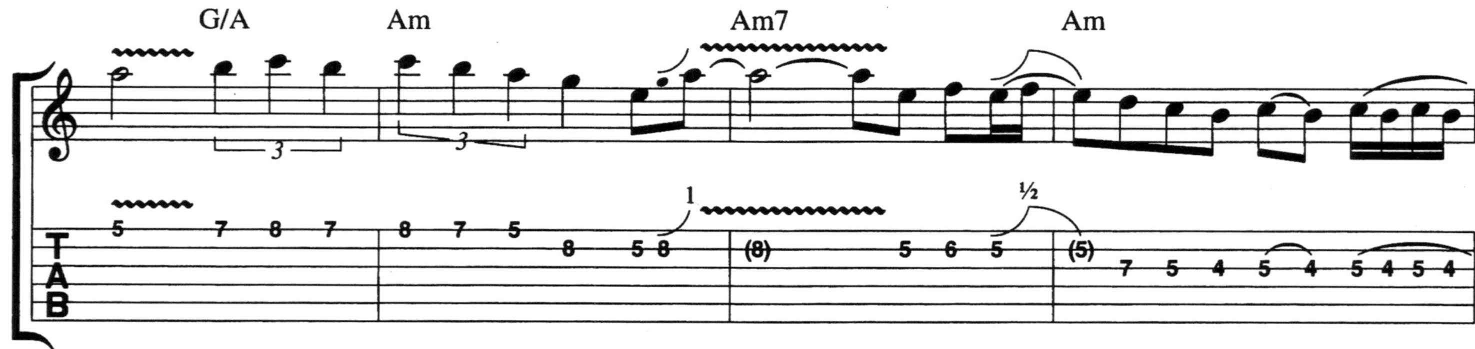

"Now try your own solo, using the A minor scale over this progression."

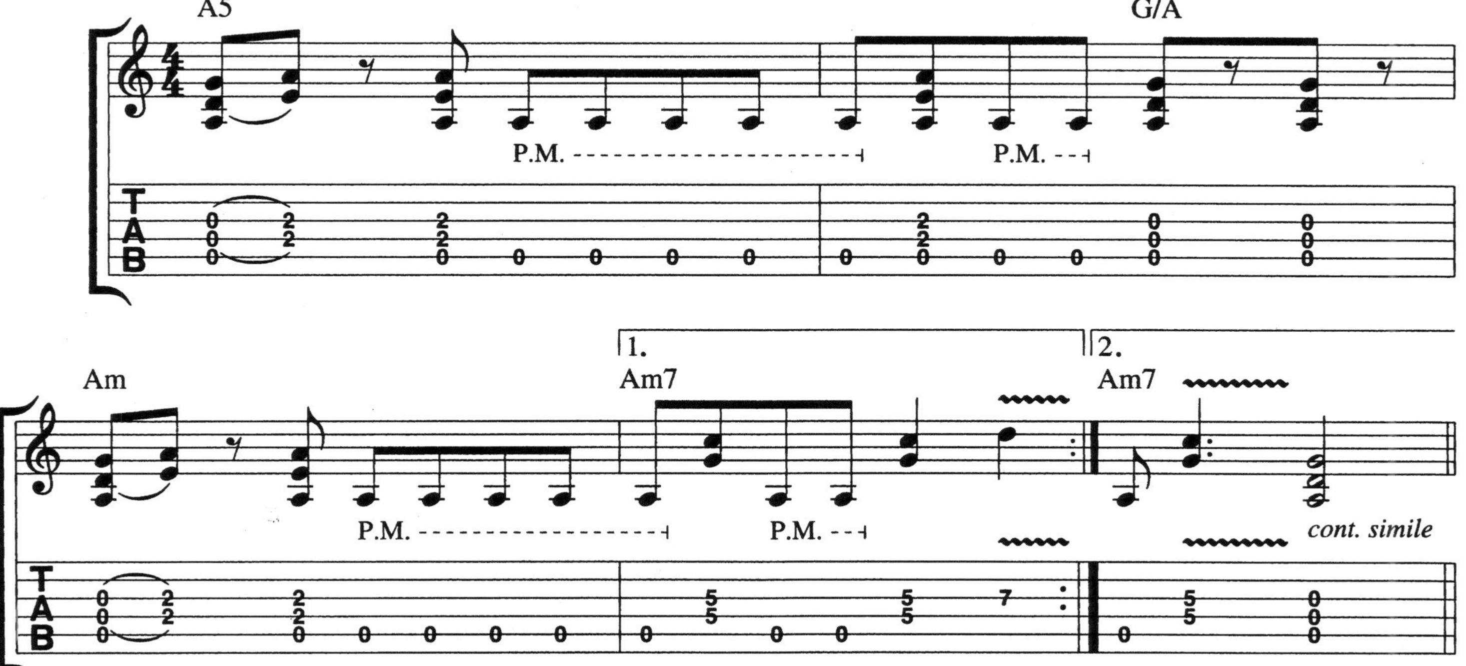

SECTION 17: NEW LICKS

Example 128: A Minor Pentatonic

Try to approach this lick as an A minor lick, and then try to hear it as an A minor pentatonic scale with the B and F added.

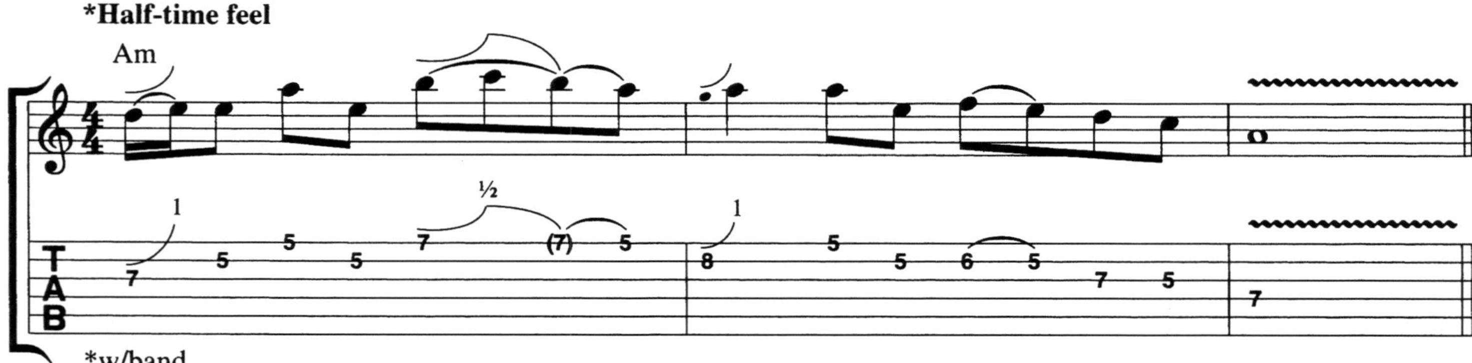

*w/band.

Example 129: A Minor

This A minor lick employs pull-offs, a sequence and then a combination of a bend and release to a pull-off. Since it resolves to A, it sounds like an A minor lick.

Example 129A

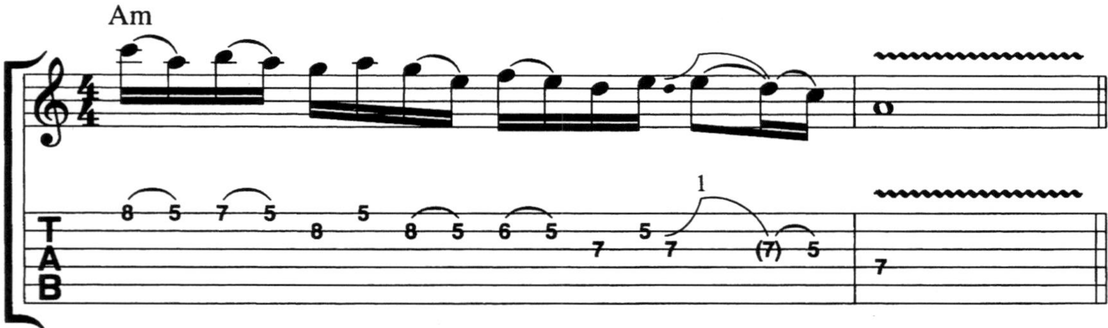

Example 129B: C Major

If you want to make Example 129A a C major lick, make your last note C.

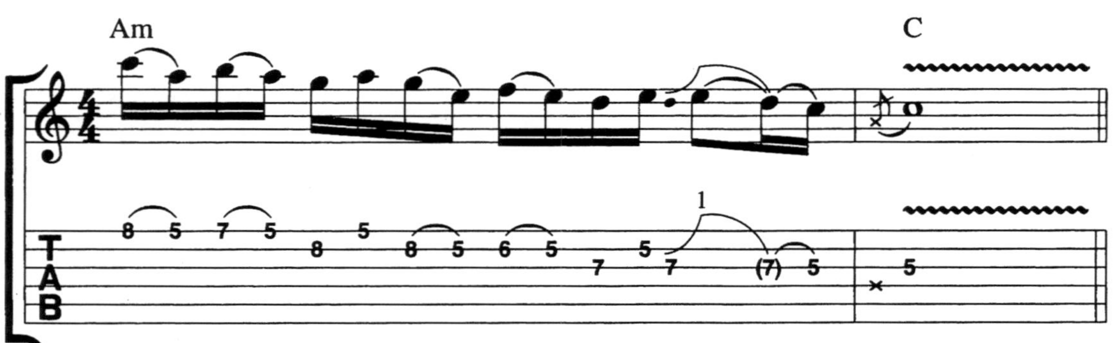

Example 130: Three-Note-Per-String Fingering

Remember that patterns and fingerings are a convenience not a rule. Sometimes it is easier to "displace" a couple of notes. Here the C that is usually played on the 6th string is displaced to the 5th string, and the 5th string F is played on the 4th string. By adding a G to the 6th string, you end up with three-notes-per-string which makes it convenient for rhythmic patterns and slur patterns.

Three-Note-Per-String Scale

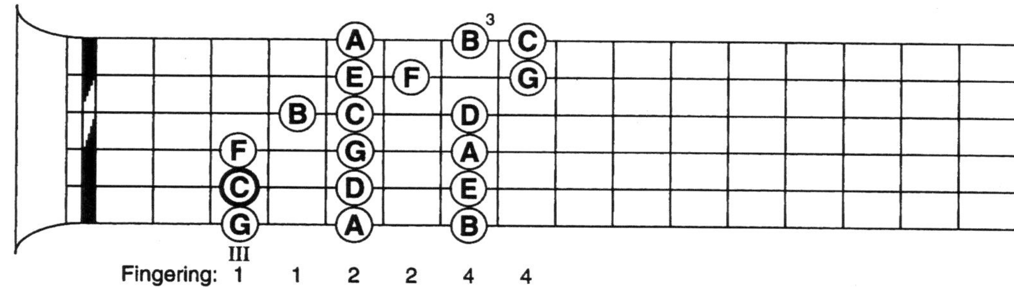

Example 131: Three-Note-Per-String Lick

WRAP UP

Where do you go from here? One thing is to keep listening to your favorite guitarists. If you can, find a good teacher. There are also plenty of good books and videos, but nothing will replace the experience of playing with other musicians. Get together with your friends and jam a lot or even write your own tunes. Good luck!

Alfred